HYSTERIA
in Performance

JENN COLE

HYSTERIA
in Performance

MCGILL-QUEEN'S UNIVERSITY PRESS
Montreal & Kingston | London | Chicago

ISBN 978-0-2280-0556-8 (cloth)
ISBN 978-0-2280-0557-5 (paper)
ISBN 978-0-2280-0720-3 (ePDF)

Legal deposit third quarter 2021
Bibliothèque nationale du Québec

Printed in Canada on acid-free paper that is 100% ancient forest free (100% post-consumer recycled), processed chlorine free

This book has been published with the help of a grant from the Canadian Federation for the Humanities and Social Sciences, through the Awards to Scholarly Publications Program, using funds provided by the Social Sciences and Humanities Research Council of Canada.

Funded by the Government of Canada | Financé par le gouvernement du Canada | Canada

Canada Council for the Arts | Conseil des arts du Canada

We acknowledge the support of the Canada Council for the Arts.
Nous remercions le Conseil des arts du Canada de son soutien.

LIBRARY AND ARCHIVES CANADA CATALOGUING IN PUBLICATION

Title: Hysteria in performance / Jenn Cole.
Names: Cole, Jenn, 1983– author.
Description: Includes bibliographical references and index.
Identifiers: Canadiana (print) 20210147598 | Canadiana (ebook) 20210147873 | ISBN 9780228005568 (cloth) | ISBN 9780228005575 (paper) | ISBN 9780228007203 (ePDF)
Subjects: LCSH: Hysteria—France—History—19th century. | LCSH: Theater—Psychological aspects. | LCSH: Theater—Philosophy. | LCSH: Women—Mental health—France—History—19th century. | LCSH: Women—Institutional care—France—History—19th century. | LCSH: Charcot, J. M. (Jean Martin), 1825-1893. | LCSH: Salpêtrière (Hospital)—History—19th century.
Classification: LCC RC532 .C65 2021 | DDC 616.85/24—DC23

CONTENTS

Figures *vii*

Acknowledgments *xi*

Introduction *3*

ONE | Looking without Seeing *14*

TWO | The Hysteric as Scapegoat *54*

THREE | Hysterical Discourse *101*

FOUR | Hysteria in/as Performance *131*

FIVE | Hysterical Strategies in Contemporary Performance *174*

Conclusion *198*

Notes *207*

Bibliography *227*

Index *235*

Figures

1.1 Augustine, *Attitudes passionnelles : Crucifixion*. Plate XXV, Désiré Magloire Bourneville and Paul Régnard, *Iconographie photographique de la Salpêtrière* 2, 1878. *16*

1.2 Augustine, *Attitudes passionnelles : Érotisme*. Plate XXI, *Iconographie photographique de la Salpêtrière* 2, 1878. *27*

1.3 *Electro-Physiologie, Figure 64*. Photograph by Guillaume-Benjamin-Amand Duchenne de Boulogne and Adrien Tournachon, 1854–56. The Metropolitan Museum of Fine Art, 2021.140. *29*

1.4 Oscar Rejlander, *Surprise and Astonishment*. In Charles Darwin, *Expression of Emotion in Man and Animals*, 1872. *30*

1.5 Albert Londe's Twelve-Lens Camera. Albert Lalonde, *La Photographie Médicale*, 1893, 113. *35*

1.6 Albert Londe, *Attaque d'hystérie chez l'homme*, 1885. Reproduction of album page, location unknown. https://thecharnelhouse.org/2013/03/30/hysterical-materialism/londe_12_pictures-3/. *35*

1.7 Augustine. *Attitudes passionnelles : Menace*. Plate XXVII, Désiré Magloire Bourneville and Paul Régnard, *Iconographie photographique de la Salpêtrière* 2, 1878. *40*

1.8 Augustine. *Hystéro-Épilepsie : État normal*. Plate XIV, Désiré Magloire Bourneville and Paul Régnard, *Iconographie photographique de la Salpêtrière* 2, 1878. *41*

1.9 Augustine. *Début de l'attaque : Cri*. Plate XV, Désiré Magloire Bourneville and Paul Régnard, *Iconographie photographique de la Salpêtrière* 2, 1878. *42*

1.10 Augustine. *Attitudes passionnelles : Menace*. Plate XVIII, Désiré Magloire Bourneville and Paul Régnard, *Iconographie photographique de la Salpêtrière* 2, 1878. *49*

2.1 Robert Fleury, *Pinel Orders Removal of the Chains of the Mad at the Salpêtrière*, 1876. Oil on canvas. Wikimedia Commons. *57*

2.2 André Brouillet, *Une leçon clinique à la Salpêtrière*, 1887. Oil on canvas. Wikimedia Commons. *59*

2.3 Édouard Manet, *Olympia*, 1863. Oil on canvas. Wikimedia Commons. *62*

2.4 *To the Feminist Congress! Le Grelot*, 19 April 1896, front page. *66*

2.5 Pierre-Auguste Renoir, *Bal au Moulin de la Galette*, 1876. Oil on canvas. Wikimedia Commons. *71*

2.6 Edgar Degas, *Le Café-Concert aux Ambassadeurs*, 1876–77. Oil on canvas. Wikiart. *72*

3.1 Augustine, *Lethargy: Muscular Hyperexcitability*. Plate XIV, Désiré Magloire Bourneville and Paul Régnard, *Iconographie photographique de la Salpêtrière* 3, 1879. *107*

3.2 Paul Régnard. *Catalepsy Provoked by the Sound of a Drum*. Engraving based on photograph in Paul Régnard, *Les maladies épidémiques de l'esprit*, 1887, 263. *108*

3.3. Augustine. *Attitudes passionnelles : Appel*. Plate XIX, Désiré Magloire Bourneville and Paul Régnard, *Iconographie photographique de la Salpêtrière* 2, 1878. *117*

4.1 [a and b] *Figure 81: Lady Macbeth, moderate expression of cruelty* and *Figure 83: Lady Macbeth, ferocious cruelty*. Photographs by Guillaume-Benjamin-Amand Duchenne de Boulogne and Adrien Tournachon. The Metropolitan Museum of Fine Art, 2013.173.44 and 2013.173.46. *148*

4.2 [a and b] Albert Londe, *Suggestions by Senses in the Cataleptic Period of "Le grand hypnotisme."* Photograph series for an article by Georges Guinon and Sophie Wolkte. Plate VI, Société de neurologie de Paris, *Nouvelle iconographie de la Salpêtrière*, 1891. *150*

4.3 Albert Londe, *Suggestions by Senses in the Cataleptic Period of "Du grand hypnotisme."* Photographic series for an article by Georges Guinon and Sophie Wolkte, Plate VIII, Société de neurologie de Paris, *Nouvelle iconographie de la Salpêtrière*, 1891. *151*

4.4 Elizabeth Robins as Hedda Gabler, 1891. Photograph: Elliott and Fry. *153*

4.5 Publicity photograph of Bernhardt in Racine's *Phèdre.* Originally published in *La Revue Illustrée*, 1 July 1895. Reproduced from: John Stokes, Michael R. Booth, and Susan Bassnett, *Bernhardt, Terry, Duse : The Actress in Her Time*, 50. *153*

4.6 Photograph of a re-enacted home therapy in Nardò. Photo by Franco Pinna, 1959. Michaela Schäuble, "Images of Ecstasy and Affliction: The Camera as Instrument for Researching and Reproducing Choreographies of Deviance in a Southern Italian Spider Possession Cult," https://doi.org/10.4000/anthrovision.2409. *168*

5.1 Dayna McLeod, Diagram of *Uterine Concert Hall*, 2016. Courtesy of the artist. *186*

5.2 Monique Mojica in *The Strange Case of Izzie M.: The Alchemy of Enfreakment*, 2018. *196*

Acknowledgments

To all the ones who held my baby while I wrote: Steven Martin, Caitlin and Bernard Martin, and Phaedra Muirhead. To Tom who has taught me so much about how knowledges move and who, in his arrival from the star world, taught me how to sink my teeth into a good, guttural sound. To the ones who supported me in the research, especially Stephen Johnson. Also: Tamara Trojanowska, Pascal Michelucci, Julie Salverson, Nikki Cesare-Schotzko, and Catie Thompson. To the students of my Feminist Psychologies classes over the years who have diligently thought through, with me, what it means to radically listen in psychiatric and psychological contexts. Ev Smith and jessi beauchamp especially for help with the book. Chi meegwech to Jonathan Crago and Kat Simpson for editorial support. For V and her pressurized speech full of love and plants. For all the ones institutionalized against their consent, in the past and right now, especially those Indigenous to Turtle Island. For all the disabled and non-disabled teenage girls and non-binary and trans and 2S youth who scream, kick up a fuss, dance their faces off. And for the quiet ones too.

HYSTERIA
in Performance

INTRODUCTION

In the late nineteenth century, Jean-Martin Charcot, director of the Salpêtrière hospital – Paris's asylum for hysterics, epileptics, women, and children – compiled the largest archive on female hysteria in the Western world, a work that aimed to rationalize the hysterical body and that, at the same time, served not only to describe and document hysteria, but to popularize it, quite spectacularly. The weekly lecture series at the Salpêtrière amphitheatre were eerily paradoxical: the "starlet" Augustine, or a patient like her, performed her symptoms under hypnosis or by way of ovarian compression as Charcot methodically described her body's articulations with medical gloss. During the Tuesday and Friday lecture series, the patient's body gesticulated wildly while her performance was narrated by Charcot, the self-professed great patriarch of medicine, popularly called the "Napoleon of Neurosis."[1]

Charcot and the hysterics' audience were predominantly male and upper class. In an era marked by the popularization of medical and anthropological scientific spectacle, the audience was also, not surprisingly, made up of as many extra-medical elites as medical professionals. Physicians and medical students, as well as journalists, authors, personal friends of Charcot, painters, philosophers, and politicians attended the famous hysteria shows.[2]

The broader project of Charcot and the doctors at the Salpêtrière was to categorize, chart, name, and regulate the hysteric's gestures, distilling French women's particular madnesses to a singular and general "grande hystérie." In the amphitheatre, Charcot's pedagogical lectures were largely nosological – he named phases of the attack as they occurred as he drew continual attention to their regularity, saying "it is always the same thing."[3] Charcot's reasonable description of hysteria was supported by a body in dramatic contortions, impressive acrobatics, and emotionally riveting poses. The spectacular gestural presence on stage of the hysteric in pain – almost always a woman – served to advance Charcot's fame for having "discovered" hysteria.

It was a very particular aesthetic embodiment of illness with which the women at the hospital were afflicted. The hysterical attack, with its distinct phases, seemed (primarily) to exist only at the Salpêtrière during Charcot's lifetime and appears to have vanished once he died. Hysteria was highly stylized and produced astoundingly specific attacks, beginning with large and rapid movements; then acrobatics, often featuring what Charcot called the "famous" *arc-de-cercle*, a backbend from foot to crown that patients could sustain for periods of minutes or hours; and finally, a period of hallucination, often erotic and/or violent, before the attack resolved. As well, Charcot asserted that hysterics were especially susceptible to hypnosis. Indeed, hypnosis experiments, mini-dramas in which patients would react to the invisible dangers of snakes and fire, catch out supposed murderers in the audience and kiss hospital statues, became a highlight of the pedagogical spectacle. Hysteria, incidentally, according to Charcot, was inherently theatrical, capable of great copy-catting, and prone to both mimesis and fakery. Somehow, the director managed to unearth an illness that lent itself to self-stylization while simultaneously remaining physiologically located in the neurological structures of the body. Charcot asserted continually that hysteria was an organic and not a mental illness. That the body might adopt somatic formations and dynamics with no somatic logic was one of hysteria's many mysterious traits.

Outside the amphitheatre, offstage, in her room, the hysterical patient continued to perform. To live at the Salpêtrière was to exist without privacy, in a state of perpetual surveillance. As she experienced attacks in her bed, physician Désiré-Magloire Bourneville recorded the patient's movements and utterances during attacks, alongside her medical history, her bodily excretions and temperatures, her responses to experimental treatments, injuries incurred in the hospital, and her attempts at escape or her eventual passage from the institution. These appeared in hospital publications called the *Iconographie photographique de la Salpêtrière*. In these theatrical documents, the hysteric appears in dozens of photographs and drawings meaning to illustrate hysteria's symptomatology and the attack broken down into phases. In the photographic images, patients are exposed in most vulnerable moments of recurring hallucinated memories of events of rape and violence, of bodily pain, of emotional upheaval. The photographs are kinetic, poignant, and disturbing. They seem to cry out for interpretation. The images in the *Iconographie* riveted the French public, and were prolifically reproduced in many popular novels, etchings, caricatures, and in both café-concert and avant-garde performances. The *Iconographie* images also act as traces of the violence of looking, cautioning the contemporary researcher to examine what her own looking might mean.

In *Illness as Metaphor* Susan Sontag writes that "any important disease whose causality is murky, and for which treatment is ineffectual, tends to be awash in significance."[4] This book, focussed on the strange appearance of hysteria in France in the nineteenth century, represents a plurality of significations around an illness that already challenges the powers of description and classification. Hysteria was, and is, inundated with significance. The illness had no known singular origin, no known cure, and produced a myriad of symptoms from anaesthetized limbs, contracted tongues, and auditory hallucinations to coughing and delirious masturbation. Hysteria, it was reported, occurred mostly in women and could be caused by or activated by a traumatic event, by too much time in cafés or too much time reading books, by disappointment with one's lot in life, or by any number of social phenomena related to anxieties around a turbulent urbanism and renegotiations of what it meant to be a woman in the modern era. For Charcot, hysteria was hereditary and neurological, located in a lesion somewhere in the body that he never found nor was able to prove. Though the director of the hospital asserted that both men and women could suffer from hysteria, he never fully separated the illness from its connection with the uterus and in many of his pedagogical demonstrations he provoked attacks by pressing on patients' ovaries and breasts. Experimentation and demonstration reigned in Charcot's hysteria ward but no cure was found or, arguably, even sought. Despite the specificity of its symptomatic attack, hysteria was a murky illness. Hysterics could rise to stardom in Charcot's lecture series, the hysteric could become a provocative French icon, but no one could say for sure how hysteria operated.

The women who lived with hysteria and its diagnosis, though documented prolifically in the medical literature and more popular cultural iterations, are even more evasive. Time in the hospital archives leads to medical histories with some biographical detail, transcriptions of words uttered in hallucination, descriptions of bodily movements, and photographs. Perhaps only one patient, cabaret performer Jane Avril, wrote about her time in the hysteria ward at the Salpêtrière after leaving, and patient Blanche Wittman's comments on her experience as a Salpêtrière starlet appear as mediated through the raconteur-style writings of medical professional Baudouin. As is so common across representations of institutionalization, patient narratives do not proliferate. The medical or official documentation is excessive but reductive, pointing always to its inability to convey the personhood and the private experiences of the female patient. I too can only access the hysteric superficially. She reserves her privacy despite and because of her iconographic status.

This work is about the violences of representation, and it is also about representation's limits. My work on hysteria is often figurative. The patients become absorbed into a work that is full of celebrations of their illness and moments of resistance to the patriarchal dominance of medical reason and that is also full of conjecture and poetic association. It is nearly impossible to resist the iconographic stature of the hysteric, to have hysteria signify for this or that and in the meantime to lose sight of the real women who lived in Charcot's hospital. What is undoubtedly a methodological weakness may also be an inevitability. To recognize the unknowable spaciousness of the other – her impossible capture and her ability to shrink from and overflow representational media – is to find oneself coming to grips with an ethics of the human subject and to encounter a tenuous relationship to responsibility.

Writing and researching, the more time I spent with the medical literature, the more the hysteric seemed to resist my optic and epistemic capture. Nearly everywhere, I found her resisting in practical ways: tearing off her straitjacket, running away, aggressively turning on her audience and the doctors, screaming her protest at being provoked into attacks in the middle of a lecture, even shooting a physician. Her resistance also seemed to appear symbolically in ways that were more subtle but no less forceful.

She seemed to undermine the possessive power of the photograph, overflowing the medium with the uncatchable immensity of her personhood. The most famous paintings of the hysteric, by Robert Fleury and André Brouillet, seemed overwrought in their representation of the hysteric as docile and voluptuous. In fact, they seemed to reveal more about a cultural anxiety around female sexuality and autonomy than about the hysteric herself. Why was Brouillet's painting so flat, when the hysterics themselves seemed to be so vivacious? The painterly style chosen by Charcot to frame his lectures was banal, rational – a curious mode of rendering an imaginative, gestural, impassioned illness. And what about these lecture series? It seemed strange that Charcot, who valued the simple transmission of material facts via explanation and description, would choose a medium so theatrical for his project. The lectures were pedagogical, but also spectacular – indeed they were so aesthetically astonishing that rumours began to circulate that Charcot and his hysterics were faking, merely putting on a show. Indeed, one of the main symptoms of hysteria in the nineteenth century was theatricality. Doctors and actresses criticized hysterics at Charcot's hospital for being too dramatic – for giving themselves over to bodily expression of intense emotion, for responding to the invisible content of their ecstasies and hallucinations with theatrical gestures, for embracing passion over reason, for chattering in a delirium of speech and inarticulate sounds. Hysterics screamed, overreacted, erotically displayed themselves, and spoke in relation to invisible counterparts, layering experiences of the past into their present realities in the hospital. More complicatedly, hysterical symptoms – the physiological disorders of speech, muscular movement, and sensation – were simulations of illness. Symptoms were really and truly experienced and produced by the hysterical body, but without any clear etiology. Diagnostically, to be a hysteric was to live with a body that revelled in simulation. This, alongside the theatrical lectures – Charcot's grand rhetorical presence and the hysteric's supplementary resplendent attacks – made sussing out the authenticity of her performance difficult. And then, the hysteric seemed to point to the limits of legibility in other ways. Her manner of speech – poetic, condensed, erratic, fragmented – and her manner of integrating sound and gesture – in a compendium of cries, breathing irregularities, squelched noises, contortions, contractions, and diverse bodily and vocal expressions – challenged the positivist language employed by medical scientists in a way that reorganized my own way of reading and listening, and that caused me to marvel at the possibilities of inarticulate language.

Above all, my understanding collided with the patient's alterity, and her means of making her alterity known within the confines of the medical documents and associated cultural texts. Something alarming occurred: once I began to look for the hysteric, to try to listen to her, I found not only that I could not see or pretend to hear her clearly, but also that she was nonetheless speaking. The hysteric has conventionally been represented as paradoxically noisy and mute. Her attacks made her positively verbose; she cried aloud; she tore at her sheets and gestured frantically. She also acted as an onstage prop, a bodily instrument through which Charcot's pedagogical monologue was realized. Charcot's use of the patient is a glaring feature of the transcripts of his lectures. Nonetheless, though he was disinterested in the value of the patient as an interlocutor, though he dismissed and explained away her interjections – in the archive, *a dialogue is taking place*. Or, if dialogue is cut off, it is not the fault of the hysteric, her so-called unreasonable speech, her illogical symptoms. Her incitement to acknowledge one's failure to recognize her and her vital but elusive presence are provocations to discover oneself in relation to her. The hysteric breaks through the documentary apparatus of capture continually, only to disappear again. But her documentary presence, no matter how opaque, is *insistent*.

This book could be taken as a series of potential dramaturgical readings or as a portrait of ambiguity. I ask the question, primarily: what kind of performance is the hysterical attack? And what is the nature of hysteria in and as performance, as it occurred at the Salpêtrière in the nineteenth century? The Salpêtrière hysteria project was a medical one, but also a theatrical one. The manner in which Charcot transmitted his research requires dramaturgical reading, because each medium – the lecture-show, onstage hypnosis, photography, the condensation of movements into a choreographed attack, the bedside scripts of patient hallucination – is a piece of performance operating dynamically and distinctly.

The work is a series of *potential* dramaturgies, because any one of the possible readings of the theatre of hysteria could be accurate, and because the aim of this work is, in part, to trouble the value of accuracy. My readings are gestures towards discovery, but undermine it, drawing attention to the limits of the process of reading. The hysteric resists legibility and writing about this resistance is somewhat difficult. How to engage in a knowledge project on hysteria that tries to make a case for marginal narratives and performances of secrecy, for the value of gnostic surrender and unstable spectatorship: how to write about unknowing? The form of the writing cannot replicate its content, though I do aim to avoid the positivist trappings of reduction by naming, belief in a single material reality, belief in the power of my reasonable discourse over the discourses of unreason or belief that there is such a binary. Each chapter presents a dramaturgical reading of the medical spectacle of the female body in pain, and each reading rests alongside a potentiality, a hysteria that signifies not A or B but somewhere in between. The chapters could also be read as counter-diagnoses – of photography, of nineteenth century heteropatriarchal medical culture, of scientific language, of power structures produced through spectacle. Hysteria was defined in specific ways in its time, but even then it applied pressure to the means employed to define it. Charcot, and the hegemonic structures that he represented – medical positivism, scientific reason, the valuation of sight over blindness, articulacy over inarticulacy, men over women, and so on – came under pressure when brought into contact with the hysteric. The theatrical modes intended to explain hysteria, and to devalue the hysteric's characteristics – autonomous female sexuality, impassioned poetics, unreasonable discourse, indulgence in theatricality, illegibility – perform contrarily to their intentions.

Photography of her most vulnerable moments, transcription of her involuntary confidences, demonstration and explanation of her embodied suffering and pleasure in the onstage lecture shows: these are representational modes of violence. Charcot and other members of the medical institution exposed, reduced, muted, and made use of young French women living in poverty. The photographs, transcripts, and lectures also represent a theatre of hysterical grappling with medical modes of capture, a public power struggle in which the essential privacy of the patient, her alterity, was a force that injected the spectacle with the dangerous potential of reflexivity and momentary or symbolic destruction.

Hysteria did much more than it was purported to. It did not just take female bodies and bend them into theatrical attacks or render them susceptible to masculine hypnotic suggestion. Hysteria showed bodies to be locales of memory, desire, and will. A woman suffering from hysteria engaged in creative language production and the mobilization of an inevitable but also dynamic ambiguity. Her public appearance was a continual ethical provocation, pointing not only to the vulnerability of her person, but the unstable position of her spectator. The book is an attempted "Portrait of Ambiguity," because the work drives at rendering a portrait of the hysteric but finds her to be capable of delightful caprice. Also, by trying to learn about the hysteric through representational media surrounding medically diagnosed hysteria, we find out more about ambiguity itself, and its ethical horizon. The hysterical patient appears in so many photographs, rose to effective stardom on the Salpêtrière amphitheatre stage, and yet this work, which aims to find her, cannot pin her down long enough to render a good portrait. The chapters that follow are careful effervescences, attentive scrawlings: in short, poor representations. Where I have aimed to catch her, I have caught, instead, my own tenuous relationship to her alterity. This book is a trace of our entanglement.

Chapter 1 traces the forced performance of hysteria on stage and above all for the camera as an expression of institutionalized violence, tied to other modes of scientific spectacle in the late nineteenth century in France. The chapter also takes up the photographic document of the hysterical patient as a theatrical medium, and the relationship of the historical researcher to the photographic archive itself as somewhat hysterical. The researcher leans on the document to render an accurate picture of the past, enters into a reciprocity with photographs and their supporting language that is contingent, precarious, and full of possibility.

The photographs published at the Salpêtrière signify excess and invisibility at once. The photograph points to the practice of documenting so many painful bodily and psychic phenomena, and to the essential privacy of the patient rendered, whose imaginary combatants and lovers fail to appear in the glass plate impressions. Analyzing the photograph is an exercise in suspense. In reading the *Iconographie*, I open myself to the other, and with no certain outcome. My work occurs in a state of contingency. Roland Barthes' *Camera Lucida* takes residency in this chapter to delineate reading the hysteria photographs as phenomenological. Barthes' work on the photograph as iconographic and/or indexical locates the photographs of the hysteric in the *Iconographie* as indexical traces of violence committed within the Salpêtrière against the hysterical patient – the violences of spectacular exposure and reduction – and also as indexes of the patient's evasion of representation, her ability to signify the limits of the photographic medium. Emmanuel Levinas' work on the ability for a person to overflow signification, and his identification of the face as the site at which ethics is formed and enacted, is relevant here. When considered alongside readings of other nineteenth century texts that focussed on categorizing the face but found themselves challenged by dynamic subjectivities, we are able to see the hysterical patient as forceful, despite the doctor and photographer's efforts to enclose her.

Chapter 2 lies very close to Hélène Cixous and Catherine Clément's work on the hysteric as a figure pushed outside of the social order, but only ever so far as to be contained and subjugated within its structures. The chapter also follows Cixous and Clément's assertion that the practice of exclusion of the feminine has historically been compensatory, repressive, and ineffective. Resting on a reading of two important set pieces in the Salpêtrière amphitheatre, built for Charcot to parade and explain his hysterics – the paintings by Brouillet and Pinel – this chapter performs a feminist psychoanalysis of the lecture series. In a chapter that reads the medical spectacle of women's bodies in pain and women in the impressionable sleep of hypnosis as a symptom of masculine anxieties around the shifting role of women in fin-de-siècle France, the lecture series come to resemble a symptom – not of sick women but of sick doctors, doctors whose ambivalent relationship to women is enacted weekly in a complex theatre of desire and disgust.

Chapter 3 is an inquiry into the force of inarticulacy, especially in the event of the human cry. Positivist language pairs against the language of the hysteric. In the false binary of discourses imagined by psychiatric professionals from the nineteenth century onwards, false because inarticulacy is part of language and not its opposite, the cry, in this chapter, comes to express the strengths of what cannot be known. I perform close readings of some of Augustine's delirious babblings and a moment in which, in a public lecture, a patient cried out and momentarily interrupted the confident eloquence of Doctor Charcot. Hysterical language appears as a welcome intervention to the positivist regime.

The fourth chapter deals with the numerous reports advanced in Charcot's time that the hysterics, and that he himself, might be faking. I assert that truth and falsehood are especially difficult to trace in performance, and that authenticity is not necessarily opposed to willful fakery. One of hysteria's primary diagnostic traits was theatricality. Add in multiple performances of the same culturally specific symptoms, a body that symptomatically simulates, and the generic overlap between contemporary theatrical traditions and hysteria becomes a site ripe for accusations of a form of acting rather indistinguishable from, if not nefariously linked to, duping. The chapter presents an odd performance history that remains undecided as to whether hysteria is most like the dance mime precedents in melodrama or more like the handful of cheerleaders in New York who collectively fell to stuttering and flailing fits for a brief period in 2012.[5] Playing hysteria generically against popular theatre traditions does not produce a clear genealogy of acting techniques or aesthetic tropes but does produce a working theory of how performance may have been at work in Charcot's hysterics. Hysteria, the chapter concludes, in so many ways, is performance.

Chapter 5 asks in what way contemporary performances are hysterical. Taking up twentieth and twenty-first century works that cite the French hysteria archive explicitly, or that parallel the modes of performative disruption that the nineteenth century hysteric exemplifies, I explore the territory of new feminist performance, concluding with Indigenous performances more locally and more currently. These recurrences of finding the hysteric continually cropping up from the past and asking performers to respond invites us to consider why the hysteric continues to return, why she has such an allure for contemporary scholars and art makers, and why we can't seem to stop addressing her. The chapter also looks at acts of performance that summon the spectator to respond by making noise, turning the spectacular medium to produce something unexpected, showing up in places one shouldn't, representing the female body in a series of non-medical displays of anatomy, and indulging in personal emotion as something valuable, all theatrical tropes the hysteric has taught me to look for and to pay attention to. Many of these works mark performance as a site for the ethical imposition of very particular human encounters.

Making use of the parameters of spectacle allowed the hysteric to challenge the power/knowledge imbalances between herself and the Salpêtrière medical community. On the amphitheatre stage and in the *Iconographie*, Charcot and his colleagues aimed to make sense of hysteria by employing hysterics' performances as supporting elements in the scientific spectacle. Charcot's project of demonstration of knowledge *via theatre* created opportunities for the female patient to resist her reductive capture, her use as metaphor or as example, her exposure without consent, exactly through theatrical interventions. The hysteric intervened at the level of spectacle by withholding information, by altering the course of the show, by dramatizing her life in a manner that overflowed empirical style and, as Foucault says, by using the scenario to "cram in all her individual life, sexuality and memory"[6] into what was supposed to be a representation of her illness. Her audience could and cannot help but jut against the limits of knowledge and the potential of performance. The hysteric points to the fraught and exciting nature of theatrical representation, continually drawing out dilemmas and unexpected dynamics of witnessing the suffering of others. Charcot created a unique mixture of drama and science in his transmission of his findings about hysteria. The hysteric made the medium express beyond expectation.

ONE

Looking without Seeing

The Image's Betrayal and Provocation

My inquiry into the dynamics of the medical spectacle around hysteria occurs somewhat awkwardly in the absence of a sound or moving image archive. Still, what historical documents remain are telling. Augustine's life at the Salpêtrière, her symptoms, her memories, her attacks and pains were made public in the late nineteenth century and remain so today via the hospital's fastidious record keeping and its inclination toward highly aestheticized publications. Because Charcot and his medical entourage published as prolifically as patients were documented, what evidence of the hysteria project existed then is mostly available to us now. Charcot's lessons were published as a series of lectures, in handwritten transcript format, giving the reader the impression that she is taking notes during Charcot's performance as he methodically conveys his medical observations. His rhetorical style and his performance methodology, against which the hysterical patients appear as secondary characters or kinetic objects of description, are uniquely preserved in these documents. Nineteenth century medical journal publications present a range of medical perceptions of Charcot's work from firsthand intern accounts of the Tuesday lectures to comparisons between hysteria as it was demonstrated at the hospital and depicted in cultural works like Flaubert's *Madame Bovary*. Is Emma a true hysteric? Flaubert, on fad, eventually claimed he was.[1] Charcot and Richer's *Les Démoniaques dans l'Art*, a work that interprets paintings from the sixth through seventeenth centuries and retroactively diagnoses the possession depicted therein as hysteria, and other hospital publications carry more general descriptions of the physicians' perceptions of hysterics. With the help of his colleagues, neurologist Désiré-Magloire Bourneville, physician-photographer Paul Régnard, photographer Albert Londe, and artist/physiologist Paul Richer, Charcot published several volumes on the hysterical patients at the Salpêtrière. Most notable is the *Iconographie photographique de la Salpêtrière*, four hefty volumes (preceding the *Nouvelle iconographie*) in which Bourneville describes the physiological symptoms of patients in hysterical attack and some of their utterances, sounds, gestures, and cries. In the *Iconographie*, alongside Bourneville's detailed bedside accounts, Régnard's photographs and Richer's drawings of patients in the dramatic phases of hysterical attack appear in support of Charcot's description of la grande hystérie. It is the *Iconographie* that this chapter addresses primarily. Turning to these visual records as a way of accessing a theory of hysterical resistance is a documentary necessity. But it is also strategic, for the nineteenth century cultural valuation of empiricism and observable truth presents one of the epistemological structures that the hysteric troubles, exactly by resisting representation.

The tone of the *Iconographie* documents is at once aloof and intensely personal. The distant gaze of the objective professional butts against the palpable pain of the patients. The photographs, records, and transcripts are excessive in their exposure of the patient's personal sexual and emotional experiences, their bodies, their agonies, and their desires, while simultaneously neglecting to address these intimacies in the medical analysis or diagnostic labelling. One easily reads the medical literature and its artistic supports assertions of scientific power realized through the pain of the patient's body. Or, one could go as far as Georges Didi-Huberman has and suggest that the historical documents convey "hatred made into art."[2] From the coquettish photographs to the onstage medical narration of the relived experience of her rape, one has the sense that no one looked carefully enough at Augustine, no one asked her where it hurt or how they could help and that somehow, at the same time, everyone looked too much, too often. This violence of looking without seeing, for which the doctors, the modern audience, and the contemporary researcher are all accountable

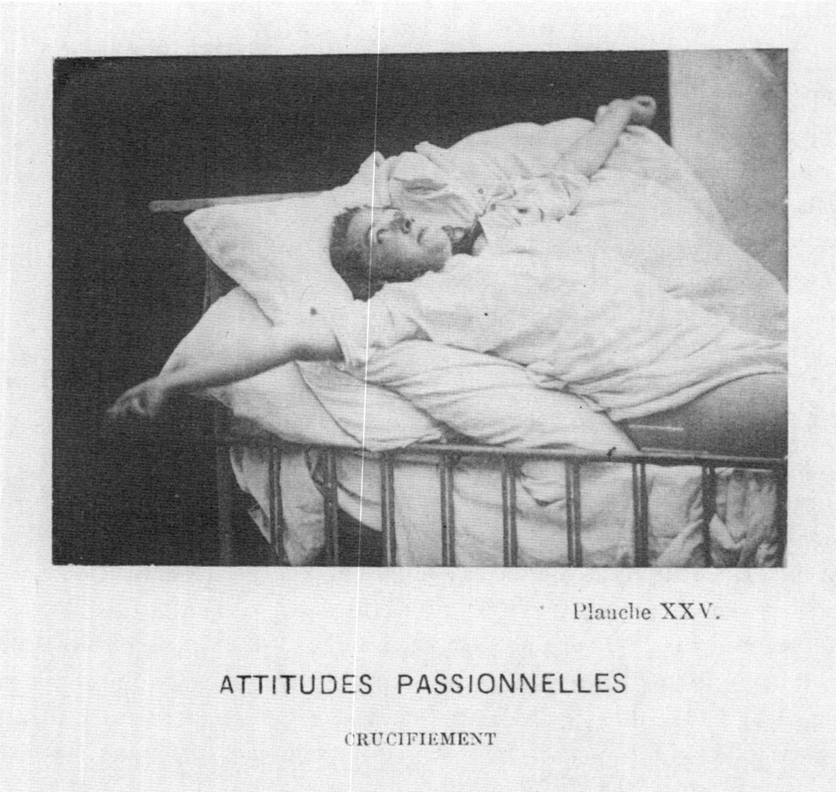

1.1 Augustine, *Attitudes passionnelles : Crucifixion*. Plate XXV, *Iconographie photographique de la Salpêtrière* 2, 1878.

to varying degrees, characterizes the performances of the Salpêtrière hysteric and her doctors. At the same time, an analysis of this violence at the sites of theatrical trans/inscription indicates a blatant inadequacy in these modes of looking. While power undeniably resided in the hands of those with privileged rhetorical apparatuses, a lack emerges when one engages in looking at the cultural documents they distributed. This lack appears acutely against or via an excessive element in the documents themselves – the patient, so alive there, coming to us as though through a glass darkly, never comes into focus, but persistently haunts the image. There is an aporia in this life overlooked, an indeterminable element that cannot or will not fully appear despite its ubiquitous reproduction. A stubborn personhood, undermining the scaffold of every well-made description, every carefully placed label. In every photograph of the patient Augustine's condition, there lies an Augustine. Thus begins her disappearance.

KNOWLEDGE/VISION
Looking without Seeing

The motto associated with the anthropological exhibits of the World's Columbian Exposition of 1893 indicates the fascination of an era: "To see is to know."[3] The phrase applies to so many modern phenomena – to spectacles of so-called primitivism in travelling exhibitions, to the fairground invitation to see for oneself the bodily pathologies of the local or foreign freak and, especially, to modern medicine.

The urge to typify that which otherwise signified irrationality produced a host of strange spectacles in nineteenth century Paris. Spectatorship of the pathological body appeared most poignantly in the public demonstrations of Indigenous peoples from places Europe was in the process of colonizing. Eli Clare vividly expresses how easily fascination for viewing freaks of any kind allowed distinctions of ethnicity, impairment, physical anomaly, or rare bodily talents to blur through enfreaking gazes.[4] Raymond Corbey, in his article *Ethnographic Showcases: 1870–1930*, relates the popularity of the ethnographic showcase to the celebration of European empire and also to the "wider context of the collecting, measuring, classifying, picturing, filing and narrating of colonial Others during the heyday of colonialism."[5] According to Corbey, such displays of Indigenous people from the French colonies at the Paris world fair of 1878 inaugurated a standard for the display of foreign Others, repeated by Western European nations in subsequent world fairs and exhibitions.[6] Corbey notes further that, "The stagewise development from savagery through barbarism to civilization was suggested by organizing museum and world fair exhibits into evolutionary sequences."[7] A direct correlation was posited between colonialism and the civilization of the "savage," a correlation the modern spectator was prepared to make given his exposure to the notion of the human type as portrayed via popular sciences. An "old Indian in shabby traditional clothing next to his son in a new suit"[8] read clearly to European citizens, who could readily interpret the image through the increasingly popular narrative of social Darwinism and degenerative heredity theory as developed by Charcot and propagated in popular literatures. As Guna/ Rappahannock performing artist Monique Mojica, who situates herself in a long line of performers, including Spiderwoman Theatre but also sideshow performers at American fairs, says, "We were there to provide the contrast and the savagery."[9] Charcot drew upon colonial narratives of progress to refer to the advanced research practices at the Salpêtrière. For instance, his invocation of the phrase "pots de terre, pots de fer" (earthenware pots, metal pots) presumptuously marked positivism's departure from so-called outdated modes of being in the world.[10] Charcot's medical posturing often relied on and circulated the othering discourse of fairgrounds.

The violence of the turn-of-the-century gaze in the context of the combined fairground sideshow and medical production of the same harmful and vindicating narratives of colonialism, racialization, and enfreakment – and the casual and celebratory tenor in which these narratives were delivered – cannot be underestimated. There are strong and under-researched connections between colonial genocide and institutionalization of racialized people. On Turtle Island, on the heels of medical sideshows that blurred the distinctions between "feeble-mindedness" and "primistivism," Indigenous people and people of colour were falsely diagnosed, locked away, and abused in federally funded psychiatric institutions against their consent in alarmingly high rates for decades.[11] Eugenics and sterilization practices accompanied the forced internment of racialized people who threatened the colonial project in the US and Canada. It was these practices that were being propped up and justified under the guise of entertainment through discourses of medical curiosity in both the sideshow and the medical spectacle.

In Europe, the case of the famous "Venus Hottentot," a South African woman whose name was Sara Baartman, also exemplifies the harm done by mixing medical authority and the spectacle of curiosity. Baartman was exhibited in England and then Paris in the early nineteenth century and described according to so-called objective classifications and descriptions. The anatomical features of her large buttocks and labial measurements were of particular interest to a public that included but was not limited to anatomists and doctors.[12] These physical "anomalies" were orated by an "expert" as part of the Venus anatomical-colonial exhibit, in which she appeared as a foreign "natural historical specimen."[13] According to Lydie Moudileno,

> Her most exciting features were her alleged "steatopygia" (a condition resulting from the accumulation of fat in the buttocks) and the presence of the (mythical) "Hottentot apron" (the elongation of the genital labia). The fascination with her anatomy continued post-mortem when her corpse was given over to the French scientist Georges Cuvier for scientific observation. Cuvier performed two very symbolically charged procedures, producing a plaster cast of her entire body and then removing her brain and genitalia in order to preserve them for display at his own private Musée d'Histoire Naturelle, and later at the Musée de l'Homme.[14]

The casts and preserved organs of Baartman's body remained on display at the Musée de l'Homme until 1974, after which they were put in storage.[15]

Charcot, in his amphitheatre, featured French teenage girls and young women, often arriving from conditions of poverty and always hysterical, and in this way fell into a modern French tradition of exhibition as a theatrical expression of power and entitlement. Quasi-scientific rhetoric seeped into these spectacles of domination, validating a gawking at the pathological, the monstrous, the foreign, the Other. How white teenage girls came to bear the burden of needful gazes caught in discourses of civilization, dominance, and intelligence over irrationality is, of course, of interest. As Clare states, citing Rosemarie Garland-Thomson, "Perhaps the freakshow's most remarkable effect was to eradicate distinctions among a wide variety of bodies, conflating them under the sign of the freak-as-other."[16] In the nature of the sideshow promise, in Charcot's lectures, to see was to know, and the itch to know, venerated in nineteenth century French culture, absolved the onlooker. Looking was power, a power associated with empiricism and with spectatorship, a combination Charcot strategically deployed.

It could be argued that Charcot, on stage with his hysterics, was not unlike Dr Caligari at his fairground tent. Dr Caligari, a 1920 film doctor-hypnotist-fairground showman-murderer-bad guy, presents a cinematic nightmare that was occurring even more nightmarishly in the real and seemingly innocuous positivist figure of Dr Charcot. Villain par excellence, Caligari (especially in the early script version of the film, before the editorial decision was made to make the narrator, not Caligari, a raving 'madman' and the doctor the compassionate hero)[17] is marked by three things: his power to convince (especially the hypnotized Cesare), his theatrical hospitality – "Step right up folks!" – and his unrestrained authority.[18] Charcot found himself a celebrity in Paris and in other parts of the continent, people drawn to his theatrical persona and rhetorical muscle, as well as to his hypnotized hysterics. Charcot's appeal, "We have hysterics, who are the hysterics of Rubens!"[19] certainly presents in bravado what it lacks in objective tone. As Pierre Janet writes, Charcot "resembled certain religious orators, barristers, or politicians who, while giving the impression of improvising, nevertheless have written out their speeches in advance and memorized them."[20]

Furthermore: "Everything in his lectures was designed to attract attention and captivate the audience by means of visual and auditory impressions. The much-discussed dramatizations of his lectures on hysteria were not at all confined to hysteria. These dramatizations were present to the same degree in his lectures on multiple sclerosis or tabes dorsalis. The patients who were selected and presented, whether individually or in groups, whether similar or dissimilar, the schematic figures on the blackboard, the graphic résumés, the projections, the entire show had been designed and arranged for teaching purposes."[21]

There may have been particular persuasive force in stylistically combining anatomical presentation, carnival sideshow and positivism, since they similarly promise to show a person everything or to demonstrate something unique, available only through the singular spectacle they advertise. Behind Caligari's curtain lies a secret, one he will share if you can pay the fairground fee. Charcot's amphitheatre too was a site of privileged information, and his lectures an exercise in the hegemony of sight. Charcot once said in a lecture: "Voila la vérité. Je n'ai jamais dit autre chose; je n'ai pas l'habitude d'avancer des choses qui ne soient pas expérimentalement démontrables. Vous savez que j'ai pour principe de ne pas tenir compte de la théorie et de laisser de côté tous les préjugés: si vous voulez voir clair, il faut prendre les choses comme elles sont"[22] (Here is the truth. I have never said anything else; I am not in the habit of advancing things that are not experimentally demonstrable. You know that I hold dear the principles of not considering merely theory and of leaving aside all prejudices: if you want to see clearly, you must take things as they are.) There you have it – truth, demonstrable, easily conveyed. In the hysteria spectacle, one is assured of medicine's ocular and linguistic authority. Logocentric and thus reliable, the physician's speech can only tell the truth. In the fleshy display of the female body, narrated in accordance with Charcot's firm grasp of real, visible facts, the spectator is guaranteed that she sees both the most possible, and the most clearly.

Michel Foucault describes the nineteenth century medical era (paradigmatically begun at the end of the eighteenth century) as determined by "revealing through gaze and language what had previously been below and beyond (its) domain."[23] Alongside a historical account of cutting through the skulls of children to examine their brains, which Foucault sets as the exemplary event in the dawn of modern medicine obsessed with looking, Foucault notes, no less graphically:

> Medical rationality plunges into the marvellous density of perception … The eye becomes the depositary and source of clarity; it has the power to bring a truth to light; as it opens, the eye first opens the truth; a flexion that marks the transition from the world of classic clarity – from the 'enlightenment' – to the nineteenth century … The gaze is no longer reductive, it is, rather, that which establishes the individual in his irreducible quality. And thus it becomes possible to organize a rational language around it. The *object* of discourse may equally well be a *subject*, without the figures of objectivity being in any way altered … One could at last hold a scientifically structured discourse about an individual.[24]

Foucault presents a harrowing account of the medical gaze's power to move beyond description to actively constituting the subject, the individual. His is a portrait of the nineteenth century doctor that Charcot's regime supports. In their rational medical practice, doctors at the Salpêtrière found qualitative similarities from body to body, reducing the subject to their visible parts. A decisive project of Charcot and the doctors at the Salpêtrière was to categorize, chart, name, and regulate the hysteric's gestures, distilling French women's particular madnesses to a singular and general grande hystérie. At first glance, it seems that, above all, hysteria was the object of Charcot's discourse. But of course, the other discursive object is in fact a subject, the female patient. A person.

One can sense the tension between the female subject and her role as hysterical object in Charcot's description of the typical attack. The hysterical attack of la grande hystérie or hysteria major,[25] as famously determined and labelled by Charcot, is described by the director and his colleague Paul Richer in their *Démoniaques dans l'art*. Portrayed there as an unfolding drama,[26] a description that refers to the physiological complexities and visually astonishing gestures of the hysteric's body more than to her experience of the illness or its manifestations, the complexities of memory, longing, motivation and other privacies fall from attention while the symptomatic body comes into view. Under the empire of the physician's eye, the body appears as a series of visible gestures, divisible into recognizable types, renderable via description.

In summary: The first phase of the attack, the *période épileptoïde* is subdivided into three distinct phases: 1. *tonique* 2. *clonique* and 3. *résolution*. These, combined, often take only minutes, and involve large and rapid movements, twitching, and acrobatics enviable by professionals.[27] The second phase, depicted as "une dépense d'énergie exagérée de force musculaire"[28] (an exaggerated expenditure of energy by muscular force) is called, perhaps for its gymnastic movements, perhaps because of Charcot's love for the circus,[29] the *période de clownisme*. While classifiable, the movements and cries as they occur in this part of a hysterical attack resist concrete description. In clownism, the strength of the patient who may appear demure is "bien faite pour étonner le spectateur" (may astonish the spectator) and "[l]es contorsions consistent en des attitudes *étranges, imprévues, invraisemblables*" (the contortions consist of strange, unexpected, unbelievable attitudes or gestures). They are "illogiques."[30] (illogical). It is in this phase that the patient often makes the famous arc-de-cercle.[31] The acrobatics, Charcot and Richer note, are often interrupted by involuntary cries.[32] The following phase, the *attitudes passionnelles*, is marked by hallucination, in which "il est facile de suivre toutes les péripéties du drame auquel elle croit assister et où elle joue le principal rôle"[33] (it is easy to follow all of the incidents in the drama (s)he believes to be witnessing or where (s)he plays the principal role). The hallucinated drama ends in a *période terminale* where the patient "vient de retrouver son équilibre normal"[34] (comes to regain her normal state), regaining consciousness or awareness. As patients emerge from an attack, they can't believe the positions or contractions of their bodies, "sur lesquels leur volonté n'a aucune prise"[35] (over which their will has no hold). This description from *Les Démoniaques dans l'art* is of a typical attack, though Charcot and Richer note that the attacks are subject to variation; they can skip a phase, run phases out of order, etc.[36] Nevertheless, these subdivided phases occur with enough regularity to make up Charcot's definition of a standard hysterical attack, a descriptive phenomenon for which he was and is most well-known. A type had been distilled from the multiple corporeal and experiential variations of hysteria.

The photographs, bedside transcripts, and public demonstrations of attacks iterate this systematic view of the hysterical experience repeatedly.

The real pain the hysteric may experience is alluded to in the *Démoniaques* text, which even seems to suggest that physicians had pity for the patients. However, this pity makes a temporary rhetorical appearance and seems primarily used as a device to elicit interest from the reader. As the patient recovers from the attack, the doctors record, "des cris de douleur déchirants; elle supplie les assistants de la soulager"[37] (harrowing cries of pain; she begs the assistants to soothe her). Terrible cries punctuate the visible phenomena of the attack. These cries present "un cachet de souffrance tellement horrible que les assistants, même les plus habitués, ne peuvent se défendre d'une pénible émotion"[38] (a mark of suffering so horrible that the assistants, even the most accustomed, can't help but give in to a difficult emotion).

There are few documented facts that support this thesis of medical sympathy.[39] The number of images of the patients' bodies in pain, classed, labelled, and reproduced for the medical and non-medical public, points to a violence of looking that was made more brutal by the medical failure to clearly see or worse – its having turned its head, not acknowledging the patient's pain. Charcot's brief words about the patient's pitiable condition, not pursued in any attempts at symptomatic relief or treatment, only make him more accountable for his violations. More than this, knowing that the patient was in pain, hearing her cries and finding them worthy of note, Charcot and his colleagues continued to provoke hysterical attacks for the purposes of demonstration. Many lectures centred around applying pressure to varying zones of the patient's body in order to produce attacks. Alleviation of symptoms was part of the performance, but doctors aimed, most of all, to activate hysteria's most dramatic symptoms in order to describe them. They were responsible, above all, for pioneering what Didi-Huberman describes as a "dreadfully effective outbreak of images."[40] The patient, under Charcot's regime, became charged with the task of experiencing and performing her pain before a live audience, before the camera lens, before the poised pen of Doctor Bourneville, who sat ready to record her "involuntary confidences."[41]

These confidences, words uttered in the patient's delirium, portray a real life, marked by what others in the nineteenth century, most notably Sigmund Freud, would call trauma. In her attacks, Augustine would often deliver a fragmentary account of her past. Lovers would appear and disappear; she would see and be afraid of the eyes of cats. She saw and fended off her stepfather who assaulted her. She cried out against the administration of drugs.

One must ask, how does one quantify this:

> *Période de délire.* – Regard effrayé: « Attrapez les rats! » – L … s'assoit. La tête est incliné à droite; regard et geste mençants; elle a de la sputation. « Pardon! Laissez-moi. » Elle respire très vite, comme si elle manquait d'air[42] (*Delirious Period.* – Terrified look: "Catch the rats!" – L … sits. The head is inclined to the right; menacing look and gesticulation; she spits. "Excuse me! Leave me be!" She breathes very quickly, like she cannot get enough air.)

or this:

> « Ah! Mon cou! Ah! Mon cou! » Puis elle crie et perd connaissance[43] ("My neck! Ah! My neck!" Then she screams and loses consciousness.)

or this:

> « Et je ne te vaux pas? … tu n'étais pas digne d'être aimé! … » Effroi. « Les rats au derrière! … Ils me mordent! … Maman! » Elle rejette brusquement les bras, découvrant ainsi les fesses. « Chameau! Pignouf! Vaurien! »[44] ("Am I worthless to you? You don't want me? … you were not worth loving! …" Fear. "Rats in the ass! … They are biting me! … Maman!" She throws back her arms brusquely, uncovering her breasts. "Scoundrel! Lout! Brute!")

One wants to resist rationalizing the experiences that these troubled and fiercely individual utterances present. In fact, one must acknowledge the impossibility of doing so. Augustine's hallucinated past and her repeated responses to it while in the asylum present a raw subjectivity, igniting the rigidly descriptive documents with a quick vulnerability. Her personal past and her relationship to it differ from the other hysterical patients' experiences and conveyances of their lives. This fact may seem obvious, but Charcot overlooked this gleaming individuality, reducing the entirety of Augustine's life before she came to the Salpêtrière to the popular objective concept of heredity or to the generic category, of "delirium." Medical notation veers, at this point, in this typifying name, away from neutrality.

Charcot insisted, "It's not something out of a novel: *hysteria has its laws* … I can assure you that it has 'the regularity of a mechanism.'"[45] He aimed to make good on his word. Onstage, the director made certain that he could conjure various symptoms of hysteria with precision. Experimentation with ferronization, electroshock, brutal touch, and hypnosis ensured that the patient could perform her hysterical body on command. These experiments were replicated for Bourneville and Régnard's major photographic project, in association with resident photographer Albert Londe, the *Iconographie*.

Charcot and Augustine's audience was predominantly male and upperclass. In an era marked by the popularization of medical and anthropological scientific spectacle, the audience was also, not surprisingly, made up of as many extra-medical elites as medical professionals. Charcot's "evening receptions on Tuesdays in his private mansions, 217 Boulevard Saint-Germain, were of course attended by high society: the elite of medicine, politicians (Waldeck-Rousseau), the most famous painters and sculptors, architects, men of letters, art collectors, police chiefs (Lépine), and even cardinals (Lavigerie)."[46]

Didi-Huberman's account of the Tuesday lectures begins as follows: "And this was Charcot's great clinical and pedagogical promise, continually renewed: 'In a moment I will give you a first-hand experience, so to speak, of this pain; I will help you to recognize all its characteristics' – how? – 'by presenting you five patients' – and he would have them enter the stage of his amphitheatre."[47] On stage, the hysteric's body was harmed continually in order to produce symptoms of hysteria for medico-spectacular ends: the body was called into hysterical presentation by caresses, aggressive touch, sudden noises, penetration and mechanical pressure, provocations to induce symptoms to be described by the hospital director. To produce pain. After having a nurse dress or undress and groom a patient for the stage, Charcot might hypnotically suggest pains to her or bring on an attack by pressing on her ovaries. Contorting, seizing, falling into paralysis, and hallucinating to the interest, if not delight, of spectators in the nature of a fairground show, the woman on stage was a spectacle of pain alongside Charcot's explanatory presentation.

In reference to the hypnotized patient Augustine, Charcot says (in the true form of a ringmaster): "What we have here before our eyes is truly, in all its simplicity, the man-machine dreamed up by La Mettrie!"[48] He further remarks that he has yet another trick; her body can be articulated at will: "Her head is pressed against the back of a chair, then the muscles of her back, thighs and legs are rubbed, and her feet are placed on a second chair: the rigid body remains in this position for a rather long time ... it is possible to place a weight of 40 kilograms on the stomach without causing the body to bend."[49] On top of the host of spectacular physical symptoms on display, female patients at the Salpêtrière were expertly manipulated into hysterical attacks, based on the traumatic experiences from which their symptoms most likely stemmed, for the purpose of show. In a public performance, Augustine would *actually experience* the emotional and physical pain of traumatic memory. In this situation: "In front of everyone, on stage, in front of the lens, there could be a replay of the 'shameful action,' the 'affair,' the 'abuse' ... here, a rape ... And is it hard not to imagine that Augustine, through her memory of such assaults, must have found it terrifying to see the faces of the public all around her, undressing each of her *attitudes passionnelles* over and over."[50]

Author and critic Mirbeau, in *Chroniques du Diable*, describes a scene he believes his readership is already familiar with, due to the popularity of the lecture series:

> Vous connaissez la scène; elle a déja été peinte cent fois. Tout à coup, chez la malade, la vue s'altère, l'oeil prend une expression d'angoisse. Les membres se contractent en tous sens. Puis ce sont des grands mouvements, des soubresauts brusques qui courbent le corps en arc de cercle. Succèdent d'étranges attitudes dramatiques ou comiques (quel comique!). Elle a peur: elle voit des fantômes, des gens qui veulent l'emmener. Soudain, ce sont des anges, des figures riantes, et elle leur sourit. Elle est en extase; elle murmure des paroles sans suite; parfois elle serre entre ses bras un être imaginaire. Enfin, c'est l'abattement, l'épuisement, la profonde mélancholie. Et c'est tout, la pièce est jouée.[51]
>
> (You know the scene; it has already been painted a hundred times. All of a sudden, the patient's vision alters, the eye takes on an anguished expression. Her members contract in all possible ways. Then there come the giant movements, brusque spasmodic leaps that twist the body into the arc-de-cercle. Strange dramatic or comic attitudes follow (what a comic!). She is afraid: she sees phantoms, people who want to take her away. All of a sudden they become angels, laughing figures, and she smiles at them. She is in ecstasy; she murmurs disjointed words; sometimes she embraces an imaginary being. Finally, it is depression, exhaustion, profound melancholy. And that's it, the scene is played.)

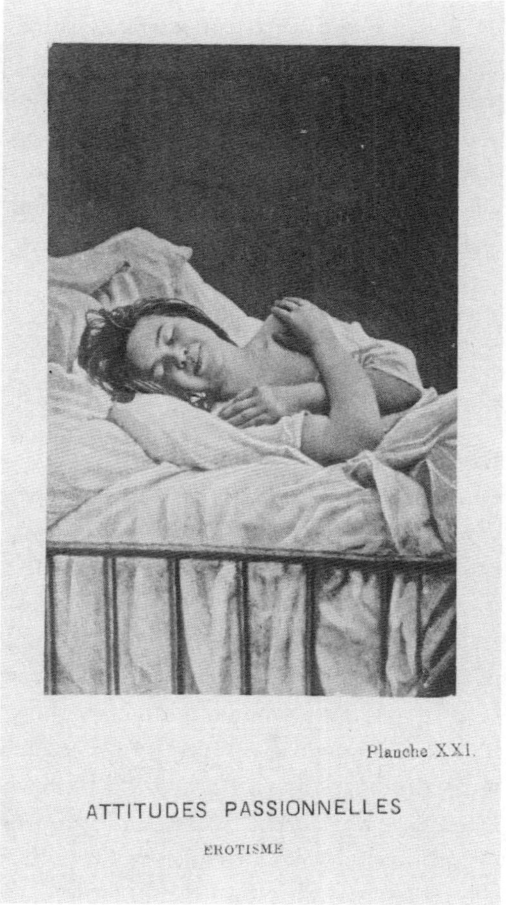

1.2 Augustine, *Attitudes passionnelles :* Érotisme. Plate XXI, *Iconographie photographique de la Salpêtrière* 2, 1878.

Anguish, fear, ecstasy and its deflation, a body in agony – private hallucinations so potent they leave the patient exhausted and depressed. These were enacted before the unrelenting gazes of male witnesses. The descriptions are troubling, and the mobilization of medical power based on the visibility of the subject who despite her wildly articulating body, is systematically ignored as the object of a morbidly curious audience's gawking, reads obviously in Didi-Huberman and Mirbeau's descriptions. But what is witnessed?

Representation is always suspended in a tenuous relationship to both power and sight. Being visible, in the medical spectacle, is not the same thing as being recognized. Being looked at is not the same thing as being seen. Being audible is not the same thing as being listened to or heard. Similarly, being described is an inadequate mode of appearing. Salpêtrière patients who became objects for description did not, as in the narrative commonly associated with Pinel, languish in their cells in darkness and obscurity, but they were nonetheless obscured by way of spectacle. The wildness of human experience, the raw emotional symptomatology of hysteria – agony expressed gesturally – these became shadowed under the superficiality of medical rhetoric.

LIVING REMAINDERS

Exemplary of his wider project of rationalizing the irrational body, Charcot created a synoptic table that recorded and typified the most expressive movements of the female body in hysterics. Everything was charted, from postures to excretions and temperatures, from menstrual cycles to the "cries from the alcohol flames used in 'thermocautery.'"[52] As Salpêtrière photographer Albert Londe writes in his *La Photographie Médicale*, images of patients must be taken and compared rigorously, in order to deduce a typified symptomatology: "Certain modifications of the face that by themselves were not recognized as constituting in isolation a clear indication of a particular illness took on a very great importance when they were found over and over in similar sufferers. Unless one happened by chance to have patients show the same expressions at the same time, they might go unnoticed. However, with close-up photographs of them, one can make comparisons between a number of examples and deduce the typical modifications of different aspects."[53] While such corporeal reduction is the foundation of medicine's practice of differential diagnosis, it is impossible to conceive that any translation from multidimensional subjectivity to flat, interpretable objectivity can occur without producing an insistent living remainder.

The tension between type and individuality played out in other modern projects concerning the face and the photograph.[54] As Tom Gunning writes, tracing the "gnostic" impulse of nineteenth century physiognomy via photographic and film media, "the study of the face possesses its own history, as well as its own ambivalent relation to systems and methods of knowledge."[55] Most notable among scientific physiognomical works are Duchenne de Boulogne's *The Mechanism of Human Facial Expression* and

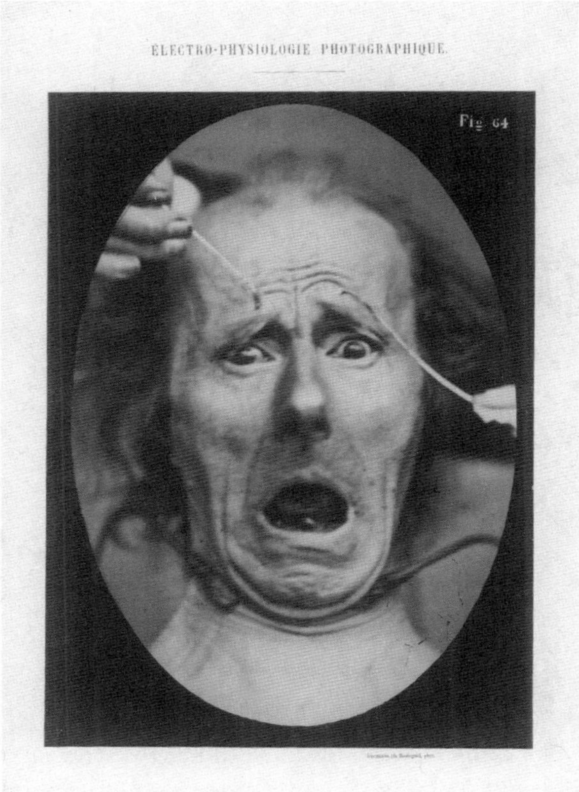

1.3 *Electro-Physiologie, Figure 64*. Photograph by Guillaume-Benjamin-Amand Duchenne de Boulogne and Adrien Tournachon, 1854–56. Also known as *Fear and Horror* and reproduced as part of a composite Plate 7 in Duchenne de Boulogne's *Méchanisme de la physionomie humaine, ou analyse* électrophysiologique *de l'expression des passions*, 1862. Subsequently also reproduced in Charles Darwin, *Expression of Emotion in Man and Animals*, 1872.

Charles Darwin's *Expression of Emotion in Man and Animals,* which feature the rigorous classification of the errant elements of human emotion and spontaneous gesture. Phillip Prodger compares Darwin's process of photograph collecting for the volume to his collection of specimens documented in the *Voyage of the Beagle.* However, while dead specimens were mostly satisfactory for Darwin's earlier work, when, in the 1860s, Darwin turned his attention to emotional expression, finding the right specimen

1.4 Oscar Rejlander, *Surprise and Astonishment.* In Charles Darwin, *Expression of Emotion in Man and Animals*, 1872.

became more complicated, Prodger notes, for, as he says, "Expressions are fleeting, complex behaviours, not simple things that can be sampled in a conventional way."[56] Prodger paints a rather sensuous picture of Darwin visiting English shops that dealt in photographs in order to look for the perfect photos to illustrate his volume.[57] Leafing through photos, looking for expressions that functioned properly as examples that would signify obviously to readers the emotional states he described, Darwin found himself caught between the curatorial itch for the perfect image and the scientifically motivated desire for truth. His notebooks are scrawled with notes on the legitimacy of expressions; some photographs are marked as genuine and some are marked as inauthentic or staged, like the "sham laughter" that occurs in one of the pages of Duchenne de Boulogne's *The Mechanism of Human Facial Expression*.[58] In fact, Darwin sought photographs of infants and mad people on several occasions, believing these more 'primitive' sets of humanity incapable of performing inauthentic versions of spontaneous, universal emotions. In the end, Darwin's editorial mode of selecting his illustrations from the collections accumulated by the commons was discarded in favour of a collaboration with photographer Oscar Rejlander, who appears in six of the photographic plates in Darwin's

Expression. Though Rejlander was a famed portraitist, Darwin decided that his staged emotions read much more conveniently and obviously to the spectator. Rejilander's mouth agape, eyes wide and hands thrown up in feigned surprise is particularly delightful; it conveys a fine representational approximation of astonishment.

For his book, Darwin also used several of Duchenne de Boulogne's electrically configured facial expressions from the experiments with the musculature of facial expression famously undertaken by the physician. Mechanically arrived at via electrical wands, these expressions were reliably classified according to their physical muscular arrangements. Grimaces, considered beyond the scope of typification or regular human expression, were provocatively excluded from Duchenne's systematic work.[59] Not every emotional experience could be conjured or adequately represented, however sophisticated the technology. Feelings are inconveniently honest and tricky to capture. While Duchenne aimed to treat the human face as a mechanism, humans stubbornly continued to produce expressions that were unclassifiable. In Darwin's *Expression* as well, it seems, authenticity was overthrown and pedantic staging embraced. Sham emotions resembled more closely the authentic typological expressions Darwin wrote about.[60] And real human expressions, as they presented themselves in photo shops, were too ambiguous to serve a work on expressive typology. In scientific works of the nineteenth century that sought to pin down emotions, faces, it seems, were always getting in the way.

In the 1840s, a literary fad emerged wherein Parisians were divided into various types, their manners and lifestyles ostensibly coded in their facial structures. "Physiognomy became a popular social science in nineteenth century Paris, where it provided a visual means to order the diverse and anonymous masses that surrounded the urban dwellers."[61] The unhinging potential of modern life in the city was a topic explored in detail by culture-makers and physicians-turned-social-commentators at the turn of the century. Being exposed to a diversity of people in city spaces was one of the documented causes for hysteria; it was a potential threat to the mental health of all genders. Physiognomical literature may have acted as an antidote to the psychological strife people like sociologist Georg Simmel asserted was at the heart of modern urban life. He wrote that "if the unceasing external contact of numbers of persons in the city should be met by the same number of inner reactions as in the small town, in which one knows almost every person he meets and to each of whom he has a positive relationship, one would be completely atomized internally and would fall into an unthinkable mental condition."[62] The healthy, necessary, but detrimental response to excessive external stimulation, according to him, was to form a rational organ on the consciousness, to build up a layer of crust, so to speak, to filter the otherwise staggering amount of stimuli. The modern urban setting – busy streets and dense population – could force a "mutual strangeness and repulsion."[63] To isolate oneself in the metropolis was to protect oneself from being psychological annihilated by the onslaught of potential, yet unachieved relationships. For survival, things must be kept on the surface. The alienated individual was forced into further alienation to protect herself from psychological implosion. Tragically, this almost always resulted, for Simmel, in a "blasé outlook."[64] In fact, Simmel writes, "there is perhaps no psychic phenomenon which is so unconditionally reserved to the city as the blasé outlook … The essence of the blasé attitude is an indifference toward the distinction between things … They appear to the blasé person in a homogenous, flat and gray colour with no one of them worthy of being preferred to another."[65]

One can see how the state Simmel describes could be comfortingly countered by a system of human classification, a codified manner of dividing up the immense volume of faces one encounters in the urban environment. The modern French citizen, plagued by too much looking, could rest his mind by diminishing his focus. In the caricature of the human type as it appears in social physiology, it is not the particularity of the individual that is sought after, but a category. This suits the person afraid of losing his bearings because of his overwhelmed perception, saturated with too much particularity, with too many living subjectivities. All those unknown faces in the crowd become too much; grouping them to reduced types offers a simple but inadequate solution so that, despite its efforts, physiology acted as an extension of the visual reduction that took place in the blasé outlook. The hysteric was one more type, appearing in the black and white tones of the photograph, constructed by a barrage of classifications that aimed to level her particularity. The reduction of women to symptoms was not simply a response to the democratization of madness made possible across genders by urbanization, though the productive force of literatures that aim to classify the spectrum and range of experiences of human being does indicate a certain anxious response to what cannot be rationalized. One wonders, and I will indeed address, especially in the coming chapters, why so much classifying and typifying work occurred at this moment in Western European history. And why so much work was done to contain women and girls.

In a paradoxical move – for hysteria was, symptomatically, distinctly corporeal, three dimensional and erratic – Charcot enacted his "medical dream" of relegating the "'case' into a two-dimensional space of simultaneity and tabulation, into an outline against a ground of Cartesian coordinates."[66]

The two-dimensional synecdoche of Charcot and Richer's table can equally be elaborated into three-dimensional space, for Charcot touted that, at the Salpêtrière, they were "in possession of a kind of *living pathological museum*."[67] In a statement that brings to mind the image of the aesthetic and dismantleable wax figure, the *Venus Specola*, Charcot called the hypnotized hysteric, upon whose body precise symptoms could be teased to the surface and held for any length of time, a "tableau vivant"[68] (a living tableau/a living table).

Charcot spoke proudly of being in charge of a hospital he had equipped with the technology to adequately document and demonstrate hysteria and its host of intriguing bodily manifestations. Preceding the preface to Salpêtrière photographer Albert Londe's *Photographie Médicale*, a mutually affirming performance between director and photographer berates the reader with the merits of medical photography, in the form of correspondence. Londe's letter to Charcot appears first, and he writes:

> Cher Maître … Cet Ouvrage, fruit des travaux des recherches que j'ai pu faire grâce à votre bienveillant appui, montrera, je l'espère, les nombreux services que la Photographie peut rendre aux Sciences médicales, services que vous avez si bien pressentis en créant le premier laboratoire officiel de Photographie dans les Hôpitaux. Veuillez recevoir, cher Maître, l'hommage de ce livre. Trop heureux si j'ai pu contribuer, pour ma modeste part, à l'oeuvre de l'École de la Salpêtrière dont vous êtes le chef si vénéré et si aimé.[69]
>
> (Dear Master … This work, the outcome of the research that I have done with your kind support, shows, I hope, the many services that Photography offers the Medical Sciences, services that you enabled by creating the first official laboratory of Photography in the Hospitals. Please accept, dear Master, the homage of this book. I am only too happy if I could contribute, in my small way, to the work of the School of the Salpêtrière of which you are the revered and loved director.)

Charcot replies in an equally ingratiating and simultaneously self-aggrandizing manner:

> Mon Cher Monsieur Londe,
> J'accepte avec grand plaisir la dédicace de votre intéressant Ouvrage sur la Photographie médicale, car ce m'est une occasion d'insister sur les réels et importants services que la Photographie est destinée à rendre aux Sciences médicales … je vous souhaite bien sincérement à votre bel et bon livre tout le succès qu'il mérite d'obtenir[70]
>
> (My Dear Mr Londe,
> I accept with great pleasure the dedication of your interesting work about medical photography, because it is an opportunity for me to insist on the real and important services that Photography is destined to provide medical science … I sincerely wish you well with your beautiful and good book and hope it receives all the success it deserves.)

The praise for one another and the institutions each represents – medical science and photography, the Salpêtrière and its photographic studio – is accompanied by praise for the pairing of institutions. In the guise of a sincere exchange of letters, the overture to Londe's volume does not let the reader forget that photography and medicine are destined to be valuable and exciting partners. Londe elaborates the specifics of this relationship in the manual; the accuracy and longevity of the photograph provides medical science with the optimal visibility required for its observational practice. The photograph is more reliable than the human eye, capable of registering great detail. And the photograph lasts longer than the physician's gaze, making it most useful for analyzing that detail after the instant in which it occurs has passed. Photography is also reproducible, so that a single case can be replicated as much as desired and even sent abroad – say, to smaller communities where doctors lack access to diagnostic resources.[71]

Londe, hired at the Salpêtrière in 1878 by Charcot, was an innovative and experimental photographer. It was as the hospital's resident photographer that he developed his chronophotography processes and mechanisms that would contribute to early film technologies. Artistically and technically adventurous, Londe worked on a nine-lens camera that could take sequential photos, powered by electromagnetic energy and triggered by a metronome.

1.5 Albert Londe's Twelve-Lens Camera.

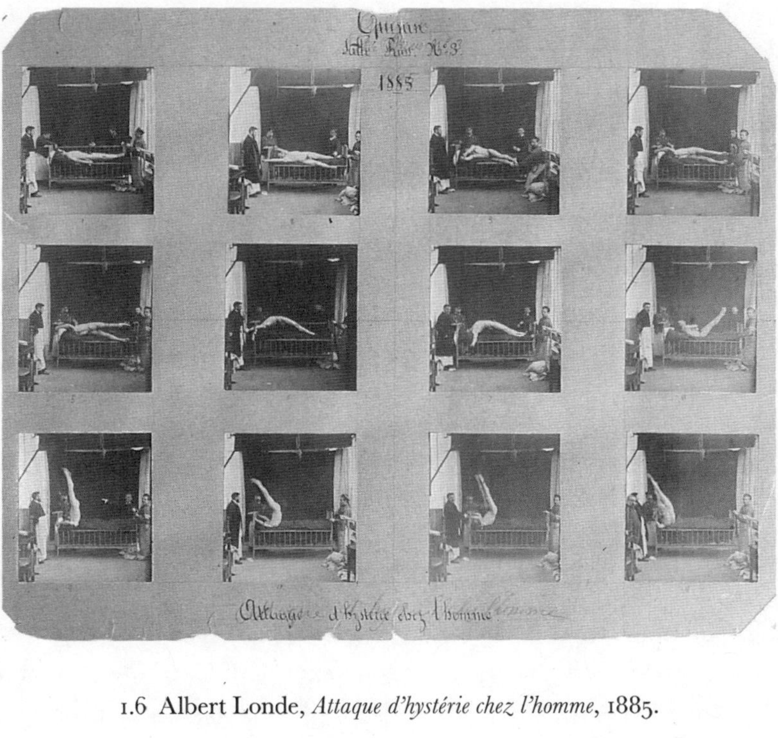

1.6 Albert Londe, *Attaque d'hystérie chez l'homme*, 1885.

He later refined his apparatus, reducing the amount of time it took to capture images and increasing the number of lenses to twelve.[72] The results are rather astonishing, resulting in a series of images that convey some of the dynamism of the hysterical attack, though they also stutter its presentation.[73]

Figure 1.6, produced in 1885, was published in *La Nature* in 1893, the same year Londe published *La Photographie Médicale.* An aesthetic and technological achievement, the photographic series is also instructive. The theatrical backdrop points to the image's technical construction, the "natural" setting of the sickbed to the supposed ability for the camera to capture from nature, only better than the natural eye. The contorting body confirms that the swiftness of the attack transcends the power of the eye to pin an image in place. But competing with the kinetic hysteric and overcoming the weaknesses of the eye is the camera, accurate and able to freeze passing time. Able to freeze the vulnerable body. Why? To be able to look at it. Segmented, sequenced, laid bare.

The printed photographic plates of hysterics taken by Londe correspond hauntingly to the mechanism itself. The image of the camera, and its miniature captures of the hysteric's body, taken together, form a strange technological echo. The machine imprints itself on the form of the body, and on the medical setting, its hegemonic processes altering its associated subjects. Where, in advance of the camera, the eye would see one body, in movement, it now sees the body replicated according to the mechanism's grid of lenses. The body tabulates. One sees the moment, the whole scene, indelibly marked by the machine itself. The patient, in duration and body, is both repeated and cut up or cut off. Looking at this naked body – in this case that of a male hysterical patient, jolting from twist to turn in twelve precise squares – one can't help but see the cameras technical mastery here.

Londe's volume, which is a description of his photographic methods, is part technical user manual, part celebratory sales pitch for the photographic medium and it never forgets to venerate Charcot's hysteria project while it promotes the value of extreme visibility. Charcot did not fail to reciprocate. Structurally, the hospital was fully equipped with tools for observation and presentation. Charcot boasted, in a lecture: "We have an *anatomo-pathological museum* with a *casting* annex and a *photographic studio*; a well-equipped *laboratory of anatomy* and of *pathological physiology* … an *ophthalmology service*, an essential complement to any institute of neuropathology; the teaching *amphitheatre* where I have the honour of receiving you and, which is equipped, as you can see, with all the modern tools of demonstration."[74] Charcot's students rightfully commented that he had raised the image "to the rank of the first order."[75] Whether fractured into rigid tabulation or paraded before a live audience, medical subjects under Charcot's direction became objects for the purpose of medical looking, appearing as classifiable bodies around which to construct a rational medical narrative. The photograph is a distinct stage upon which the theatre of reduction via representation took place. The patient became the picture of hysteria.

While looking was integral to the director's empirical medical process, in the following example, one can sense its blatant inadequacy. An intern described Charcot's analytical process:

> He sits down near a bare table and immediately has the patient to be studied brought in. The patient is then completely stripped. The intern reads the 'observation,' while the Master listens attentively. Then there is a long silence during which he gazes; he gazes at the patient and drums his fingers on the table … Then he instructs the patient to move in a certain way, makes her speak, asks for her reflexes to be measured, for her sensitivity to be measured. And again he falls silent, Charcot's mysterious silence. Finally he brings in a second patient, examines her like the first, call for a third and still, without a word, compares them.[76]

Didi-Huberman remarks that these accounts given by Souques and Meige "suggest that Charcot could nearly forget traditional questions like 'What is the matter?' or 'Where does it hurt?' For he seemed to *have always already seen*."[77]

Taking note of the importance of physiological examination, Jules Claretie, director of the Théâtre Français and author of the novel *Les Amours d'un Interne*, described Charcot as one who symbolically furrowed his brow.[78] Pierre Janet, a student of the director, emphasized Charcot's "talent *d'observer* et la minutie de ses *observations*" (31) (His talent of observing and the minutiae of his observations). Even Freud referred to Charcot primarily as a "visuel" and described his experience of the doctor's method, uncritically, as being akin to "watching Adam name all the animals."[79]

The predominance of the value of medical visuality is strikingly obvious in the case of the physician who defined hysteria and his medical colleagues. Still, Charcot's presumptuous claim of that sight straightforwardly promised clarity was occasionally, if not consistently, undermined. Looking is its own kind of violence, a violence worth examination. Especially since the physicians under Charcot's direction were not at all interested in cure but rather invested their energies in demonstration, the implications of their observation demand ethical judgement. At the same time, we must ask: how could looking, charting and naming ever be enough, even according to the terms set out by medical science, in the face of such an incoherent condition, in the face of such stubborn personality?

Charcot was famous for uttering statements about the ease and obviousness of his method of seeing – statements, it is worth noting, that seem oddly casual given his commitments to empiricism. He said, quoting Molière, "A ceux qui me rapprochent de toujours parler de l'hystérie, et avant de m'expliquer plus complètement à ce sujet, je répondrai par ce mot de Molière: « Je dis la même chose, parce que c'est toujours la même chose »; je constate, et rien de plus"[80] (To those who reproach me for always speaking of hysteria, and before I explain myself completely on this matter, I will respond with these words from Molière: "I say the same thing because it's always the same thing"; I state what I see, nothing more). The director seems to have been saying, innocently, that all he does is state what he sees. He is simply a medium of transmission. This flagrant assertion that aims to connote Charcot's positivist position may have indeed had a practical root; after becoming director of the Salpêtrière, Charcot never treated a patient in medical rounds.[81] He was *only* one who saw without touching, described only his objective and thus limited observations. Without spending time with these patients offstage, Charcot still believed that he was able to diagnose them accurately, and to describe their symptoms causally and with precision.

But how does one reconcile what Mireille Dottin-Orsini describes as "L'*Iconographie* avec ses cinq observations et ses quarante clichés de femmes hystériques"[82] (The *Iconographie* with its five observations and its forty clichés about female hysterics) with Claretie's much more dire characterization of the Salpêtrière as the "Versailles de la douleur"[83] (Versailles of pain)? Charcot said, "Pouvoir reproduire un état pathologique, c'est la perfection"[84] (To be able to reproduce a pathological state; that's perfection.) How does the Salpêtrière project of picturing the hysterical body alongside well-made description and rigorous categorical terminology stand up against real pain and real personhood?

SPECTACULAR RESISTANCE

The photographs in the *Iconographie* are a record and an extension of the Salpêtrière's theatre of pain and power. To photograph a patient like Augustine was to watch and record her suffering so that it could be looked at again. The *Iconographie* photograph is above all a reproduction of pain and an index of violence.

In the *Iconographie*, we see the same woman over several photographs in poses indicating pleasure, defiance, helplessness, combat. We are aware at once of the *physicality* of the woman in the images. We see, expressed in Augustine's musculature, tension in the sinews of her neck, the rigid contraction of her arm as it forms a fist to fight her brother or stepfather as they appear to her in her delirium. The strength and stamina required for the feat of the arc-de-cercle astonishes the viewer. Her mouth, set in a cry, expresses what we can only imagine is a gasp or a scream, the ambiguity leaving us wondering why the mouth gapes, and for or at what. As she surrenders to her own embrace, features softened, we nearly sigh in relief with this woman, whose body, the photographs indicate, labours intensely as it gesticulates in accordance with her private agonies, seeming to genuinely rest only infrequently.

Formally, the medical photograph, as it appears in the *Iconographie*, seems structurally incongruous with its content. This is precisely because its content is contestable. Is the subject, in fact, what is described in the caption or is it something else? Read anatomically, the *Iconographie* photograph is divisible into an upper and a lower half. Above the line, the body contorts and releases. Here, at the level of the photographically rendered body, "flesh (is) in the foreground."[85] Flesh – the tactile planes and surfaces of the kinetic body, and also the elusive living personhood of this body in particular – fools us, perhaps, into thinking we are getting to know Augustine. Below the line, the medical curators of Augustine's private experience impose a scaffold of quasi-information. There, Augustine appears under several names – X, L, Louise, Augustine. The multiplicity of names can be taken as a refusal by the Salpêtrière doctors to see or transmit Augustine to the public as an autonomous singularity, a person with a name, recognizable as herself. In the authorial "signing" of Augustine's name as a multiplicity of letters and designations, the woman as referent is replaced by a play of ambiguous signification and referentiality. The name as identification disperses and drops out and what becomes consistent,

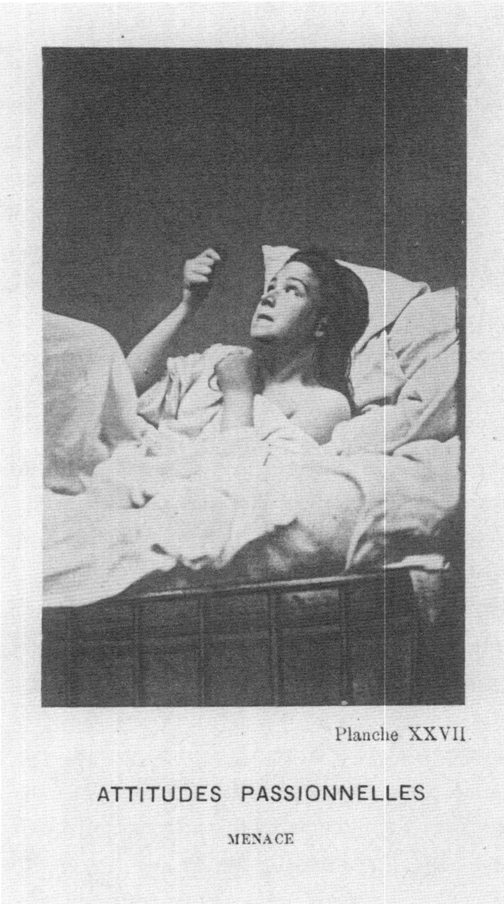

1.7 Augustine. *Attitudes passionnelles : Menace.* Plate XXVII, *Iconographie photographique de la Salpêtrière* 2, 1878.

instead, is the tyranny of classification employed self-consciously at the Salpêtrière. What we see is labelled "Attitudes Passionnelles" or "Extase" or "Clownisme." The condition or phase of the attack, rigorously consistent, takes precedence over the patient. Sometimes the woman Augustine is not even identified.

The medical intention regarding the potency of the label over the patient's own person is not merely implied by the iconographic document; Charcot also spoke to the relationship between corporeal image and description, saying, "Seule la parole suggestive donne corps au symptôme"[86] (Only evocative speech gives body to the symptom). In the director's view, the body does not even have corporeality until it has been

1.8 Augustine. *Hystéro-Épilepsie : État normal.* Plate XIV, *Iconographie photographique de la Salpêtrière* 2, 1878.

justified by the interpretation of the physician. The doctor's speech, not the hysteric's body, has "puissance"[87] (power). This is what ideologically and methodologically underlies the compilation of images and labels for the *Iconographie.* In one photograph, Marquer points out, the patient Rosalie appears, in all visible ways, to be normal and healthy. The doctors, though, can see that she's a hysteric. This privileged knowledge is indicated at the rational level of the label. Marquer calls this a demonstration of the "indispensable médiation du regard du savant"[88] (the indispensable mediation of the savant's gaze).

However, we know that the pairings of description and image are not always as objective as they appear, despite the clean aesthetic the label provides. Sometimes, they are utterly false. Didi-Huberman notes one such artistic lie. In the photograph of Augustine in her *état normal*, Baudelaire remarks that she is posed in contrived modesty.[89] This is an easily palatable image, one of a sort of ideal domestic woman, happy to be looked at.

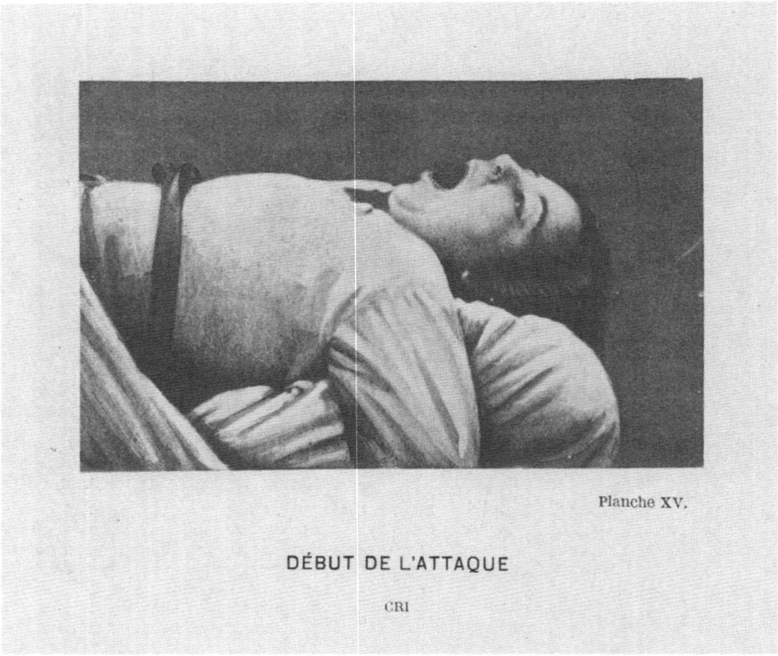

1.9 Augustine. *Début de l'attaque : Cri.* Plate XV, *Iconographie photographique de la Salpêtrière* 2, 1878.

It is tempting to think, alongside the other photographs, especially the neighbouring plate of Augustine crying out at the onset of an attack, that this must be the original Augustine, the authentic one.

However, in the "normal" image, Augustine's image has been heavily constructed. The hand holding her head so softly, creating an aura of civility is, in fact, her paralyzed hand. It has been placed by an intern or by the photographer.[90] Here, the photographers and doctors at the Salpêtrière have not only photographically constructed their particular brand of madness; they have also (re)constructed "normalcy." This example of an overt curatorial construction of the body, conveying only the most desirable visual information in order to bolster the hysteria project, points to a lack of honesty that is always already present in the structure of the photographs of patients in the *Iconographie*. In these visual fractions where the corporeal and personal sit above a label, the descriptive anchor tries to covertly undermine its remainder. Looking becomes overlooking.

Patients expressed their objections to the Salpêtrière's photographic procedures. They complained to doctors that they disliked the way their images were being used, but their medical superiors discounted their apprehensions, instead insisting that being photographed was "therapeutic" for the patients.[91] As physician Joseph Delboeuf remarked after his visit to the Salpêtrière: "Par parenthèse, les jeunes filles à qui j'ai parlé se plaignaient de l'abus qu'on faisait de leurs images. On comprend ces plaintes. Mais, quand on va au fond des choses, cet abus est plus imaginaire que réel. Qui, en dehors du monde scientifique, se procure ces recueils si chers et dont le texte est si rébarbatif?"[92] (Parenthetically, the young women I spoke to complained about the abuses we make of their images. We understand these complaints. But, when we get to the bottom of things, this abuse is more imaginary than real. Who, outside the scientific community, procures these precious anthologies for which the accompanying text is so imposing?)

The parenthetical nature of his remark is telling. The patients' complaints are dismissed as being imaginary since, really, it is only the scientific community that makes use of the photographs. The excuse that the pain and humiliation of patients is morally passable because it is of interest to the monolithically valuable institution of medical science pervades the entirety of Delboeuf's "Une visite à la Salpêtrière." The same excuse appears continually in Charcot's lectures and other written work and the work of his colleagues. Sometimes Charcot addresses the issue head on, explaining that while each patient presented as a case on stage requires treatment, what will help them in the long run will be the outcomes of a nosological and anatomical clinical practice.[93] Other times, the dismissal of patient distress occurs in a strangely celebratory manner. In one case, Charcot delights being spared the trouble of provoking an attack because the patient's feelings about appearing publicly will cause her to succumb to hysterical fits: "Now look at this patient. It will not be necessary for us to intervene, for the emotion that she has experienced at finding herself before so many people in the lecture room will save us the trouble of provoking an attack. In the first phase, rhythmical jerkings of the right arm, like the movements of hammering occur. The patient has her eyes closed."[94]

Susan Sontag, in *Regarding the Pain of Others*, considers the violence implicit in looking at images of suffering and in taking such images. She writes: "Photographs objectify: they turn an event or a person into something that can be possessed."[95] And elsewhere, "Les photographies sont une façon d'emprisonner la réalité, que l'on conçoit comme rétive, impossible à saisir: elles la font se tenir tranquille"[96] (Photographs are a way of imprisoning reality, unruly, impossible to grasp: they make it quiet itself). Sontag indicates a violent and compensatory nature at the heart of the photograph, its power to seize or capture a life and render it a mere object or thing. In this way, she is not terribly far from Walter Benjamin, whose suspicions of the photograph lie in its material destruction of the quality of presence.[97] The photographic practices at the Salpêtrière were reductive, assumed ownership over the patient and her image, were violent in their ruthless exposure. And yet, were they entirely objectifying? Is it possible that the photograph, too, presents a site in which the patient Augustine injected nothing less than her own life, a wrench in the anthropological machine, via the very medium that aimed to seize her? What, indeed, is going on in that alluring space above the line in our anatomical division of the *Iconographie* image?

Londe's photographic manual, written with examples from his work at Charcot's hospital, advises that a detailed close-up photograph can only be taken if the patient remains still. If she, however, as is common in hysteria, moves rapidly or with large gestures, the cameraman must move backward from her, creating distance between camera and subject (67). It is because of the difficulties that arise in photographing a patient who gestures too much and too often that other modes of generating bodily stillness, like hypnotically induced catalepsy, become so valuable to the medical photographer.[98] Augustine's refusal, as a photographic subject, to keep still causes her to literally recede from view, and analogously, forces distance between the photographer and the subject he intends to capture. The mechanics of distanciation as it occurs in photographs of Augustine are both pragmatic and symbolic.

Roland Barthes recognizes the awkward foresight of the photographed subject who poses stiffly, already feeling themselves becoming object.[99] But the thing or person photographed, in Barthes' *Camera Lucida*, refuses to stay still, persistently asserting itself. While Barthes tries to uncover the essence of the photograph, he finds that photography continually disappears against the "something" or "someone" featured in the photograph. The irritant is as follows: "a photograph is always invisible. It is not it that we see."[100] The photograph always carries the referent with itself, is contingent upon the referent.[101] Part of the dilemma that we aim to resolve in the images of Augustine is that while the Salpêtrière patients, whose visages were relentlessly documented in the modern age, "shine blindingly" but "with a dark light," they appear to us only because of the obsessive coercive photography project of Charcot and his colleagues.[102] It becomes impossible to weigh the cost of visibility. And yet, these photographs rely on the patients; the photograph hangs on Augustine. As Barthes says, in photography, a pipe is always a pipe.[103] "In short, the referent adheres."[104] Because of its dependence on Augustine and her fellow patients, their bodies, their illnesses, the *Iconographie* photograph is, after all, "pure contingency."[105]

What's more, the referent is unstable. Its tottering between subjectivity and objectivity makes it a locus of activity that points to "*the impossible science of the unique being.*"[106] After his mother died, Barthes looked through piles of photographs of her, trying to locate one in which he could really *recognize* her.[107] Many photos passed through his hands, producing near likenesses – "That's *almost* the way she was!"[108] – but only one photograph, the winter garden photograph, transmitted "the truth of the face of the one [he] had loved."[109] Part of the photographic subject's agency lies in her power to elude or to appear suddenly, catching the viewer by surprise. In a strange turn of Darwin's failure to find an archetypical example amongst too many rogue human photographs, Barthes was able to find only one photograph in which his mother really appeared to be herself, as he knew her.

He is upfront about the subjective quality of his assessment. For Barthes, photography is subjectively anchored in reciprocity. Phenomenological relationships to photographs can be classified as belonging to either the domain of *studium*, general interest or commitment, or *punctum*, a sting, cut, or accidental little hole.[110] Even in the photos of his own beloved mother, most of the images passed as studium for Barthes, lacking the power to arrest his attention and to prick him unexpectedly. Only one photograph produced the perceptual wound called punctum. Punctum occurs in several other unexpected places for Barthes. In one photograph, it is a pair of shoes, in another, crossed arms. A wide collar, a finger bandage – these are the elements that sting him beyond the general interest aroused by the photograph's historical or contextual circumstance.[111] The punctum can occur out of great tenderness or great mischief. He says, for instance: "William Klein has photographed children of Little Italy in New York (1954); all very touching, amusing, but what I stubbornly see are one child's bad teeth."[112]

I would like to suggest another level of punctum. For in the images of Augustine, whose flesh, desire, fear, erotic surrender, and rage are spectacularly figured in the *Iconographie,* the punctum for me is what drops out, what fails to appear. It is the photographs of hysteria that comprise studium, but the punctum is that remainder that the Salpêtrière physicians aim to dismiss that captures me, bothers me, will not let me rest. In short, it is Augustine, slipping from view despite her iterative figuration, who pierces through my general interest in the *Iconographie* images.

The theatre of hysteria at the Salpêtrière presents us with four distinct scenes. In the medical photograph, all scenes layer up. The photographic reader encounters a packed context of layered theatres of exchange between the hysterical patient, her life, her observers, and their volatile and impotent scrutiny. The most obvious, the most public, is the hysteria show or Charcot's lecture series in the amphitheatre. This medical spectacle designed for public consumption took place in a theatre equipped with chalkboards and electric projection used for visual aids relevant to Charcot's lectures on hysteria, epilepsy, anatomy, or neurology. Stagehand physicians or nurses held or manipulated the patient's body, rolled her bed on or off stage, caught her when she fell into a state of catalepsy, hypnotized her, or articulated her rigid body into impressive and startling postures.

The second is the scene of writing. Bourneville, whose transcriptions of Augustine's words, physiognomy, postures, and symptoms appeared in the widely distributed and popular *Iconographie photographique de la Salpêtrière,* is one actor at the scene of inscription, a figure in a pair of authors. One author speaks, gestures, evades; the other witnesses and writes it "all" down. The dialectic of inscription here is complicated. Augustine embodies the hysteric who writes without inscribing anything that sticks, figures without leaving a clear trace. Or, she writes without inscribing anything legible, leaves traces that bring the trace itself into question.

The third scene, the scene of the photograph, is an icon of medical power, of the force of the physician's gaze and constative authority. It is, as mentioned, an index of perceptual violence and systemic use of the image to ensure the notoriety of Charcot's hysteria project. It is also an index of attempted erasure of the woman who also happens to be a patient, the exposure, and simultaneous nullification of a body belonging to someone. Thus, it is always also an index of the female patient's resistance to capture. Her image is more slippery than it first appears. Partly, this "significative evasion"[113] takes place at the level of a fourth scene in this theatre of pain and representation.

For the fourth is a scene more remote, one from the past: the scene of the crime or the scenarios Augustine repeats in her states of delirium. A scene of sexual assault, her intimate encounters with her lovers, fights with her brother or her parents: domestic scenes of trauma from the patient's earlier life outside the hospital, enacted in the gestural theatre at the site of the patient's body.

Londe said that "la plaque photographique est la vraie rétine du savant"[114] (The photographic plate is the real retina of the scholar). A. Meneut, who published *Le passé, le présent et l'avenir de la photographie* in 1861, wrote that photography is "l'expression la plus réelle de la nature. C'est la vérité, même"[115] (the most realistic expression of nature. It is even truth itself). These two statements present stunning faith in this relatively new medium to accurately transmit truth. And yet, from French spectators at the Tuesday lectures to contemporary readers of the *Iconographie*, what audiences to Augustine's hysterical attacks witness is, ultimately, this fourth invisible scene. But how? At odds with documentary evidence, a site of secrecy, the image's real content is irreducible to the visible record.

The living memory, enacted in the body through a complex symptomatology, resists the modernist documentary hunger that Benjamin calls the ever-growing urge "to get hold of an object at very close range by way of its likeness, its reproduction."[116] As Freud would note, several years after his apprenticeship under Charcot, every sign is a symptom open to a series of differing meanings: "The hysterical symptom does not carry this meaning with it, but the meaning is lent to it, welded on to it, as it were; and in every instance the meaning can be a different one, according to the nature of the suppressed thoughts which are struggling for expression."[117] The hysteric's body is a field of meaning and a field of possible meanings.[118] It is partly because of the gap between what is represented and its impossible portrayal as evidence that the nosological captions under Augustine's images become imperative.[119] The label aims to anchor the subject of an unwieldy image. It is compensatory, saying "You see – this fraction of an attack, this particular display of the musculature, this grimace is like so many others. What you see, this is merely an *example* of *clownisme*. It is but a feature of la grande hystérie. It is an outcropping of terminology." But, as Jean-Luc Nancy says, speaking of quite another body: "But we certainly feel some formidable anxiety: 'here it is' is in fact not so sure, we have to seek assurance for it. That *the thing itself* would be there isn't certain. instantly, always, the body on display is foreign, a monster that can't be swallowed. We never get past it, caught in a vast tangle of images … This, this … *this* is always too much, or too little, to be *that*."[120]

And what could we call the remainder of Augustine's experience? What can we name the inarticulable pain of the suffering other? Incapacity to name, Barthes insists, is a good indication of having been wounded by punctum. Likewise, the incapacity to name adequately, suggests the force of a punctum beyond the scope of naming. In his study of psychiatry's capacity to identify normalcy and abnormality, David Rosenhan poignantly suggests that labelling is what we do when we reach the limits of our knowing. Labelling is an indication of our having come to the edge of knowledge.[121] The label can never be enough, cannot cover the multitude of memories, sensations, or symptomatic relations at work in the woman Augustine. Nor can it capture Augustine herself. Her absence asserts itself persistently, both imagistically and at the level of the nosological text affixed to the image.

Charcot and Richer described the hysterical attack as an unfolding drama.[122] So too, the photographs of hysterics appear to be representations of an unfolding theatre of the body. The images are theatrical in several ways. They are "dramatic," in the sense that they exceed the mundane, rely on gesture to communicate, convey emotion and action through an expressive body. Especially, one can also begin to fill in the gap that exists on either side of the still photographic image. A temporality that exceeds the "instantaneous" quality of the photographic medium presents itself via the expression of the body in the photographic moment. If it is a moment, it is one among many, for photography, as Didi-Huberman says, points to time as much as it points to its imagistic content.[123] It "has to do with an instant, but it is furrowed with duration."[124] Or, to quote Barthes, "the punctum has the power of expansion."[125] One senses temporality extending in both directions from the photographed patient, especially because of her the personal theatre of her illness – its gestures, its recurring memories, its likelihood for repetition without cure. The photographed hysteric kinetically transcends static two-dimensionality as she durationally floods the image. She infects the image with time and movement, above all pointing to the elsewhere outside the black and white confines.

A seized moment of a woman resisting with her body, elbow out, face terse, suggests scenic possibilities that lie outside the frame. She turns away from and gives her defensively poised arm to what one can only imagine is another person. Clearly the person against whom she reacts with such tension, such defiance, has violated her personal limits in some way. Because

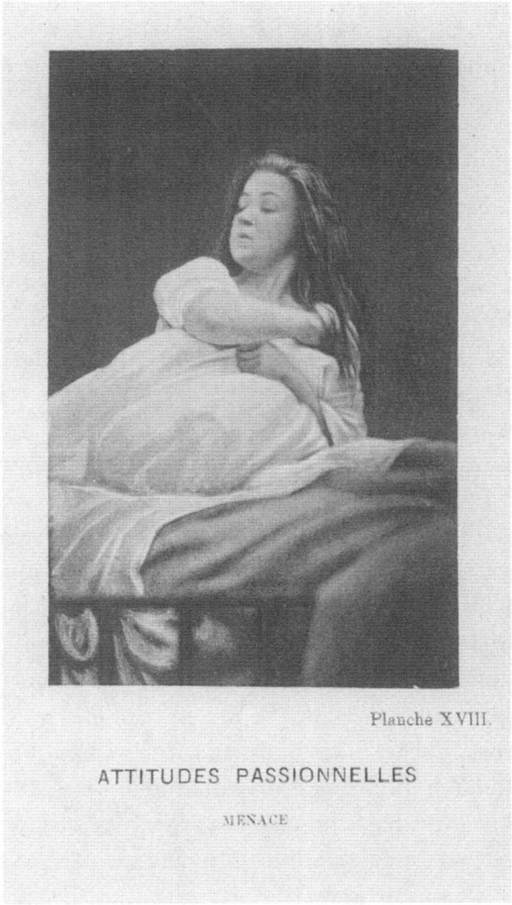

1.10 Augustine. *Attitudes passionnelles : Menace.* Plate XVIII, *Iconographie photographique de la Salpêtrière* 2, 1878.

of the transcripts of Augustine's utterances in her hallucinogenic states, we may assume that this person is her mother, brother, lover, or stepfather, all implicated in her reenactments of past memories in particularly turbulent ways. Durationally, the photograph moves backward into the unknown of what came before. The memory may also recur in Augustine's body in a temporal layering of multiple experiences. She may not be fighting either her mother *or* her stepfather. Many people and many tenses may affect her mind and body at once. In the attitudes passionnelles, the distinction between violent and sexual experience was often distorted[126] and in a hysterical attack, it was quite possible for a hysteric to play both the man and the woman of her hallucination. Freud writes that "in one case which I observed, for instance, the patient pressed her dress up against her body with one hand (as the woman) and tried to tear it off with the other (as the man)."[127]

The volume of photographs of Augustine published alongside this one suggests that the outcome of this defiant gesture also has multiple possibilities – Augustine may give in to her lover, and orgasm in the bliss of imagined intimacy. She may feel what she describes as rats in her genitals and fall into unconsciousness or overwhelmed thrashing. She may continue this way for awhile, hauling insults at her mother. She may find her attack has resolved and go for a walk in the garden. Action can be imagined preceding and following the gesture that the camera has recorded as an instant. And it is in both the photograph and on the body that duration is borne and appears to us. Indeed, after more than a hundred years, the "live" element of the body persists via the document. And ultimately, the body is illegible. The flesh in the foreground of the medical photograph guards a secret; under close scrutiny of the image, this secrecy is what we discover. Picturing the hysteric, squeezing her into the confines of a classification, causes a resilient subjectivity to slip through the cracks of the gestural body. Personhood overflows the structure of the nosological photographic plate. Strangely, the images of Augustine's publicized personal theatre, her body disseminated and iterated in photographic reproduction, prompt a durational imagining in which the essential privacy of her experience transmits as much as her corporeal generosity. We look at her repeatedly and begin to feel the gaps in our looking.

Benjamin has famously said that the photographer, like the surgeon, aims to penetrate reality.[128] But Londe, the Salpêtrière photographer, cannot help but overlook and thus to fail to picture that persistent privacy that Augustine's life, over time, presents. Charcot's statement, "je ne suis absolument là que le photographe; j'inscris ce que je vois"[129] (I am nothing but a photographer. I inscribe what I see), here, can be interpreted in two ways. One, Charcot, believing in the straightforward transmissive power of the photograph, the undoubtable accuracy of the camera's eye, thought the comparison between himself and photographer apt – he simply inscribed and relayed what he saw. In his nineteenth century context, in accordance with dominant views of the photograph, Charcot believes that he transmits unquestionably like the scientific retina of the transparent medium. But we know the apparatus to be unstable, transgressive. In another light, considering the limitations and turns of the medium of photography, Charcot in effect outs himself in this statement as being absolutely nothing but a photographer. He is *only* a photographer, acting within the limited capacity of the camera's mode of looking. When Charcot says, "I am but a photographer," his presumed power to show everything about the hysterical patient is undermined by the medium of photography and by the patient's relentless subjectivity. In "photographing" Augustine, he also refigures her persistent absence from within the frame, and her simultaneous vivacious secrecy indicated there.

Didi-Huberman writes: "Are you looking for the image's secret? Then take another look at plate 14. *Its secret is written beneath it*, in capital letters, its secret is its legend; HYSTÉRO-ÉPILEPSIE."[130] We know that part of Charcot's allure was his presentation as medical seer, a privileged eye, who could label an opacity of gestures with clinical finesse. We also know that other covert operations live at the nosology below the line in the Salpêtrière photograph, an attempted disavowal of the complexities of the photographic medium and most importantly the person Augustine, who was never asked to pose according to her intentions or desires, who was never consulted about the proliferation of her image through Western Europe and beyond. No one asked Augustine if she wanted to share the secrets of her past or her body's painful betrayal. Nor did anyone ask her if she had a personal secret she would like to share with her imposed public. And while this violence perpetrated via the dissemination of images and public spectacle can be classified as a violence of looking, always looking, but never seeing, the demonstration that failed to take into account its remainder may have been paralleled by a secret refusing to make an appearance. A resistance to representation through representation.

Augustine's strangeness, her alterity, appears to us in a face that we can look at dozens of times in its documentary reproduction. Hers was, alongside a small group of women, the face of Charcot's hysteria. It is also possible that this face, so naked and susceptible to violence, produces a cataclysmic incision in the medical power Charcot and his audiences took for granted. For as humanist philosopher Emmanuel Levinas explains in his work on the ethics of alterity, "The face is present in its refusal to be contained. In this sense, it cannot be comprehended, that is, encompassed."[131] Again, "The face resists possession, resists my powers."[132] This ungraspable epiphany of the face opens a new dimension – the unknown element of the person I encounter, her radical alterity, is ungraspable and overflows the paradigmatic moment – Levinas calls this totality – with

Infinity, or the thing that lies beyond the bounds of the knowable. Thus, attempting to possess or describe the other as though I comprehend her is a form of violence, as anyone who has felt the sting of being misunderstood or misconstrued realizes. Also, it is a futile effort toward an impossibility. "The expression the face introduces into the world does not defy the feebleness of my powers, but my ability for power."[133] The face, like the photograph, carries the signification of its inability to fully produce the referent. What's more, the face always functions like a punctum, puncturing my general interest. Before Augustine's face, we and her audience are not rendered more powerful by our looking. We are pierced through by the call and imposition of the visage. As Levinas explains, the transcendent event of the face-to-face encounter, flooded by the infinite, is the original site of ethics. Augustine's face opens an ethical dimension, provokes an ethical possibility. She, like each person, resists knowing and cannot be grasped and still demands that I take responsibility for one I cannot understand or grasp. As Barthes teaches, looking, whether the subject of our gaze can look back or not, is a reciprocal event. It is precisely Augustine's vulnerability that violates my potential ignorance. For, "the epiphany of the absolutely other is face where the Other hails me and signifies to me, by its nakedness, by its destitution, an order. Its presence is this summons to respond."[134]

Contemporary research juts awkwardly against knowledge of what it was like to be Augustine or to witness her hysteria. While images of the woman during her time as a patient at the hospital pervade our cultural imagination, Augustine still remains remote. The photographs of faces in the physiognomic projects of Darwin and Duchenne have demonstrated the way in which real life collides against knowledge at the level of the face. Régnard and Londe's photos of women at the Salpêtrière also capture the subject's evasion precisely as they aim to pin her down. Likewise, the clarity of an image does not indicate transmission. The image above, of a cry or gasp, of a mouth widened in what seems like horror, does not lack detail. We see muscular distress, taut back muscles aiming to arch off the surface of the bed, Augustine held down firmly by leather and fabric restraints. We see an open mouth, a face, arms thrown back, and eyes looking at something other than the photographer. The movement and sound that obviously accompany this moment where gesture is captured on a glass plate – a few seconds – present a durational challenge of the referent to the photographic sign. But more than this, this face eludes me precisely in its obstinate vitality, its palpable exposure.[135] Augustine's face, "captured" by the camera, relentlessly challenges us, appeals to us. Part of the resistance of the woman in the image is in the facial phenomenon of the enigma, the aporia of her personhood. Augustine herself resists capture, acts out an autonomous and forceful resistance par excellence, calls to us, makes a provocative sound despite her wordlessness. I am helplessly moved by her. Any attempt for my eye to be neutral is punctured by her ulterior presence. For, again, "*The epiphany of the absolutely other is face where the Other hails me and signifies to me, by its nakedness, by its destitution, an order. Its presence is this summons to respond*" (*Humanism* 65, emphasis mine). If Augustine is present at all in the medical photograph, if she reveals anything, her presence is a command to reconcile myself to my perceptual limits and accountability. Her revelation is of my own ethical responsibility, here tied inextricably to her visibility and my impossible mode of looking.

Charcot said that the photo of the patient was both artful and instructive.[136] Putting ourselves in the position of nineteenth century spectators, we feel ourselves to be voyeurs of human pain, and witnesses to and perpetrators of violating exposure, seeing far too much. Simultaneously, we encounter our ocular and gnostic limitations, find ourselves steeped in the agony of unknown women, who appear only to reveal an unrelenting privacy. The *Iconographie* is an artifact of both harrowing violence and beautiful insufficiency. What we learn from the documents that survive the Salpêtrière hysteria project is that to look at photographs of Augustine is to experience, if not come to terms with, the withdrawal of the human person from capture, her giving herself only to expose the unknowable that illuminates her expression.

TWO

The Hysteric as Scapegoat

Why was the violent exposure of female patients at the Salpêtrière essential to the theatrical lure of the medical lectures? Was violence a crucial component of the lectures' popularity or simply (but not innocuously) a "medical inevitability?" Can such violence ever be addressed at all adequately? To examine the audience stake in the hysteric's performance, it is revealing to turn to nineteenth century questions of femininity and especially masculine anxieties about the shifting roles of women and adjacent redefinitions of the feminine. The lecture series and its hypnosis mini-dramas were charged sites for working through French masculine anxieties about women. The stage was constituted by a complex interplay of public and private: Charcot's fame, the audience's gaze, the hysteric's internment and her simultaneous radical public exposure, her onstage embodiment of the subdued domestic woman and her spectacular gestural frenzy, often an expression of her most private pain and memory.

As women in France literally and symbolically ventured from domestic spaces, appearing more frequently in public and in spaces formerly designated as male (places of employment and entertainment, nocturnal places, places of intellectual work, etc.), women were interned at the Salpêtrière for precisely these spacial transgressions. To be diagnosed as a hysteric was often to be diagnosed as being the wrong kind of woman, a woman guilty of appearing where she ought not to. Her punishment was to be tucked away behind hospital walls, and to appear in public under strict conditions, in which she appeared as a pathological woman, one whose symptoms consisted of being too womanly, or not womanly enough. As Didi-Huberman has written, "hysteria never stopped calling the feminine guilty."[1]

Feminist scholars Hélène Cixous and Catherine Clément write that:

> In their attempt to define the cultural function of the *anomaly*, both Lévi-Strauss and Sartre, who elsewhere contradict each other, seek to situate it in the fault lines of a general system where some correlative structures do not successfully harmonize all their correlations. Societies do not succeed in offering everyone the same way of fitting into the symbolic order; those who are, if one may say so, between symbolic systems, in the interstices, offside, are the ones who are afflicted with a dangerous symbolic mobility … And more than any others, women bizarrely embody this group of anomalies showing the cracks in an overall system.[2]

Investigating the margins of French society –in this case, women –as they were moved to the Salpêtrière may reveal aspects of French culture that are frequently omitted from conventional histories. Daring to view the hospital patients as repressed material from dominant modes of perception and social organization plumbs not just what is remembered in history, but what is forgotten. The surrealists tried to retroactively claim Augustine as the poetic emblem of an era, an icon for a poetics of the nineteenth century. This chapter will claim that she already was. By doing so, I hope to give new light to the cracks in the system. By looking at the way the hysteric was constructed as a scapegoat for broader cultural phenomena, the lecture series appears to be a theatre where masculine ambivalences about women and anxieties about themselves were able to play out under the guise of reasonable scientific inquiry. In a theatre where the hysteric was made to play a host of femininities desirable to her audience for one reason or another, the show was actually, more often than not, about the men who witnessed her.

INSTRUCTIONAL SET PIECES
Two Paintings and the Bodies between Them

Hanging in the amphitheatre where patients performed in Charcot's lectures were two paintings. On the walls surrounding the stage, Robert Fleury's 1878 artwork, *Pinel Orders Removal of the Chains of the Mad at the Salpêtrière* entered into symbolic visual dialogue with André Brouillet's 1887 *Un Leçon Clinique à la Salpêtrière* (figures 2.1 and 2.2). Bernard Marquer argues that the assembly of the two paintings, as a frame for Charcot's lectures, presented a tale of progress, from the inhumane treatment of the insane who were once chained like animals to the more scientific treatment of patients and disease at the Salpêtrière under Charcot's directorship. Not only did the pairing of the paintings set Charcot in the lineage of a paternal hero like Pinel, it also situated Charcot as the next radical visionary at the hospital, his hysteria project a revolution in medicine. Even Freud did not miss the connection between Charcot's work and the rendering of the 1780 liberation of the madwomen from their chains. Remarking on the painting, he said, "In the hall in which he gave his lectures there hung a picture which showed 'citizen' Pinel having the chains taken off the poor madmen at the Salpêtrière. The Salpêtrière, which had witnessed so many horrors during the Revolution, had also been the scene of this most humane of all revolutions."[3]

Taken together, the Fleury and Brouillet paintings bear interesting similarities and provocative differences, especially when one considers that Charles Louise-Muller's 1849 painting of Pinel ordering the chains removed from the insane, with its masculine counterparts experiencing liberation, is far less well remembered than Fleury's feminized version.

In Fleury's scene, the eye is first drawn to the woman being freed from the waist manacle that still binds the women to her left, where her limp arm gestures. Though Pinel is the hero of the tale, the woman is the most prominent figure in the painting. Her gaze is slightly blank, her mouth is in a half smile. These could be indications of a history of pain combined with relief and disbelief at being freed, or the features of lunacy. The intrigue around this feminine expression multiplies because this woman is indecipherable for the reason that she is mad. The hospital wall, with its many windows, would have been familiar to Charcot's attending public. Pinel and the already mythologized event of the liberation would have been equally recognizable. But the perceptual reality of the centre

2.1 Robert Fleury, *Pinel Orders Removal of the Chains of the Mad at the Salpêtrière*, 1876.

figure, clues to her personhood, are concealed by her downcast eyes and what we know to be her mental condition. While her expression resists interpretation, her dishevelled hair and her lax comportment point to the fatigue generated by a life spent in distress. And more: her dress falls off her shoulders as she is disrobed of her metal chains, giving her a sensual air. Pair her against any of the other women in the painting – the woman tearing open her shirt, writhing on the ground with breast bared; the old woman reaching with a hard face; the woman rushing forward, mouth agape in desperation; the woman crouched in some kind of private horror; or the one kneeling to chastely and gratefully kiss the hand of Pinel – and she begins to look demure. Cultural historian Sander Gilman notes that Fleury's painting "portrays several stock figures in the tradition of asylum art: a woman (on the ground) tearing at her clothing, two huddled melancholics, a tense maniac, and a woman (at right) with a vacant stare chained to the wall."[4] But who is this woman at centre? Elaine Showlater's reading of the piece is less generic. She writes that the "division between feminine madness and masculine rationality is further emphasized by the three figures at the centre. In the foreground is a lovely, passive and dishevelled young woman, her eyes modestly cast down, upon whose exposed bosom an erect and dignified Pinel gazes with ambiguous interest."[5] Showalter's reading of modesty on the face of the young woman in the painting may be liberally interpretive and Pinel does not at all seem to be gazing at her bosom, but Showalter's inclination to picture the woman as the object of masculine desire is based on other cues in the artwork. After all, even though Pinel may be looking elsewhere, we, the viewers of the painting *are* gazing at the madwoman's breasts. Stock figures or no, the woman at the centre of the painting evokes our sympathy more than any other. She is the tragic heroine of the scene, and her madness does not lift from her an air of desirability. She draws us in. Her limp arms and exposed white skin leave her body open to the touch of our eye. Her gaze is comparable to the dreamy, far away look of the nude, that "dreamy offering of herself, that looking which was not quite looking."[6]

The hysteric in Brouillet's painting is a strange echo of the Pinel madwoman. The woman pictured here is not a stock figure at all but is painted after the real Salpêtrière patient Blanche Wittman. Still, her ability to resemble the semi-dressed voluptuousness of the Pinel archetype is impressive. Charcot commands the framed space; Wittman's torso leads the eye to Charcot's hand, raised in a gesture of authoritative explanation. Wittman falls into a catatonic state under hypnosis, breasts aloft and luminous, while Charcot narrates her symptomatology to the masculine upper-crust who look on with neutral or interested expressions, their position as spectators much more institutionally constructed than in the Pinel painting, where onlookers do not have a weekly seat to the drama of the triumph of rationality over madness. Wittman's body is reclined, slung over Doctor Babinski's arm in half-sleep. Her pose amongst the male spectators prompts Didi-Huberman to have Charcot ventriloquize Mallarmé: "No sign will treat you to the interior spectacle, for there is now no painter able to give even its sad shadow. I bring you, living (and preserved through years by sovereign science) a Woman of bygone days. Some naïve and original madness, an ecstasy of gold – I know not what! – that she calls her hair, folds with the grace of cloth around a face illuminated by the bloody nudity of her lips. In place of vain garments, she has a body [...] from breasts lifted as if they were filled with eternal milk, their tips to the heavens, to smooth legs that retain the salt of the first sea."[7]

2.2 André Brouillet, *Une leçon clinique à la Salpêtrière*, 1887.

Painted for the salon in 1887, Brouillet's *Une leçon clinique à la Salpêtrière* is an image that haunts our impressions of the history of madness. The painting was widely distributed in print publications in the late nineteenth century, "reproduced endlessly in black and white etchings," and was well known to French citizens.[8] Freud owned one. In the many novels written about Charcot's lectures, this scene in particular, of a patient collapsed into a doctor's arms in the hysterical sleep of hypnosis, inscribes itself repeatedly, generating a cultural memory trace of the hysteric as a woman subdued by the forces of masculine reason. As Dottin-Orsini writes in her book on fin-de-siècle misogynist representations of women, "Finir dans les bras de Charcot, c'est une belle fin pour une femme de roman"[9] (To end in Charcot's arms is a beautiful ending for a woman protagonist).

The proliferation of the Brouillet image in French culture, and its relation to the Pinel legacy, already well known by the people of France, made this image of the hysteric in the physician's arms an indelible representation – *the* representation, it could be argued – of hysteria.

Moreover, the Brouillet painting, often in conjunction with Fleury's rendering of Pinel and the madwomen, is reproduced in nearly every contemporary historical or popular work on the Salpêtrière hysterics. Both the Fleury and the Brouillet painting persist as mnemonic icons for interpretations of nineteenth century femininity and hysteria.[10] Their persistence, I would like to suggest, is not simply because of the inevitable or innocent continuation of their popularity. Rather, their appeal in the nineteenth century was based on a complex range of masculine desires and anxieties that caused the images to hold fast to the imaginations of the French. The hysteric, viewed as a subdued, seductive woman, was an irresistible image. Her embodiment of masculine ideals of the feminine and her pathologized assaults on these ideals were easily symbolized in the image of a womanly body draped over the arm of a doctor. Thus, the paintings made perfect set pieces for a drama of projection and scapegoatism.

The pictorial figures of the hysteric produced an ideological and literal frame for the hysteric on stage. Sometimes the woman performing in direct citation of the Brouillet image was Blanche Wittman herself. But any hysteric could be easily substituted for the one in the painting, because the lecture show so often resulted in a similar scene. Of course, Charcot was always there on stage as well, the masculine dialectic to the voluptuous pathology of Womanhood represented in the artworks and in the body of the performing female patient.

Fifty years after hysteria's inception as a popular diagnosis for all kinds of errant femininities, André Breton and Louis Aragon called Augustine "delicious."[11] It is not without significance that Dottin-Orsini, when describing the Brouillet painting, identifies the Wittman figure as being made of the stuff of dreams: "[U]ne belle fille demi-nue qui s'abandonne, l'érotisme de son partiel déshabillage, et des auditeurs strictement vêtus, d'un sérieux total, en troupe nombreuse, regardant Charcot comme si *elle* n'était pas sous leurs yeux – comme si elle n'était qu'une projection de leurs rêves"[12] (a beautiful woman, half-naked, in a sate of abandonment, the eroticism of her partial undress, and the auditors, strictly clothed, altogether serious, a numerous crowd, watching Charcot as if *she* wasn't there, under their eyes – like she was a projection of their dreams). As we shall see, the performing hysteric, like the one in the painting, came to embody the projections of male fantasies, from sexual savant to manipulable marionette. She, herself, was a dream.

PROSTITUTE, FEMINIST, HYSTERIC
A Threat Too Public, Too Private

One last painting. One that never would have appeared in the amphitheatre alongside Brouillet and Fleury, although its subject is not unrelated to hysteria, it poses an interesting alternative portrait of womanhood, one that, in the end, may be better suited to the patients at the Salpêtrière. T.J. Clark's exploration of the controversy over Manet's salon painting *Olympia* exposes a common fear of the autonomous woman with a sexuality her own. Clark describes the scandal that *Olympia* created amongst the public and art critics alike following its salon viewing in 1865. The controversy was not over the representation of a prostitute – nearly every year since the salon's inception, there were several depictions of prostitutes. The trouble with *Olympia*, Clark suggests, was that she was not a nude – instead, she was utterly naked – and there was an important distinction between the two. The nude was traditionally most often represented without a pubis. In place of this absence of genitalia, Manet's *Olympia* had what countless critics objected to – the shameless contraction of a hand over her vagina.[13] Worse, hers was a *particular* sexuality.[14] Historically, the nude was represented in a way that depicted that "dreamy offering of herself, that looking which was not quite looking."[15] *Olympia*, rather, was looking right at the viewer, depriving him of his usual anonymity in voyeurism. He was caught in the act of witnessing. Challenged. Manet's Olympia, accused of "masculine cynicism" and being the kind who must smoke cigarettes, her forehead "bulging with the force of (her) own obstinacy,"[16] was not, as the traditional nude was, an object of male desire. This particular sexuality, this ownership of her body is what caused critics to find Olympia dirty. She was so filthy, according to several journalists and critics, that she was literally decomposing.[17] She was diseased, and dangerously able to spread her decay.

During the latter half of the nineteenth century, shifting roles of women provoked a ferment of questioning around what women were and who they ought to be. As historian Ruth Harris, explains, "the era was experiencing a transitional period in sexual relations, one manifested by the growing concern over the 'women's question' during the Third Republic."[18] Feminism was a minority activity, even by the end of the nineteenth century, but because feminists were very vocal, and in part because of the impressive (perhaps disproportionately vitriolic) anti-feminist backlash,

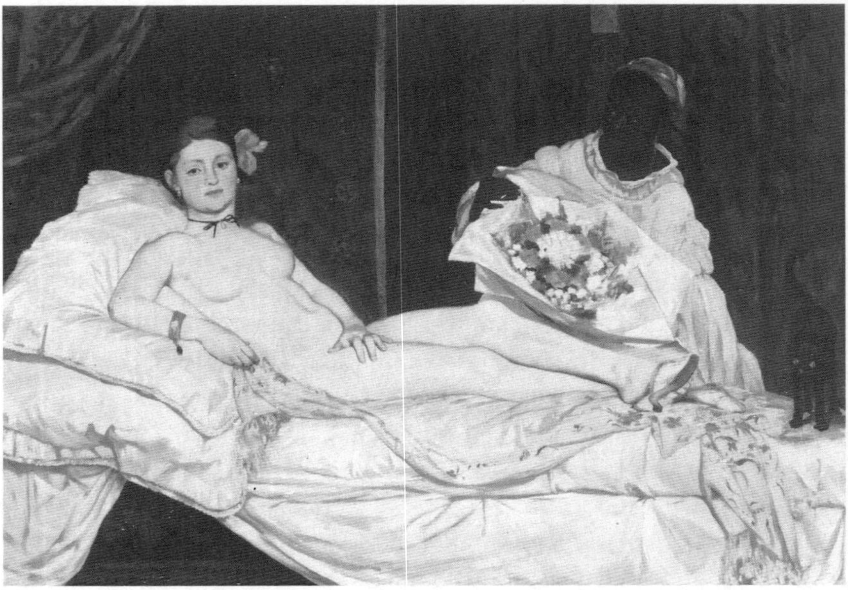

2.3 Édouard Manet, *Olympia*, 1863.

feminism received a lot of attention in the press, ensuring that "feminist ideas were in the air."[19] "Regular feminist congresses – at least eleven between 1878 and 1903 – provided a very public forum for discussion of the major issues: the suffrage, reform of the profoundly sexist legal code … equality in education, employment and equal pay, the recognition of maternity and domestic labour as socially important functions, the reform of the laws on prostitution."[20] At the same time, many French women who were not feminist activists began all the same to appear in domains formerly conceived of as masculine. The presence of "the feminine" in public consciousness presented a challenge to conventional notions of women as occupants of private space or creatures of the interior. For according to anthropologists, authors, doctors, politicians, and a host of other male figures, a woman was supposed to be married, domestic, matriarchal, and therefore feminine. Dependent.[21]

Historian Jules Michelet, in 1859, wrote that "The worst destiny for a woman is to live alone."[22] Uzanne, the French writer and journalist, wrote, in his history of Parisian women, *La Femme à Paris, nos Contemporaines*, that women should be such fundamentally interior creatures that they should, lacking need for outward ordainment (they were not rushing off to any public events, so needed not dress the part) ordain themselves instead in undergarments of extreme finery and softness for their husbands sole enjoyment.[23] Jozé, a well-known Parisian writer who specialized in "psychologically sophisticated novellas" said that men and women's fundamental differences could be categorized as the public world of action and the private world of emotion and maternity, respectively. Female heroines in Émile Zola's works were described for a reviewer for *La Fronde* as being reducible to "les hanches larges et un grand coeur"[24] (large hips and a big heart).

Also, fears of the decreasing populations in France compared to other European nations caused childbearing to become a question of nationalism.[25] As such, the woman using birth control or the unmarried woman, not committed to making her share of French citizens, was often described as anti-nationalist or anti-social.[26] The prostitute and the feminist were both chastised for their meagre childbearing. Women who neglected their infants or avoided pregnancy were labelled "patriotically irresponsible" by physicians.[27] In Théodore Jordan's antifeminist nationalist 1905 annual diatribe, *Le mensonge du féminisme*, he railed, "Feminism, like Socialism, is an anti-French malady!" He objected to feminism, he said, "because it allows women to envisage happiness as independent of love and external to love." This emphasis on the value of love seems ironic, given Jordan's hatred for women, for he also opined: "In reality, if not in law … good households are those where the man considers the woman as an object made for his own personal pleasure and well-being and where the woman believes she ought to please her husband, to serve him, and applies herself exclusively to that end."[28] Comments like Jordan's indicate how conservative ideals of woman as domestic wife and submissive matriarch, bolstered by the discourse of national responsibility, could become systemically expressed in French law. Some women, like Nelly Roussel, argued against the national mandate to produce children, refusing to create what they said amounted to more canon fodder for France's military exploits or more subjugated women, who would be born into a state that punished women for being women: "Beware, oh Society! The day will come … when the eternal victim will become weary of carrying in her loins sons whom you will later teach to scorn their mothers or daughters destined – alas! – to the same life of sacrifice and humiliation! The day when we will refuse to give you, ogres, your ration of cannon-fodder, of work-fodder, and fodder for suffering! The day, at last, when we will become mothers *only when we please*!"[29] And yet, David Harvey describes that "Legally considered a minor under the Napoleonic Code, it was difficult though not impossible for a woman to make her own way in life, economically or socially, without some kind of protection from her father, husband, kin, lover, pimp, institutions (like convents and schools), or employer."[30] If women were not living with their fathers or husbands, working for a man became an alternative to the lack of financial and judicial stability female independence presented. It isn't coincidence then, that domestic employment was the most sought-after job for unmarried women in the second half of the nineteenth century. It offered adequate food and appeared more like the conventionally acceptable family structure. But the hours were long (ranging from fifteen to eighteen hours per day) and female employees were at their employer's whim. Sometimes this involved sleeping with sons in the household to prevent them from seeking fulfillment in less "honourable" (less private) ways.[31] Perhaps it was also no coincidence, then, that to be "a well-endowed widow" was a coveted position among women.[32] According to Harvey, the "protection" that was offered to a young female minor by a domestic position was "open to all manner of abuse."[33] The wages of being a domestic were also insufficient to meet even basic needs most times and this, according to Harvey, lead women to two choices: to supplement their income by developing a liaison with a male, or by engaging in prostitution. Domestics out of work often turned to prostitution.[34] Senator Edme Piot's institution of state-awarded medals for motherhood seems a rather weak compensation for such demoralizing and dangerous legal subjugation.[35]

A swath of literature from the era continually classified women who transgressed conservative masculine ideals of femininity, acting outside boundaries of marital duties and the space of the home, as hysterics or prostitutes, both signifiers for the morally bereft, antisocial, mentally and physiologically ill, and pathologically errant. Medical literature publicized the same misogynist drivel, with authority. At a time when resistance to changes in the modern French cultural landscape was particularly anxious and hostile, the terms feminist, prostitute and hysteric overlapped so frequently that they produced a nearly singular derogatory discourse. One became interchangeable with the other, the crimes of each related to female autonomy enacted in ways that threatened misogynist conventions.

According to Harvey, there was, in Paris, a "pervasive fear in bourgeois circles, that of the unsubmissive, independent woman."[36] This fear rose, in part due to the new, truly modern phenomenon of the woman in public.

Baron Haussman's new Paris created an unprecedented environment for public travel and visibility. Replacing the meandering, largely unlit avenues of pre-modern Paris, widening the streets of the city and directing pedestrian traffic along major commercial arteries allowed female *piétonnes* to travel too.[37] The modern emergence of department stores and arcades created an environment in which women were not only employed as salesclerks, but also encouraged to travel, to be *shopeuses*, a kind of female parallel to the typically masculine *flaneur*.[38] The design and mass manufacture of the bicycle offered women a new "freedom to roam."[39] Sarah Bernhardt provocatively described women on bicycles as "devouring space"[40] and criticized them for flouting domestic life, a critique that was echoed in the caricature of the nineteenth century *hommesse*, taking off on her *vélo* to attend a woman's congress, leaving her husband in a chaotic mess of kids and dishes.

Furthermore, the newly installed gas lighting of Paris allowed for "a more extroverted form of urbanism"[41] and something Parisians had never shared before: a public nightlife.[42] Modern Paris saw the beginning of the café-concert – along with it, its crude and stunning entertainment, cheap drinks, and diverse patronage. The café-concert became immensely popular at this time – by the early 1870s there were at least 145 cafés-concerts in Paris. Though it was a mixed crowd, "droves of respectable people" attended.[43] The phenomenon was not met without disdain. Journalists, appalled, noted that women and children spent evenings at the cafés-concerts, rubbing shoulders with questionable company: "Alongside them (the white-tied ambassadors), rubbing shoulders with them, a crowd of little people, shopkeepers, shop assistants, and maidservants; and beside them, inevitably, cranks and criminals and thugs. There can be seen here, without any barriers between them, each quite at home with the other, the woman for sale and the society lady, the ex-convict and the magistrate, masters and servants, honest men and thieves."[44] Historian Simone Delattre has noted the link between lower class and female occupation of public space as transgressive. She emphasizes that: "L'une des caractéristiques des classes laborieuses réside dans leur tendance à ne pas respecter la conception bourgeoise de l'espace et du temps. Les gens du peuple ne feraient pas de distinction entre la sphère publique et la sphère privée: "Il y a interpénétration incessante de deux espaces; la rue est bien plus qu'un lieu de transition entre l'atelier et le foyer: on y travaille, on y entend des échos des disputes privées, on s'y attarde, on s'y divertit, bref on y vit"[45]

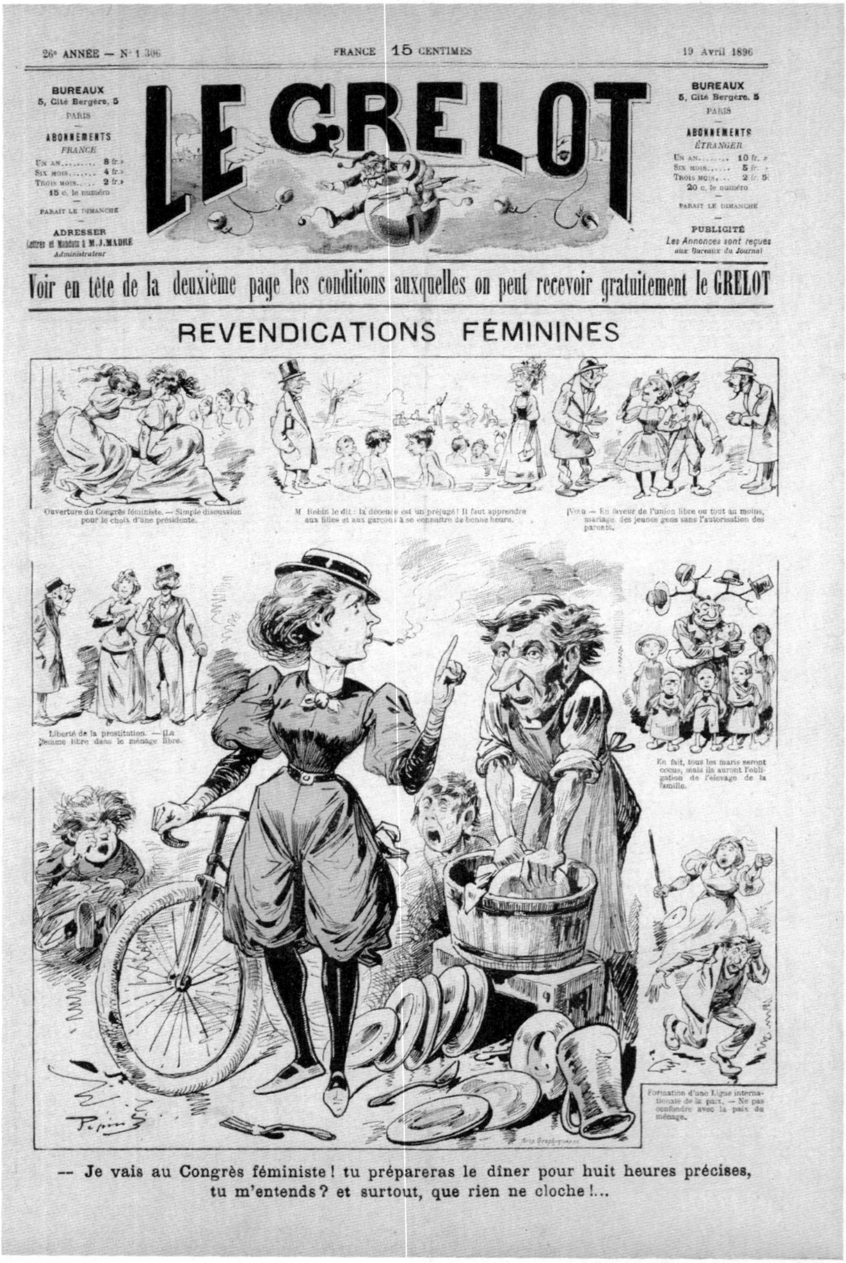

2.4 *To the Feminist Congress!* in *Le Grelot*, 19 April 1896, front page. The central caricatured figure on a page of "feminist demands" declares to her husband: "I am going to the Feminist Congress! You will prepare dinner for 8:00 sharp, make sure nothing goes wrong."

(One of the characteristics of the working class is their tendency to disregard the bourgeois conception of space and time. The lower class did not make a distinction between the public sphere and the private sphere: "There is constant interpenetration of two spaces; the street is more than a place of transition between the shop and home: they work there, you can hear echoes of private disputes, they linger, they entertain themselves, in short, they live there.")

Cassell's popular guide for warned: "one thing that will strike the stranger is the immense proportion of women in the streets as compared with men."[46] Spacial transgression was literal and symbolic of an alarming shift in female positions. Historian Silverman states:

> The menace of the *femme nouvelle*, who left home and family for a career, pervaded contemporary journals between 1889 and 1898. Ranging from the sober academicism of the *Revue des deux mondes* to the ribald caricatures of *L'Illustration*, the periodicals presented the *femme nouvelle* as rejecting woman's position as the anchor of bourgeois domesticity. Alternatively envisioned as a gargantuan *amazone* or an emaciated, frock-coated *hommesse*, the *femme nouvelle* inverted traditional sexual roles and threatened the essential divisions ordering bourgeois life: public from private, work from family, production from reproduction.[47]

As women began to occupy public spaces of employment, entertainment, education, and travel, masculine anxieties rose in a manner that brought femininity itself into question. Indeed, feminist historian Karen Offen suggests that "perhaps the greatest tribute to the force of feminist ideas and activism in fin-de-siècle France was that it precipitated a major public debate and gave rise to a vitriolic antifeminism that forced men to take a position on the woman question."[48] As Dottin-Orsini explains, "(les) oeuvres littéraires, les ouvrages médicaux ou philosophiques … à la même époque, tentent de théoriser le féminin, de le définir, de le fixer"[49] (literary, medical and philosophical works … in the same era, attempted to theorize the feminine, to define it, to pin it down).

Uzanne, in language resembling that of the scientific discourse around hysterics and prostitutes, "equated feminism with a dangerous unleashing of social and sexual inversion" and he advised young men to avoid the ornamental women seen decorating herself for public, to avoid, "educated, 'ambitious females' who 'could solve mathematical problems'" and to choose instead 'a young lady who does not despise crocheting, whom tapestry interests, and who loves embroidery.'"[50] Uzanne's equation of social with sexual inversion was a popular one. In fact, the general term, *femmes isolées*, stood for the handful of those independently employed female schoolteachers, seamstresses, and craftswomen as well as for prostitutes. Harvey, quoting E. Thomas, writes: "For the bourgeois, the term *femmes isolées* signalled 'the domain of poverty, a world of turbulent sexuality, subversive independence and dangerous insubordination ... In their association with prostitution, these women carried 'the moral leprosy' that made large cities 'permanent centres of infection'; they permitted expression of or simply expressed those 'tumultuous passions' that, in the time of political upheaval – as in the revolution of 1848 – threatened to overturn the entire social order."[51]

The French state clamoured to regulate female financial and sexual independence, the labour activities of all women, including prostitutes were legally hemmed in. "In 1892, after considerable controversy, the French legislature broke with its noninterventionist principles to pass a law regulating the employment of adult women. The new law not only restricted the daily hours of women's work in industry but forbade women's employment at night (when work was often much better paid)."[52] Independent female employment disrupted the social order with the dangerous insubordination likened to that of prostitution. In fact, the infractions of prostitutes, in the following tidy list, could equally be listed as crimes of the *nouvelle femme*: "L'exercice de la prostitution participe de ce que les médecins désignent comme la virilisation des comportements des filles publiques, phénomène dont on trouve les fondements dans la liberté sexuelle dont elles jouissent, leur fréquentation de l'espace publiqe nocturne, leur autonomie financière et l'affranchissement dont elles font preuve à l'égard de l'injonction au marriage"[53] (Prostitution participates in what physicians refer to as behavioural masculinization of prostitutes, a phenomenon whose basis is found in the sexual freedom they enjoy, their frequenting public spaces at night, their financial autonomy, and the freedom they demonstrate against the injunction of marriage.)

Partly, it was the sex worker's occupation of public space at late hours that made her morally suspect. "Selon la morale propre à la bourgeoisie, pendant la nuit toute personne honnête doit se trouver chez elle"[54] (According to the moral propriety of the bourgeoisie, at nighttime, every honest person must find themselves at home.) Because of the equation of nightlife with immorality, any woman found on the streets at night could be arrested simply for being out of doors at the wrong time.[55] Likewise, women found out of doors nocturnally were labelled prostitutes, regardless of their occupation. Besnard recounts that in January 1874, Valérie Durand was apprehended by an Inspector Hipper after he saw her buttoning her boot and addressing some people in the street. After the arrest, it was discovered that Durand was not a sex worker at all, but a piano teacher who lived with her parents. Hipper defended the arrest by stating that Durand resembled a prostitute unquestionably – he could tell by the way she looked at men in a provocative manner. She exhibited the dangerous trait of expressing female sexual desire in public, and at nighttime, which was a punishable offence in nineteenth century France. Darkness presented an inconvenient cover for morally suspect activities when lawmakers were obsessed with keeping track of women out of doors.[56]

Tellingly, in Paris, the same committee in charge of public morality was in charge of the underground sewer system as well as prisons and public opinion.[57] The proliferation of prostitutes and women like them (like Durand) in city streets aroused a fear of contagion. There was, in Paris, a kind of terror that if the prostitute "were not analyzed, counted and controlled she would circulate in the social body, spreading disease and confusion."[58] "Good" women could easily be turned away from their maternal duties and dragged into deviant sexuality. The danger of sexual intoxication was especially acute because women were already considered to be fragile and impressionable. Not only this, women were thought to be morally corrupt, looking for any chance to flout their moral obligations to be married servants. The anxiety about women's surge outward into public individuality, a sensual one, can be inferred when Edmond de Goncourt, for instance, writes, that his *Fille Élisa* "s'était faite prostituée simplement, naturellement, presque sans un soulèvement de conscience"[59] (she prostituted herself easily, naturally, without barely a flutter of her conscience). Doctor Reuss wrote that any woman spending her time in the company of prostitutes was "une femme perdue" (a lost woman) and that she was a secret prostitute herself.[60] According to medical research, the feminine caste could simply not resist mimicking the promiscuous behaviour or the shameless self-exposure in public places that the prostitute affected. There was, as Silverman states, an inextricable link between "the problem of the 'New Woman' and the discovery of the interior world as a sensitive nervous mechanism."[61] Male experts raced to prove that women ought to return to their private domains. Legrand du Saulle elaborated the contrived pathological danger of tender women sharing public spaces with prostitutes:

> Le métier de prostituée exige, en plus des rapports sexuels, une fréquentation assidue des lieux publics tel que les cafés, les restaurants de nuit et des théâtres, qui sont perçus comme des endroits dangereux pour la santé mentale et physique en général et celle des femmes en particulier. Le docteur Legrand du Saulle, médecin et chef du dépôt et de l'infirmerie spéciale et expert auprès des tribunaux, publie en 1861 un article consacré à « L'insalubrité de l'atmosphère des cafés, et de son influence sur le développement des maladies cérébrales. » Il déplore dans cet article l'insuffisante ventilation des cafés dans lesquels un très grand nombre de personnes passent plusieurs heures de la journée. Ces endroits sont « un milieu où les lois les plus élémentaires de l'hygiène sont incessanment violées. » L'air y est confiné, vicié par la fumée de cigarette, les « miasmes animaux » et la transpiration abondante.[62]
>
> (The prostitute's occupation requires, in addition to sex, regular attendance at public spaces such as cafés, bars, and theatres, which are considered to be dangerous places for physical and mental health in general and for women in particular. Doctor Legrand du Saulle, doctor, depot, and special infirmary chief and medical expert for the courts, published in 1861an article about "The unsafe atmosphere of cafés, and its influence on the development of brain diseases." The article criticizes the insufficient ventilation of cafés, where a great number of people spend hours of the day. These places are "an environment where the most elementary rules of hygiene are constantly violated." The air is stale, polluted by cigarette smoke, an "animal stench," and profuse sweating.)

Eventually, occupation of close public spaces led to a general intoxication that caused blood to flow to the brain, resulting in the neurological troubles of general paralysis.[63] Already, the connections between prostitution and hysteria begin to entrench themselves. Being in the wrong place at the wrong time or for too long a time was not only morally corrupt and

2.5 Pierre-Auguste Renoir, *Bal au Moulin de la Galette*, 1876.

punishable, it was also medically determined to be neurologically harmful. To be a woman in public, especially at night, was a sign of illness. Maxime du Camp, equating prostitutes with the public spaces male and female French citizens enjoyed, wrote, of prostitutes, that "toute leur personne exhale un odeur infecte, étrange, presque toxique"[64] (their entire person emanates an infectious odour, strange, nearly toxic). Claims like du Camp's echo the criticism of Manet's *Olympia*, where the autonomous sexual body is associated with decay, and reveal a fear of sensual women in public as much as they disclose the common modern fear of syphilis.[65] Reports of neurologically dangerous toxicity in the cafés and the cafés-concerts are at odds with Impressionist renderings of the spaces, in which women are absolutely luminous.

From Renoir's *Bal au Moulin de la Galette* to Degas' *Café-Concert des Ambassadeurs*, women are depicted as creatures of light, spectacularly illuminating the scenes they inhabit and enjoy. One can already see how the hysteric in the Brouillet painting, so milky white against the sea of black

2.6 Edgar Degas, *Le Café-Concert aux Ambassadeurs*, 1876–77.

suits that she begins to glow, is an awkward substitute for the luminous women in public represented in the paintings of Renoir and Degas. The women the Impressionists depict seem already to possess the liveliness that the painters' brushes put down so quickly. It is perhaps for their unbearable pleasure that, as the subjects of Impressionist painting, they were dismissed as asylum inmates and compared to corpses. As Emily Apter writes, in her essay on Mirbeau and hysterical perception:

Akin to another preferred keyword of the Goncourts, *plaque* (meaning "plaster applique," "veneer"), *tache* correlated impressionist impasto with the flaky epidermis of a syphilis victim. The critic Albert Wolff evoked this image of cadaverous skin when he attacked Renoir: "Just try," he urged in his article on the second major Impressionist show (1876), "to explain to M. Renoir that a woman's torso is not a decomposing mass of flesh covered with black and blue marks and conjuring up a putrefied corpse!" The *tache* was also maligned by Claretie, who castigated Manet for his reliance on this egregiously nonrepresentational sign. Huysmans, reiterating the general reaction in his *L'Art moderne*, and availing himself of a self-ironizing rhetoric of excess not unlike Mirbeau's, saw in the Impressionist effort to paint the depth, transparency, and evanescence of light and colour nothing but opacity – a sickly pallor that clung to the surface of the canvas. Subjecting Monet's feminine subjects to a gaze both violent and violating, Huysmans, as is well known, saw these *femmes-fleurs* ("women-flowers"), with their faces congested by an infernal blush or chalky with layers of make-up, as resembling the inmates of a clinic, an intimation of his imbricated analogy between madness and impressionism. Referring to the paintings as "touching follies," Huysmans asserted that the "works derived their inspiration from physiology and medicine." Finally, he alluded to Charcot directly, despite a stated resolve not to name names: "most of the paintings corroborate Dr Charcot's experiments on changes in color perception which he noted in many of his hysterics at the Salpêtrière. They had a malady of the retina.[66]

Nineteenth century criticisms of Impressionist style rested on the critique of its female subjects, comparing both to caked make-up, putrid flesh, and hysterics. The eye of the painter comes under scrutiny by Huysmans, but so does the female subject. They are both fit for the Salpêtrière. While the woman may end up there, it is evidenced by the flat, strictly "representational" lines of the Brouillet painting, that the Impressionist does not. Repugnance for the *tache*, which was egregiously non-representational, parallel's a general distaste for the irregular that emerged in a culture in ferment and transition. The hysteria project at the Salpêtrière was a complicated answer to the "deregulation of vice that was the matter" in modern France.[67]

If woman was supposed to be a creature of the interior, the ruler of domestic order, and subordinate to man, the prostitute and the feminist were certainly among the most vile misrepresentations of the traditional view of femininity and thus to be despised.

Many of the texts that sought to define womanhood in relationship to her spacial transgressions were written by physicians. A critique and anxious redefinition of womanhood appeared in the garment of scientific typology. Thus, to flout masculine ideals of feminine nature and behaviour was to be relegated to a class of degenerates, primitives, prostitutes, and hysterics. An article in *Progrès Médical* described the prostitute as degenerate, born with a nervous constitution, low intelligence and an absence of moral sense.[68] Doctor Octave Commenge wrote that the word "pudeur" (decency or restraint) did not exist for the prostitute, for whom virginity and chastity held no value.[69] Doctors confirmed nostalgic notions of femininity by making "immorality" a diagnosable condition. Nineteenth century medicine ensured that women presenting errant femininities were also conceived as pathological. It was thought that so many prostitutes were confined in the Salpêtrière in the nineteenth century that the hospital was able to redefine itself "as the medicalized version of the brothel (for a simple step separates the hysteric from the prostitute, that of scaling the walls of the Salpêtrière, and ending up on the street)."[70]

Prostitutes admitted to the Salpêtrière between 1875 and 1886 were diagnosed multiply as hysterics, epileptics, alcoholics, manics, and *aliénées.* Approximately 33 per cent of prostitutes interned at the Salpêtrière during this time were admitted with primary diagnoses of hysteria.[71] Though, according to Besnard, the number of prostitutes who were hysterics was wildly exaggerated. While Legrad du Saulle estimated that there were fifty-thousand hysterics in Paris, many of them prostitutes and while the medical literature linked hysteria and prostitution irrevocably, the Salpêtrière and police records for the latter part of the nineteenth century indicate that six or as low as one percent of prostitutes were diagnosed as hysterics.[72] That statistically very few prostitutes were actually hysterical patients is indicative of a cultural mythology that offered so much to its believers that it overshadowed empirical reality. A widespread understanding of the hysteric and the prostitute as synonymous, connected because of their sexual deviance, their autonomous movement outside the dominant moral, social and economic expectations of the era, persisted despite the few prostitutes actually interned in the Salpêtrière's hysteria ward.

The hysteric was the perfect scapegoat for deviant femininities in part because of her easy association with female fragility – her constitution was weak and nervous – and with the offensive sexualities of the prostitute and the feminist. She refused to marry, hallucinated sexual encounters, masturbated by wriggling her hips against her pillows, orgasmed publicly. She was also susceptible to suggestion, fell into helpless sleeps, worried what the doctors thought of her appearance, and performed voluptuousness or subservient politeness on stage on command. The hysteric was simultaneously able to represent a nostalgic feminine ideal and a pathological deviation that played out in a theatre of masculine medical power. Charcot's lecture series and his investment in muddling hysteria and femininity made a hysteric like Augustine or Blanche Wittman much more provocative as an icon for failing women than the prostitute, though the hysteric never fully shook herself free form the association with the sex worker.[73]

Even as late as 1913, Hippolyte Bernheim, perpetuating the link between hysteria and errant femininity, declared that there was no vice to which the hysteric was immune, that the word hysteria had become synonymous with the terms unbalanced, perverted, immoral, irresponsible, nymphomaniac.[74] Fear found expression in a hatred expressed in terminology. The conceptual unification of hysteric and deviant woman persisted well after Charcot's heyday, proof that the female scapegoating in his medical spectacles ran deep in French imaginations. Maupassant even poked fun at the simple equation of womanly nature with hysteria in his *Une Femme*:

> Hystérique, madame, voilà le grand mot du jour. Etes-vous amoureuse? vous êtes une hystérique. Etes-vous indifferente aux passions qui remuent vos semblables? vous êtes une hystérique, mais une hystérique chaste. Trompez-vous votre mari? vous êtes une hystérique, mais une hystérique sensuelle. Vous volez des coupons de soie dans un magasin? hystérique. Vous mentez à tout propos? hystérique! (Le mensonge est meme le signe caracteristique de l'hystérie.) Vous êtes gourmande? hystérique! Vous êtes nerveuse? hystérique! Vous êtes ceci, vous êtes cela, vous êtes enfin ce que toutes les femmes depuis le commencement du monde? Hystérique! hystérique! vous dis-je.[75]

> (Hysteric, madame, here is the big word of the day. Are you amorous? You are a hysteric. Are you indifferent to passions, which all seem similarly unmoving? You are a hysteric, but a chaste hysteric. Are you deceiving your husband? You are a hysteric, but a sensual hysteric. You steal pieces of silk from the store? Hysteric. You lie at every word? Hysteric! (Lying is even the characteristic sign of hysteria). You are a glutton? Hysteric! You are nervous? Hysteric! You are this, you are that, you are like all women since the beginning of the world? Hysteric! Hysteric, I tell you!)

As Maupassant teaches, the term hysteria was so porous that it absorbed all sorts of marginal ways of being. Hysteria was a metaphoric diagnosis, as much as Charcot insisted upon its physiological basis in the neurological lesion. In fact, the ability for hysteria to persist as a catch-all term for a host of symptoms of being a modern woman, alongside its more spectacular gestural symptomatology and its continual equation with a material pathology is intriguing. Hysteria's metaphoric nature was allowed to slip by and the metaphors themselves to entrench deeply, as the term adhered to an empirical rhetoric.

What's more, in the spirit of positivist classification, the modern project of questioning and defining womanhood forced female pluralities into the shadow of a singular Femininity. As Dottin-Orsini writes, "le féminin pluriel est illusoire"[76] (the feminine plural is an illusion). The singularity of womanhood was ideological. Max Nordau wrote that "La femme est typique, l'homme est original" (woman is typical, man is original) and again that, "Les femmes différent moins entre elles que les hommes: qui en connaît une, les connaît toutes … leurs pensées, leurs sentiments et même leurs formes extêrieures se ressemblent"[77] (women differ between themselves less than men: to know one is to know them all … their thoughts, their feelings and even their external forms resemble one another). Edmond de Goncourt wrote that "l'être féminin, du grand au petit, et de haut en bas, est le même être"[78] (the feminine being, from large to small, from top to bottom, is the same being) If all women were, in essence, the same, then the hysteric could easily stand in for all women, especially if her illness was a mere embellishment of typical feminine nature. Metaphor and medical terminology, together, ensured the hysteric's iconic status as Woman.

Ultimately, it was in the body of the hysteric that masculine anxieties about the shifting position of women, nostalgia for a woman of bygone days, and ambivalence towards women converged. And it was the lecture series in which male anxieties and longings around women were brought to the fore and massaged into a false catharsis that was, in fact, repression.

TWISTED FEMININITIES

A Turn of the Private Woman in Public

If the nostalgic "gynophobie" sweeping Paris was causing a hope among certain parts of the population that a woman might not be in public at all but rather remain, "queen of the interior … what Nature ha[d] made her: an ideal woman the companion and lover of man, the mistress of the home,"[79] the lecture series was an enchanting turn of her occupation of public and private spaces. The female body was brought into the interior space of the asylum and was put on display – not as prostitutes had displayed themselves in windows,[80] or how the femmes nouvelles had shamelessly displayed themselves in public – only under the regulation, suggestion, and reasonable discursive commentary of the male medical doctor.

The Salpêtrière, since its conversion from a gunpowder facility into an asylum, was a space to store the unwanted of Paris. An enclosed space with high walls, the block of buildings and gardens housed people living in poverty, orphans, widows, alcoholics, and those considered to be mad. As early as 1656, Louis XIV charged the Salpêtrière with accommodating "les femmes et les filles … pour nettoyer Paris de tout ce qu'elle compte de miséreux"[81] (women and girls … to cleanse Paris of all its poor). As Marquer writes, "Dès l'origine, donc, les bâtiments sont conçus pour être un lieu clos, protégé"[82] (From its origin, then, the buildings were conceived to be an enclosed space, protected). A protection.

In the hospital spectacle, the hysteric rose to certain celebrity. She was often half dressed or naked, "souvent nue ou en chemise;" she pulled her clothes off and twisted in erotic ecstasy before the eyes of her onlookers.[83] Within the privacy of the little theatre of the Salpêtrière she enacted the kind of sexuality that came under harsh criticism and punishment in broader French culture. If there is another lesson to glean from the Fleury and Brouillet images, read progressively, it may be that the hysterics at the hospital were liberated, but only conditionally. No longer in chains, simply hidden away behind the walls of that great "ville dans une ville"[84] (city within a city), the hysteric was brought into public view but still imprisoned in the dramaturgical confines of the medical show. The patient's privacy, during the lectures, was always exploited.

Even the French term *camisole* carries the double meaning of nightdress and straitjacket. Sometimes, when the lecture transcripts read that the patient wore a camisole, the reader has to look for other clues to indicate whether the garment worn is the private undergarment or the cloth restraint. Contained within this euphemism is a tradition of misogynist ambivalence toward women, who seduce and please, and who need to be controlled, who may show or conceal their private parts, but who ought to be constrained for doing so out of turn.

The lack of respect for patient privacy in the hospital spectacles, and the male desire to make the patients' private pain public resulted in several hypocrisies: women suffering from hysteria were enclosed together with and often diagnosed as erotomaniacs and nymphomaniacs. They were denied "any contact with men who might fire their desires, and provoke attacks,"[85] though this caution only applied to fellow inmates. That Charcot's entire practice revolved around provoking such attacks in front of an audience of men was not considered to be an exact enactment of this very prohibition, though it was. While masturbation by a woman was considered to be both a cause and symptom of derangement,[86] doctors frequently incited hysterical attitudes passionnelles, during which the patient publicly arched, thrust, wriggled, and thrashed in orgasm. Attendants performed procedures on female patients that closely resembled manual stimulation: ovarian compression, a common procedure used to incite and cure attacks, involved "introducing the index and middle finger into the hysterical woman's vagina during the attack to 'grasp the ovary.'"[87] Female sexuality, rendered spectacle and medical property at once, was no longer a woman's personal affair to enact as privately or publicly as she wished. Along with her pleasure, the patient's pain and unconsenting paticipation was integral to the spectacle of masculine power. Indeed, as Elaine Scarry writes, "the felt experience of physical pain gives rise to ... an almost obscene conflation of private and public. It brings with it all the solitude of absolute privacy with none of its safety, all the self-exposure of the utterly public with none of its possibility for camaraderie or shared experience."[88] The same can be said of pleasure in this instance. Publicly experienced, the patient's *jouissance* was intensely private and obscenely exposed.

The hysteric's attacks seemed, sometimes, to mimic the forbidden behaviour of the autonomous sexual woman, but these attacks could be called on and halted by the director's use of ovarian compression, loud noises, magnets, or hypnosis. Her "misbehaviours" were brought forth into full view and then returned to their hidden places in her body, under the command of the doctor. The woman in hysterics was certainly no master of crocheting, tapestry, and embroidering, but she was nonetheless submissive.

Charcot emphasized the regularity of the attacks and their subordination to medical techniques, placing the patient's dangerous pathology – her womanhood – firmly at the physician's whim. Judging from medical writings, the hysteric also, as in Brouillet's painting, could appear voluptuously soft and sleepy, a passive woman in the arms of the Salpêtrière doctors and nurses, not unlike the idealized "queen of the interior." The hysteric's publicity was a strictly directed pivot of the public appearance of women that made French men so anxious. What sort of woman did doctors want to see? What feminine type did spectators desire? Charcot could bring her forth. Since she was not invited to appear publicly, but was instead coerced into doing so, her privacy and public appearance were regulated even more than that of the *femme isolée* on Paris' streets. Furthermore, the knowledge that Charcot could go home following the proceedings and that a patient like Augustine would be tucked away until needed again was an ever-present reminder that the hysteric's public appearances were limited, and that she was ultimately confined.

THE HYSTERIC AS SCAPEGOAT
A Dramaturgy of Projection

Octave Mirbeau, who attended the lectures, describes them as a theatre of coercion and submission: "(La première hystérique) entre en faisant des façons; ce monde aperçu tout d'un coup, sous la lumière rougeâtre, la gène et l'intimide. Elle a des gestes de colère, elle s'assoit en rechignant, elle ne veux pas ôter sa camisole. « Allons! Voyons! Il n'y a pas de danger, tu garderas ton fichu. » Enfin, la manche est retroussée. Le grand bras est inerte. Mais l'autre est bien vivant, et tout à l'heure … le bras est devenu de pierre: elle est vaincue. Charcot s'approche: pic! pic! pic! la longue épingle d'acier entre dans la chair! Pic! pic! pic! Elle ne sent rien"[89] (The first hysteric enters, making a fuss; seeing the audience all of a sudden, under the reddish light, makes her shy, intimidates her. She makes gestures of anger, she sits grudgingly. She does not want to take off her camisole. "Come on! Let's see! There is no danger. You will keep your head scarf." Finally, the sleeve is rolled up. The upper arm is inert. But the other is lively, and, after awhile … the arm has become stone. She is vanquished. Charcot approaches her: pic! Pic! Pic! The long steel needle enters the flesh! Pic! Pic! Pic! She doesn't feel a thing.)

The woman Mirbeau describes is at once shy, resistant, then compliant. She is made of stone and made of flesh, an uncanny figure, both woman and not quite woman. At first she feels too much, overestimates the danger of being on stage this way. Then she is incapable of feeling anything at all. She is malleable and multiple. The hysteric played a range of femininities, hosting any of the identifications an audience might need to make in her. Her soft femininity was crossed by the monstrous violence of her attack in a repeated wave of the unmannerly over the demure. Her delicacy contorted with the emotional surge of a past scene. As Charles Richet wrote for the *Revue des Deux Mondes*, "Quelles fréquentes et rudes convulsions en de si délicates créatures, et avec tant de réitération et de renforcement!"[90] (What frequent and unmannerly convulsions in such delicate creatures, and with such reiteration and increasing force). His astonishment at the violence moving through delicate bodies is clear. The pity and horror elicited in the patient's very real performance quickly turns to marvel. The hysterical woman's hallucinations are: "de toute sorte, tantôt gaies, tantôt tristes, tantôt amoureuses, tantôt religieuses ou extatiques. Chaque fois qu'une image a surgi dans l'esprit, aussitôt les mouvements des membres, les traits de la physionomie, l'attitude générale du corps, tout se conforme à la nature de cette hallucination. Ces poses, ces *attitudes passionnelles*, ont une vivacité, une vigueur d'expression qu'on ne saurait retrouver d'ailleurs"[91] (of every sort, sometimes gay, sometimes sad, sometimes romantic, sometimes religious or ecstatic. Each time that an image surges in the spirit, at once the movements of the limbs, the facial traits, the general attitude of the body, all conforms to the nature of the particular hallucination. These poses, these attitudes passionnelles, have a life, a vigour of expression that we would not know how to find elsewhere). He notes the recurring force of the hallucinogenic content once more: "Ce sont les mêmes personnages qui apparaissent, les mêmes scènes qui se reproduisent à tous les attaques"[92] (These are the same people who appear, the same scenes that reproduce themselves in all of the attacks). The hysteric's private experiences have spectacular appeal. It is the form as well as the content that astonishes.

Charcot described the hysteric as one who elicits pity and fear.[93] His lectures featured descriptions of catharsis paralleling Aristotle's descriptions of Greek tragedy. In the performances of hysteria, disorderly audience sentiments were worked upon but the cathartic effect and the lecture series' parallels to tragedy are up for debate. The Salpêtrière patient was not greater in stature than her audience members – in fact, she was thought to be the opposite. She did not take vengeance for crimes committed against her. The woman behind the hysteric was not fictional. She was sometimes more real than the theatrical structure could bear. There was, however, something of a goat song in the dramaturgy of projection. It was not a mythic theatre; it was a real theatre where something resembling the sacrificial took place. The hysteric stood in for a loathed and intriguing populace of women and was foisted onto the stage as the scapegoat for their so-called transgressions. Moreover she functioned, in performance, as the scapegoat for masculine anxieties about male positions under threat in society. As Clément writes, "Lévi-Strauss distinguishes two modes of repression … The anthropoemic mode, ours, consists in vomiting the abnormal ones into protected spaces – hospitals, asylums, prisons."[94] In some ways, though this book argues the impossibility of such a total reduction of selfhood, women like Augustine or Blanche Wittman, heaved into confinement at the Salpêtrière, came to be on stage as all women and for all men.

In 1846, Landouzy defined hysteria as "a neurosis of the woman's generative apparatus." Briquet had distilled the origins of hysteria down to two possibilities by the last half of the nineteenth century. Its source was either genital or due to sensibility – a feminine sensibility.[95] Though the common belief that it was caused by a rebellious, travelling uterus became outmoded, hysteria was still, by definition, a woman's illness. Hysteria, according to Didi-Huberman, "was the symptom, to put it crudely, of *being a woman*."[96] And, as previously stated, it "almost never stopped calling the feminine 'guilty.'"[97] According to Charles Richet, hysteria was exceedingly common and could be caused by heredity, circumstance, ambition, or being female. When women became educated beyond their social station, he noted, hysteria was frequent. According to him, the symptom of "chimeric hopes" plagued many hysterical women in France. They had trouble finding men who lived up to their dreams. Marriage became disenchanting because a life doing chores did not sufficiently fulfill a woman's fantasies. Hence misery, chagrin, and discomfort were often symptoms of hysteria. Richet concludes that hysteria has one physiological basis – heredity – and one social basis – that of reality not living up to one's dreams.[98] Richet's assessment of hysteria, like Charcot's, does indeed render it a woman's illness. Hysteria's causes and effects distinctly describe several feminine states or experiences in the shifting socio-economic terrain of the nineteenth century, wherein one could argue that social change was arriving too slowly or too quickly, depending on the gender one occupied.

Hysteria was ultimately a feminine diagnosis, but paradoxically it was also a terminological dumping ground for feminist traits considered to be too masculine – like sexual desire and ambition. Doctors manipulated the hysterical patient to produce figurative embodiments of either subservience to paternalism or confident sexuality, symbolically curating, in a real woman's body, simultaneously idealized and feared sexualized feminine forms.

The hysterical body was prone to fits of ecstasy, producing effects that doctors labelled, not without degrading judgement for sex work or female sexual autonomy, according to popular names for prostitute – *horizontal, lionne, joueuse*. Augustine was photographed in ecstatic states in poses that depicted her as both *femme fatale* and child. Representations of womanhood in documents of hysterical performance more often than not show female sexuality being demonized or dominated. What aspects of French women did deeply ambivalent physicians emphasize over others? Lying down, hysterical women fell asleep, smiling and sleepy, in the midst of hallucinated sexual relations. The asylum drama also presented women wildly tearing off their clothing, contorting in sexual abandon. Hysterics could alternately perform as demure and shy, uncomfortable with their public nudity or ignited by a self-serving desire. Sometimes the same woman played both roles in the same performance. She might be timid or even reluctant before a provoked attack that caused her to disrobe in attitudes passionnelles. Or she might be flirtatious to begin with, exuding all sorts of sass, and then find herself subdued in a hypnotically suggested performance where she sheepishly and gratefully received one of Charcot's portraits or timidly picked a bouquet of flowers, asking the director's permission to cut blossoms from an imaginary garden.[99]

The hysteric's embodiment of so-called paradoxes of sexual behaviour shows exactly how hysteria functioned primarily as a metaphor. It was a life-changing diagnosis and it was a catch-all for contradictory male perceptions of women, for a spectrum of popularly idealized and demonized femininities. Because hysteria was invented, we look to those who constructed, perpetuated, and clung to its expression for clues as to why the patient's poor body was needed so badly. Foucault states that in ceremonies of public torture and execution "the main character was the people, whose real and immediate presence was required for the performance."[100] His claim is true for the medical spectacle at the Salpêtrière as well. For the spectacle was partly of the hysteric and all she represented but was also of the people who orchestrated and watched the little theatre of sacrifice.

In lecture, Charcot's descriptions of his patients were both medical, to do with physiological traits and pathologies, and based on an aesthetics of male desire and entitlement. Blanche Wittman appeared on stage, described in relation to her physicality, her beauty, her big breasts, and also her love for the attention of men: "Blanche est grande, elle mesure 1,64 cm, elle a une forte corpulence (soixante dix kilos), elle est blonde, avec un teint lymphatique. La peau est blanche. Les seins sont très volumineux. Son intelligence atteint à peine à la moyenne. La mémoire est assez bonne … Son regard est brillant: la vue et la contact des hommes produisent chez elle une espèce d'excitation particulière"[101] (Blanche is large, she measures 1.64 cm, she is stout (seventy kilograms), she is blond with a lymphatic complexion. Her skin is white. Her breasts are very voluminous. She is moderately intelligent. Her memory is good enough … The look in her eye is bright: the sight of and contact with men produces in her a particular excitement). What the audience may glean from this description is that Blanche is buxom, barely smart, sensual. When he spoke on behalf of the women on stage, Charcot described their brain lesions (which were not apparent but rather represented by drawings of an imaginary lesion that Charcot never found) and their physicality. Speaking of ovarian compression, he described not only the process but above all, "a beautiful girl with magnificent shape and abundant blonde hair."[102] The director himself made explicit the connection between physiological femininity (the womb), womanly appearance, and hysteria, making his lectures a theatre of masculine desire. Charcot, whose language was inclusive, ensured that the audience identify primarily with him in the dramatic pairing. His, "In a moment, gentlemen, I will show you" and "I assure you gentlemen" drew the audience into his position – that of observer and orchestrator.[103] If the attack was a sexual performance, Charcot performed both sexual restraint and proprietary sexual dominance. He could call on a woman's desire, provoke her vaginal wetness, throw her into the throes of ecstasy. But he himself would remain clothed, apart. Domination poorly disguised itself as demonstration.

Charcot's perspectives on women and their societal roles were far from progressive. His persona off stage, if there was such a space for a man of such celebrity, embodied many conservative ideas about women and feminism, and his biases certainly informed his creation of the Salpêtrière's particular brand of hysteria. For instance, while it seems that the director of the hospital would avoid publicity that might undermine his objective project with false tales of intern romps with the patients, Charcot very much admired Jules Claretie, pictured in the audience in the Brouillet painting, and encouraged him to come to the Salpêtrière to research his novel, *Les amours d'un interne*.[104] Far from fearing the reputation that a salacious novel about doctors and medical students in dalliances with patients might cause, Charcot escorted Claretie to the hospital daily in his carriage. The doctor's attitudes towards medical practice and patients did not exclude fictional romantic treatment, indicating a softness for heterosexual encounters within the Salpêtrière, even if imaginary.[105]

Charcot's comments at a doctoral thesis defense caused women present to laugh at him for his outmoded ideas of gender roles. He chastised the doctoral candidate, who seemed, for him, to represent all progressive women, that women ought not to be doctors but ought to take time, instead, to care for their appearances, leaving governing the world to men.[106] Charcot and Richer both expressed what can only be described as great excitement for the way hysterics tore off their clothing in *Les démoniaques dans l'art*, regretting that certain artistic renderings of early hysterics lack this feature.[107] In the same volume, Charcot's project was to marry nineteenth century notions of hysteria with their less informed and less correct expressions in early artworks from the eleventh to the eighteenth century. Bernard Marquer has been diligent in tracing the doctor's aim to herald in a secular, positivist mode of thinking by reaching back to classical works and pointing out their similarities and errors and also his aim to validate his work at the Salpêtrière as artistic. What has been less addressed about this baroque project is how it simultaneously brought outdated modes of thinking up to speed (from demonic possession to hysteria, and therefore out of the dark ages), and made contemporary hysterics classical, on par with the beauties of Rubens.[108] One can already sense the nostalgia that accompanies Charcot's presentation of "his" hysterics. They are like artworks from the past. In fact, Charcot directly addressed the crossover between art and medicine at the juncture of the nude female body, read imagistically, in several of his lectures. He once said, "En réalité, Messieurs, nous autres médecins, nous devrions connaître le *nu* aussi bien et même mieux que les peintres"[109] (In reality, dear sirs, we doctors had better know the *nude* as well as and better, even, than painters). The remark has connotations with morbid anatomy and the medical value of being able to perceive the whole female body with accuracy. It also points to Charcot's relationship to the hysterical patient as an artful projection, as an embodiment of the exciting relationship between science and art figured in the female body displaying itself, and in the doctor observing, knowing, and rendering. The hysteric permitted the doctor to seep into the domain of art; the physician's expertise thus proliferated.

The hierarchical masculine/feminine pairing of the Salpêtrière co-stars was essential to the lectures' reception. A reasoned Charcot alongside a hysteric, inarticulate and contorting, allowed the woman on stage, and symbolically all women – hysterics were, after all, "femmes plus que les autres femmes"[110] (more women than women) – to appear as the pathological twist on the normal masculine type.[111] The patient, often hypnotized or hallucinating, bore many forms of femininity at once – often those forms most feared or most desired by the male doctors who, swollen with their own feelings towards womanhood, provoked her towards a typified state.

In the hypnosis experiments especially, doctors enacted their fantasies. They made up scenario after scenario in which the hysteric played a duped or silly woman, a sexualized woman who felt appropriately shy about her behaviour afterwards, a woman in pain whose own body seemed to be betraying her. Or else she played an ideal moral woman, acting the faithful wife, or responding to male commands – to believe her scarf was on fire or to fall into a catatonic sleep. These little dramas of fantastic projection are revelatory; in the safe territory of the "experiment," masculine ambivalences towards women, their anxieties, repulsions, and desires, could play out in a theatre of what Svetlana Boym calls restorative nostalgia,[112] wherein men at the Salpêtrière impossibly tried to recreate a woman who no longer existed.

For Elaine Scarry, spectacle is integral to the inscription of a regime's power through the bodies of the tortured. As she explains, "It is not accidental that in the torturers' idiom, the room in which the brutality occurs was called the 'production room' in the Philippines, the 'cinema room' in South Vietnam, and 'the blue lit stage' in Chile: built on these repeated acts of display and having as its production the fantastic illusion of power, torture is a grotesque piece of compensatory drama."[113]

The combination of pain and theatre that Scarry emphasizes certainly speaks to the spectacle of medical power and the power of spectacle itself in Charcot's lectures. The public quality of pain and its unfolding within a dramatic structure of positivist inquiry, of women rendered docile in hypnotism, of little scenes between doctors and patients that appear to be innocent but reek of hatred – all this points to an attempt to establish male supremacy at the unique site of theatre.

The following two scenes, constructed by doctors via hypnotism, are instructive:

> La blonde et passive Alsacienne congédiée, nous étions restés avec la brune et sémillante Parisienne. Nous fîmes alors une curieuse

expérience, à laquelle, depuis, tous nos sujets se sont prêtés sans difficulté, toujours avec plein succès. À cette expérience, on a donné le nom bien choisi de *mariage à trois*. On persuade à la jeune fille endormie qu'elle a deux maris: un mari pour le côté gauche et l'autre pour le côté droit, et qu'elle leur doit à chacun une fidélité scrupuleuse. M. Féré et moi étions ces deux maris. Nous pouvions chacun caresser notre moitié, elle accueillait nos caresses avec un plaisir marqué. Mais gare à celui qui voulait empiéter sur la moitié de l'autre; moi, dans ce cas, je recevais une tape soignée; M. Féré une tape un peu plus timide. Dès que l'un de nous approchait de l'exacte ligne médiane du corps, sa défiance était en éveil, et la main s'apprêtait à mettre à la raison le téméraire.

Cette expérience peut passer, à première vue, pour n'être qu'amusante. Mais elle nous montre la suggestion amenant le dédoublement de la personnalité. Elle peut ainsi expliquer les phénomènes si singuliers dont nous avons parlé au début, la demi-léthargie, la demi-catalepsie, le demi-somnambulisme. Elle montre à coup sûr combien l'hypnotisé est un sujet docile entre les mains de l'hypnotiseur.[114]

(The blonde and passive Alsatian dismissed, we stayed with the vivacious Parisian brunette. We then did a curious experiment, to which all of our subjects have lent themselves easily, always with full success. We gave this experiment the well chosen name of *mariage à trois*. We persuade the sleeping girl she has two husbands: one husband for the left side and one for the right side, and should give each of them her scrupulous fidelity. M. Féré and I were both husbands. We could each caress our half, she welcomed our caresses with marked pleasure. But woe to the one who wanted to encroach on the other half; I, in this case, received a precise tap; M. Féré a pat a little more shy. As soon as one of us approached the exact midline of the body, her defiance was awakened, and the hand prepared itself to restore sense to the audacious perpetrator.

This experiment may seem, at first, only to be amusing. But it shows us how suggestion causes the personality to split. It can explain such strange phenomena as discussed earlier, half lethargy, semi-trance, half-sleepwalking. It most definitely shows how the hypnotized subject is a docile in the hands of the hypnotist.)

And:

M. Charcot fit introduire ensuite une autre pensionnaire de la Salpêtrière: c'était une fille chétive, maigre, hâve et pâle, physionomie honnête et assez intelligente, bien qu'un peu extatique; mise pauvre, mais propre.

Elle salua poliment l'assistance et, avec une nuance de familiarité, M. Charcot. « Vous allez bien? lui demanda-t-il. – Très bien! – Vous avez déjeuné? – Parfaitement. – Qu'avez-vous pris? – Du lait, du pain. – C'était bon? – Très bon. – Regardez un peu vos pieds, voyez quel beau bassin et quelle eau limpide! – Vraiment! fit-elle en regardant le plancher d'un air admiratif. – Et les beaux poissons rouges? – Comme ils sont nombreux, M. Charcot, il y en a de toutes les tailles! – Montrez un peu. – Il y en a de petits comme ceci, et de grands comme cela. – Et tout autour du bassin, voyez-vous le frais gazon, semé de jolies marguerites, roses et blanches! Me permettez-vous d'en cueillir, M. Charcot? – Certainement, ma fille. »

L'hallucinée se pencha, cueillit ses marguerites, avec précaution, de-ci, de-là. Elle cherchait visiblement à ne pas faire de trop grands vides dans le gazon; après quoi elle les arrangea en un bouquet qu'elle attacha à son corsage avec une épingle. « Vous voilà bien heureuse. – Si heureuse! – C'est dommage seulement que votre jambe droite soit paralysée. – Ah! mon Dieu! »

Et la pauvre fille donna des signes de la plus profonde angoisse, essaya de remuer sa jambe, elle tombait si l'on ne s'était empressé de la soutenir. « Voyons! ça va mieux, voilà votre jambe remise. – Bien merci, M. Charcot. – Malheureusement, vous avez mal dans le dos. – Ah! que j'ai mal! » Et elle se tord, manifestant la plus vive souffrance.

Moi à M. Charcot: « Est-elle endormie? – Je ne sais pas. – Est-elle éveillée ? – Je ne sais pas. – Elle est cependant endormie ou éveillée? – C'est possible, mais je n'en sais rien. – Est-elle toujours comme cela? – Toujours. – C'est bien singulier. – Oui. – Et l'explication? – Je ne l'ai pas. » Pendant tout ce dialogue, nous avions oublié notre sujet, qui continuait à être en proie à ses douleurs. M. Charcot s'empressa de les lui enlever.[115]

(Charcot then introduced another resident at the Salpêtrière. She was a puny girl, thin, gaunt, and pale. Her physiognomy was honest and smart enough, though a bit ecstatic; she was poor, but clean.

She politely greeted the audience and, with a hint of familiarity, Charcot. "Are you doing well?" he asked. – Very well! – You have eaten lunch? – Perfectly. – What did you have? – Milk, bread. – It was good? – Very good. – Look at your feet, see what a beautiful area and what clear water! – Really, she said, looking at the floor admiringly. – And the beautiful goldfish. – How many there are M. Charcot! There are all sizes! – Show a little. – There are small ones like this, and big like this. – And all around the pool, do you see the fresh grass, dotted with pretty daisies, pink and white! Would you allow me to pick some, M. Charcot? – Certainly, my girl."

The hallucinating patient bent down, picked her daisies, carefully, from here and there. She visibly tried not to leave spaces that were too big in the lawn; after which she arranged them into a bouquet which she affixed to her blouse with a pin. "You are very happy. – So happy! – It's only a pity that your right leg is paralyzed. – Oh my God!"

And the poor girl showed signs of profound anguish, tried to move her leg. She would have fallen were we not there to support her. "See here, it's better. Your leg is well again. – Well thank you, Mr. Charcot. – Unfortunately, you have a backache – Ah! It hurts so much!" She twists, manifesting the deepest suffering.

I said to Charcot: "Is she asleep? – I do not know – Is she awake? – I do not know – She is asleep or awake though? – It's possible, but I know nothing of it either way. – Is she always like this? – Always. – It is very strange. – Yes. – And the explanation? – I don't have one." Throughout this dialogue, we forgot the poor subject, who continued to be plagued by her pain. Charcot hastened to relieve her of it.)

In the first drama constructed by the doctors, several masculine fantasies come to the fore, despite Delboeuf's claim that the experiment is for the scientifically curious only.[116] Because the hypnotized patient is open to any suggestion, that the role-play of the *mariage à trois* is repeated on several occasions makes it particularly revelatory. The hypnotized patient could be made to do anything, to be anyone, and she was made to adopt a domestic position where she desired each doctor so unequivocally that she was faithful to both of them at once. This fantasy play of the hetero-patriarchy could not be more obvious.

The language Delboeuf uses to describe the patient and to outline the experiment is based on desire from the beginning. "That vivacious Parisian" is the woman they hypnotize – not an ill woman, not a woman who is particularly easy or difficult to hypnotize – a vivacious brunette. The language is also one of possession – each man may caress "his half." The drama features a monogamous heterosexual wife who is, above all, faithful. She plays both wives perfectly, each is totally loyal to her husband, safely situated within the marital structure. When the doctors toy with her devotions, her faithfulness proves itself all the more. She will not entertain affections from the other man on the half that does not "belong" to him. That many women in the hospital were victims of sexual abuse of one kind or another and could not possibly benefit from or experience healing in a public theatre of unwanted caresses is not taken into account. Because the patient is sleeping, she is a sexual object, not actively engaging her sexual subjectivity. What becomes important is that the doctors can turn her desire and her faithfulness on and off "like a faucet."[117] The men freely caress the passively accepting woman who finds their touch pleasurable, "markedly" so. If we take into account the hysteric's unique ability to stand in for all women, then in the scene enacted with this woman, the message is clear: women do belong to men and do want their advances; they are sexually open to whatever man may assert his desires. And above all – an impossibility, of course, and this is exactly the crux of the drama – men control female desire. Delboeuf notes that the experiment may seem amusing, or that it may seem *only* to be amusing, indicating that it is – for him, and likely for the audience. While he outlines the contribution that the experiment makes to certain understandings of hypnosis, his ultimate conclusion is that the hypnotized woman is docile in the hands of the hypnotist. The greatest achievement and the biggest pleasure of the experiment, for Delboeuf, is the proof of docility. Delboeuf's triumphant conclusion follows closely the rampant antifeminist sentiment of the likes of Theodore Jordan for whom women were objects made for husbands' personal pleasure, believing they ought to please and serve them exclusively.[118]

Despite Delboeuf's position on the ultimate revelation of the hypnosis experiment, it is certain that the scenario reveals much more about the desires and fears the doctors bring to the theatrical laboratory. What becomes apparent is a deep-seated wish the doctors have for the woman with a distinct sexuality to desire *them*, and for her to feel conflicted about her desires, to be at once sexual and chaste. Wanting so much, it is no wonder the doctors must lean on hypnosis to conjure their hysteric heroine. The scene, with its Therèse Raquin come to life, presents a betrayal of the overvaluation of monogamous, quiet sensuality in anti-feminist, anti-prostitution, and medical texts on hysterical pathology. Instead, an ambivalence pokes through. The doctors revel in the possibility of having mastery over the patient's desire, but they do not want the desire to disappear or the patient to become too demure. If she can respond with pleasure to their advances and remain faithful, she embodies a sexually subservient wife or mistress, playing by the rules of the patriarchy. In the hypnosis drama, doctors can produce a woman character who is sexually available, seemingly consenting, and docile at once. This is volatile dramaturgy. Of course the hypnosis drama produces a woman who plays chastity and voluptuousness *under the male doctor's command*. That this conjuring of ideals occurs through a patient who signifies so-called errant femininities when she is fully awake and more fully herself is significant. When she is ill, she is hysterical. When she is under the doctor's care, she can be modified. For a group of men destabilized by the shifting roles of women in French society, this misogynist fantasy is safe, guaranteed, and will unravel itself at the end of the experiment, when the woman will become hospital resident once again. One thing is clear: docility is what the doctor wants to be the outcome of the experiment. The Salpêtrière experiments move Delboeuf to write that even "plus que le cadavre" (more than the cadaver) – a morbid invocation, but a revealing association – the hypnotized female patient "est un esclave qui n'a plus d'autre volonté que celle qu'on lui inspire … Il se souviendra de ce qu'on voudra, il oubliera ce qu'on voudra"[119] (is a slave who doesn't have any more will than we give her … she will remember what we want her to, she will forget what we want her to).

Delboeuf's account points to motivations that transcend the obvious desire to dominate a woman-slave. The reiterated conclusion that the hysteric lacks a will and can be made to do, remember, and forget what and when the doctors like is excessive. Occurring many times in Delboeuf's paper, the continued utterance betrays excitement but also anxiety bordering on desperation: "The patient is docile; the patient is a slave," repeated like a mantra, actually demonstrates the phrase's lack of power. It is as if Delboeuf does not believe his own words. One also wonders if the experimental emphasis on memory does not betray a similar anxiety.

What if the patient could remember all of what the doctors did to her and all of the versions of women she was made to play? Would her docility remain intact? Is her slavishness not precariously hinged upon hypnotically suggested forgetfulness? Perhaps Delboeuf already suspects, at least to some extent, that patient docility is not a fact but a contingency.

In her work on the body in pain, Scarry notes that torture plays out in a drama that is "compensatory" and that produces a "fantastic illusion of power."[120] In the Salpêtrière experiments, the doctors produce patient docility as a theatrical fulfillment of a wish and also to ensure that their fantasies, their illusions of power, can play out without intervention from the patient, who surely would not stand for the conditions of the spectacle and who could only ever point to the failures of the hypnosis drama to produce a real woman. Patient docility, then, is a diversion. A wish and a dramatic subterfuge obscuring the wish. The manifest content of the spectacle carries a latent meaning that appears due to the apparent simplicity of the scene.[121]

The ruse continues, for the doctors staged patient docility, but also pleasure. In another scene, M. Féré, having manipulated Blanche Wittman's musculature through a series of swellings, contractions, and grimaces, is "triomphant" (triumphant) after he plays her "comme d'un piano"[122] (like a piano). He takes credit for being virtuosic, when it is her body that has been through a physiologically laborious performance. And then, M. Féré makes Wittman spasm with erotic pleasure, producing orgasmic response to the bodily domination she has just experienced on stage.[123] The pleasure the doctors call out of the patient's body is a violation and a red herring. She is made to seem to bear the pleasure taken in the experiment, when it is the physicians' pleasure that is taking place. Not only is the female patient acting out a masculine fantasy of controlled sexuality, or sexuality where there is, instead, violence, but she is also made to carry the burden of fantasy herself. When she spasms erotically, her desire saturates the spectacle, as though she enjoys the version of herself she has become in hypnosis, as though she wants to be constructed this way. The patient's pleasure bears the repression of the masculine desire that produces the spectacle that occurs in her own body. It is via her pleasure – also constructed via hypnotic suggestion – that the men on stage and in the audience are permitted to forget that it is they who do not know any more "what kind of woman they want," or are entitled to have, who have to work through their anxieties and desires about female autonomy, sexuality, and identity by playing with a living doll, writing a scenography of scapegoatism.[124]

The second scene is as brutal than the first and involves physically harming a patient, a practice that was regularly part of Charcot's lectures. At first, the director plays charm and feigned interest. He asks questions a compassionate person would: "Are you doing well?" and "Have you eaten?" This chatty pretence of care only renders more starkly brutal the violence that follows. The director's attentiveness to the patient's well-being moves through tender flower picking and beautification to two acts of injury and ends with Charcot so disinterested that he leaves the patient in agony in order to chat with Delboeuf. The woman who hallucinates is, in the beginning, treated like a daughter, in a tone at once tender and diminutive. She asks Charcot's permission to pick the flowers. He paternalistically replies "Certainly, my girl." She does so, pinning the daisies she collects to her blouse, demonstrating a femininity that is easy (for some) to digest. And then he hurts her. She is in profound pain. She falls, plays out the iconic hysterical collapse that is mistaken for surrender. When Charcot makes her well again, she thanks him, although it is he who inflicted the pain in the first place. He heals her only to make her twist in back pain, to harm her once more. Then he forgets about her, while he converses with his colleagues.

This horrific scene points to the ease with which doctors inflicted pain on female patients. The literature produces many other instances of the same thing. Elsewhere in Delboeuf's report, physicians hypnotically suggest burns to patients that are so bad they leave scars.[125] Hypnotized patients produce stigmata on several occasions and swollen, red lesions that weep pus.[126] The hysterical attack itself, provoked on stage ad infinitum, could be extremely painful.

The question asserts itself: Why? Why, at the end of the nineteenth century, does this medical theatre of pain and power take on iconic status? Why does this scene occur at all? And why does Delboeuf transcribe it in such a cavalier manner? What permits Charcot to fail to heal the patient at once, and to fail to remember that she is still in agony, dismissing her experience as he talks with a doctor-fan? I cannot explain such brutality. In this age marked by misogynist panic and positivist paternalism, I cannot account for how hatred came to be enacted and proliferated in such a way.

I find myself grasping for explanations.

Perhaps it was, in part, the single-minded commitment to science that allowed doctors to discount a patient's experience of pain or to view it as a fair price to pay for medical discovery. In the hypnosis experiments, what was sought was to what extent suggestion could take hold of a patient's body. Doctors, then, wanted to see if hypnosis could leave a mark. But once it had been discovered that patients could, in fact, experience pain so bad it lead to scarring, elaborate hypnotic dramas were repeated, so much so that a patient was burned three times in one day, causing her to ask, finally, "Comment ne prend-on pas la précaution de me préserver du feu quand je suis en expérience?"[127] (How did you not protect me while I was in the experiment?) There is another side to the force of momentum of the scientific project. Its thrust was forceful in itself, as empiricism gained popularity in the fin-de-siècle, and it also acted as a vehicle for male ambivalences to play out without admitting to doing so. Scarry, in her studies on public torture, has discovered some of the "logic" at work at the Salpêtrière. She notes that torture structurally features "Three Simultaneous Phenomena," which can equally be applied to the medical theatre of female hysterics and to the doctors who injure them. These are, "the infliction of pain," "the objectification of the subjective attributes of pain," and "the translation of the objectified attributes of pain into the insignia of power."[128] On stage, Charcot and his colleagues burned, lanced, scarred, and twisted the bodies of women, but always under the guise of empirical research. Firmly in the grasp of reason, the patient's pain reflected her powerlessness against even her own body, and demonstrated medicine's power to produce, name, and quell symptoms, and also to play the hysterical woman "like a piano." It is no coincidence that Delboeuf concludes, from one experiment rife with complexities of desire and fear, that what has been proven is the docility of the patient under the power of the hypnotizer. The scientific objectification of hysterical symptoms acted as a moral cover for acts of violence that otherwise would have been called torture.

The medical spectacle was entrenched in turning private experience into reasoned description, narrating away the socially turbulent "new woman" without ever mentioning her. The terminologically inflected medical discourse described a patient without will, thus objectifying female subjectivity as a way of translating it into a fiction of positivist masculine power. As Scarry writes, "ultimate domination requires that the prisoner's ground become increasingly physical and the torturer's increasingly verbal, that the prisoner become a colossal body with no voice and the torturer a colossal voice."[129] In an era where empiricism was in vogue and where the people whose bodies came under scrutiny were often the marginalized of French culture – people from the colonies, prisoners, prostitutes, and so-called "degenerates," the Salpêtrière theatre was, not surprisingly, one where doctors spoke while hysterics' bodies were emphasized. The Fleury and Brouillet images survive partly because of their contribution to this picture of reasonable masculinity's ability to tell the story of madwomen and all women. In the scene above, with Charcot and the Parisienne, the patient's movement from chatter to silent agony marks a symbolic slide from voice to voicelessness, from active humanity, with its interests, reflections, and expression, to a body in pain, objectified to the point of being forgotten by the director. If a dramaturgical "message" based on the historical context of relationships between men and women could be inferred from this spectacle of torture, it would be that men are still superior to women, that women will do anything for men, that women have nothing of value to say, and that women are bodies without will, susceptible to pleasure or pain only at the whims of the reasonable architects of womanhood.

Women's bodies are all that matter but they also do not matter. They bear forgetting. And women appear in public so that men can exploit their most private experiences.[130] The public torture produced a spectacle of power, in which the tenuous nineteenth century categories of public and private were toyed with such that the patient's privacy was reduced to a private experience of pain that demonstrated the power of her perpetrators to control what constituted privacy and public exposure, both integral components to a particular picture of feminine stature.

In the public enclosure of the Salpêtrière dramas, the project of performing masculine power over women who are deemed without will or autonomy alarmingly parallels the broader social and political French attempts to refuse women equal personhood to men. Delboeuf, following his participation in the Salpêtrière hypnosis experiments, even expressed excitement about the social implications of applying hypnosis outside the hospital, in society, declaring that once public resistance to hypnotism has been broken, it will be "appliqué comme une force sociale d'une puissance incalculable"[131] (applied as a social force with incalculable power). For through hypnosis, "on obtient si facilement ce qu'on désire"[132] (we obtain so easily what we desire). The body of the femme isolée – feminist, prostitute, and women who could easily be classed as either for breaking a range of conventional mores – and the hysterical body shared so many signifiers that one could be written over the other. The common language of both bodies allowed for a re-inscription of the signs of the femme isolée over the hysterical body, this time under the control of the medical patriarchy and, finally, through well-organized spectacle, men in general. Furthermore, the errant, sexualized hysterical body could be rendered docile or could be punished for being so devious. Charcot and his physicians repeated hysteria's symptoms ad infinitum in order to ensure a continual and certain rewriting of the female body as being under their control and regulation. The implication of an audience in this process ensured a popular common possession of the female form. In this theatre where the hysteric played the scapegoat for all kinds of women who failed to live up to certain masculine expectations, the struggle for power sometimes took the form of punishment, the patient's body brutalized in a manner that betrayed the hatred men present at the lectures felt for women.

The records show how hypnotized patients were viewed as hyper-imaginative, infinitely flexible and, at bottom, mere representations of masculine suggestions, embodiments of fiction. For example, Delboeuf describes, several times, how even the hysteric's emotions are pliable inventions. Doctors can (and do) make and destroy her emotions. In one case with a magnet, "marvels" are produced. "Il la fait tomber de la gaieté dans la tristesse, de la haine à la bienveillance, de la colère dans la mansuétude, du souvenir dans l'oubli, de la vision en rouge dans la vision en vert"[133] (He makes her fall from gaiety to sorrow, from hate to benevolence, from anger to meekness, from remembering to forgetting, from red-hued vision to green). If any emotional state can be substituted for another, the hysteric's emotional terrain is proven to be beyond incompetent; the medical spectacle suggests that nothing she feels is real. Doctors demonstrate that what the hysteric feels can swing to any extreme. They alter her facial expressions and postures so that they seem to reveal an irrational and feckless subjectivity. Hysterics also demonstrated great feats of anaesthesia. Confusingly, maybe, the hysteric felt such a range of emotions and sensations, and with such violence, as Richet notes, but she often also could not feel anything: "On peut les piquer, les pincer, les brûler, sans qu'elles éprouvent la plus légère douleur"[134] (We can prick them, pinch them, burn them, without their feeling the lightest pain). In a great leap that only an unimaginative misogyny could permit, the anaesthesia of a limb or the ability to be hypnotized was sometimes mistaken for a subjective vacuity. Richet also notes that "il y a eu une *absence* complète: la vie intellectuelle avait absolument disparu"[135] (there was a *complete* absence: the intellectual life had absolutely disappeared). A woman with no will, no sensation, no memory – not only was her pain considered to be unreal, she herself was thought to barely be a real human subject. Torture, according to Scarry, "bestows visibility on the structure and enormity of what is usually private and incommunicable, contained within the boundaries of the sufferer's body. It then goes on to deny, to falsify, the reality of the very thing it has itself objectified by a perceptual shift which converts the vision of suffering into a wholly illusory, but to the torturers and the regime they represent, a wholly convincing spectacle of power."[136] The patient, not a real presence enough to merit being relieved of her pain in this spectacle, was nonetheless blameworthy. Doctors believed that she harmed herself, or that it is her body that harmed her. The layers of scapegoating multiply. Richet said that it is one patient's imagination, so vivid that it can turn a lie or fantasy into injury, that causes her stigmata.[137]

M.P. Richer describes the attack like this (cited in Richet): "Elle cherche à se déchirer la figure, à s'arracher les cheveux, elle pousse des cris lamentables, et se frappe si violemment la poitrine avec son poing qu'on est obligé d'interposer un coussin; elle s'en prend aux personnes qui l'entourent, cherche à les mordre, et, si elle ne peut les atteindre, déchire tout ce qui est à sa portée, ses draps, ses vêtements, puis elle se met à pousser des hurlements de bête fauve, frappe son lit de la tête en même temps que des poings … en poussant des petits cris rauques"[138] (She seeks to tear at her body, to pull out her hair, lamentable cries surge from her body, and she hits her chest so hard with her fist that we are obligated to block it with a cushion; she turns on the people around her, seeks to bite them, and, if she can't reach them, tears at everything within her reach, her sheets, her clothes, then she screams like a wild animal, hits her bed with her head at the same time as with her fists … letting go hoarse little cries.)

The hysteric, in a delirium brought on by her illness, fought off aggressors by turning on her audience, but also on herself, so brutally that the doctors had to intervene and place a pillow between her fists and her body. Female fantasy leads to her demise – was this the lesson to be gleaned? Never mind that it was the trusted doctor who offered the suggestion that the patient would be wounded in the first place. It was inferred that it was her radical submissiveness that allowed her to experience the pains suggested to her. The pain in the medical spectacle served to magnify the extent to which the hysteric would go to please her perpetrators and her audience. Despite the abuses made against her body for the benefit of her biggest fans, she still bent to them, adding to the curated notion that her deepest desire was to serve them. Despite all this, Blanche Wittman, "la placide et assez appétissante Alsacienne, non seulement mettant de la complaisance, mais trouvant un plaisir visible à se prêter à tout qu'on lui demanda"[139] (the placid and appetizing enough Alsatian, did not just show compliance, but found visible pleasure in lending herself to whatever we asked her). Wittman, later in life, spoke of her time as a Salpêtrière starlet as a painful one, saying, "ce n'était pas du tout agréable"[140] (it was not at all pleasant). The hysteric embodied fiction in ways other than the ones perceived by the physicians. The woman Delboeuf describes only exists in an environment of coercion and abuse, where the power over not only women, but over spectacle itself, rests firmly in the hands of the doctors.

Nostalgia, Svetlana Boym writes, is "longing for a home that no longer exists or that never existed."[141] The woman Mirbeau describes is at once shy, resistant, then compliant. She is made of stone and made of flesh, an uncanny figure, both woman and not quite woman. Likewise, the woman constructed on the amphitheatre stage was not an actual woman. The hysteric needed to be manipulated in order to produce the host of fantastic femininities the doctors desired. The hysteric herself was a woman so real she needed to be made to sleep or pressed into ecstasies or pains to corroborate the kind of woman the masculine medical institution wanted to present. Again, the hysteric embodied the fictional, but not the fiction of female autonomy; this time, she revealed the fictions of the spectacle itself. The lectures, read unapologetically anachronistically via psychoanalysis, turn Freud's description of hysterical symptoms on its head. Freud's work on condensation in dreams, in unconscious resistance in analysis, in the force of repression and in the potential ideational and symbolic creation of an organic symptom, indicates that sometimes a symptom needs to be read sideways.[142] A hysterical symptom does not carry an obvious meaning, nor is its meaning the one that most easily presents itself. According to Freud's description of the enigmas of hysterical presentation, the doctors, whose theatre can be read as a symptom, begin to look like hysterics themselves. The hysteric, made scapegoat for nineteenth century women, and for the ambivalences of nineteenth century men who were embedded in the patriarchy, offers a symptomatic clue – but not for pathological womanhood. Looking sideways, the hysteric, as she was constructed at the Salpêtrière, is a symptom for an unbalanced male culture. The hysteric's legacy preserves the ambivalent fantasies of desire and hatred, intrigue and repulsion, that her male counterparts injected into their theatrically constructed version of womanhood.

The spectacle of the female body in pain continually performed the notion that women were impressionable and, if sexually errant, also sexually obedient and physiologically ill-equipped for societal participation. But these cries that the patient releases into the show, this violence turned against the audience, presents a different patient altogether than the one draped over the arms of a well-dressed man, as in the iconic Brouillet image. In the attack Richer describes, the doctor poses the self-harm of the patient as the alternative to harming the spectators. The lectures were, "in part, the obsessive display of agency that permits one person's body to be translated into another person's voice, that allows real human pain to be converted into a regime's fiction of power."[143] However, when a voice contrary to the one expected rings out, the fiction in the power and the consequent obsession of the display perforate the smooth translation from one voice to another. "She turns on the people around her, seeks to bite them, and, if she can't reach them, tears at everything within her reach … hits her bed with her head at the same time as with her fists." The woman pictured in the scene above is dangerous. She screams and turns violence back on the men who watch her. Was the audience afraid of the hysteric? Were the doctors? The scene above indicates a distinct lack of submission to the dramaturgical proceedings. When the patient cries out, making her voice go ragged, she is speaking an incommunicable pain, a pain proper to her. She takes back her privacy for a moment, taking advantage of the public spectacle to sound out her singularity. She ruptures conceptions of women as stone bodies, automatons, appetizingly docile slaves. The hysteric herself threatens the feminine portrait the doctors aim to construct. And her cry betrays the scripted nature of the theatrical construction by defying the script. Her screams shatter the supposed fiction of her distress. They betray the power struggle at work in the medical show by refusing submission. The patient's cries transcend the digestible pity and horror of a neat medical tragedy with terrifying rage that damages the gentle catharsis the directors of the drama repeat in which subterranean impulses and emotions could have been excited, and then tempered in the spectator. The cathartic attempt falls short. Her screams signal that there can be no successful catharsis because the compulsion to repeat the ambivalent show of desire and violence, tenderness and brutality is compulsive, obsessive. The show is never enough to put masculine minds at ease – they continue to repeat it, like a symptom they just cannot shake. The Salpêtrière scenography, despite and because of its inclusion of the hysteric as scapegoat, betrays a compulsion to repeat repressed material, masculine anxieties, desires and hatreds churning through a medical theatre of torture. The hysteric, viewed as a symbolic vehicle for the women French men were trying to forget, magnifies the repression at play and her cries begin to uncover the dramatic strategy.

As Cixous and Clément write, "Somewhere, every culture has a zone for what it excludes, and it is that zone that we must try to remember *today*."[144] "When 'The Repressed' of their society and culture come back, it is an explosive return, which is *absolutely* shattering, staggering, overturning, with a force never let loose before."[145] The hysteric, by preserving an essential privacy that her scream illuminates, refused to be put to rest, always "came back." Her presence, required for the acting out of nostalgic masculine fantasy, also acted as a fracture in the dramatic structure, preventing a smooth Aristotelian catharsis, its own continual burial of the repressed. Catharsis of any sort resulting in resolution could not be achieved because the woman on stage continued to return with force. Her presence drew attention to the undercurrents in the show, which was less about her body, her sexuality, her autonomy, her position, her will, and more about the bodies, sexualities, and positions of the men who required her in a working through of their feeling under threat – a working through that, in part, could not be achieved because it lacked self-reflexivity.

The lecture series were a drama featuring two sets of symptoms – the hysteric's and the physician's. The hysteric, thought to be a woman who stood in for all women, was called upon to express a range of femininities in a complex spectacle that amounted to a symptom itself, one of masculine ambivalence, anxiety, and nostalgia related to the shifting cultural roles of women. "The feminine role, the role of the sorceress, the hysteric, is ambiguous, antiestablishment … Antiestablishment because the symptoms – the attacks – revolt and shake up the public, the group, the men, to whom they are exhibited."[146] When Cixous and Clément write that "In their attempt to define the cultural function of the *anomaly*, both Lévi-Strauss and Sartre … seek to situate it in the fault lines of a general system where some correlative structures do not successfully harmonize all their correlations and that "more than any others, women bizarrely embody this group of anomalies showing the cracks in an overall system,"[147] they point to the power inherent in a close dramaturgical reading of the Salpêtrière theatre, where the fault lines in a culture became visible at the site of the female body. In the case of the nineteenth century medical show, hysterical women did not just "shake up the group," they showed that the group was already shaken, destabilized by the shifting cityscape and the tidal shift in definitions of womanhood, expressed in a sea of luminous female faces. The men who acted out their anxieties via the hysterical patients were on shaky ground. The Salpêtrière drama ultimately could not make good on its promise to give the audience a live reincarnation of a woman who could be anything men suggested. The hysteric was too resistant. Their methods revealed too much about the emotional thrust of their purpose.

The Brouillet painting and its survival point to nineteenth century French culture's fascination with the hysteric. Its presence in the amphitheatre alongside Charcot indicates the director's approval of the image, of its representations of the medical theatre and the woman, Blanche Wittman. Its presence is self-congratulatory. It is a nearly life-sized painting of a sea of society men and doctors, their faces made to be recognized by the painting's audience.[148] Looking at the painting again, its lines seem too constrained for the subject matter. Where is the violence? Where is the turbulent eruption of symptoms? It makes a damp conclusion, like Delboeuf's. The patient is docile. Its subjects are static, its lamps dark. Still, Wittman hangs there, obstinately aglow.

THREE

Hysterical Discourse

What Screaming Can Do

LANGUAGE/INSTRUMENT

Charcot's Rhetorical Style

Charcot's German peer Ernst von Leyden wrote that when the doctor was on stage, he used "sharp, striking, living expressions, for example: accentuated speech, stepping walk."[1] Others were less impressed with Charcot's rhetorical style. Visiting Glasgow physician Jane Henderson observed that, though his message was of great import, Charcot's voice was quite quiet, saying, "Charcot's voice was not at all strong, so that the raised seats were too far away [for it] to be appreciated, and the majority of the students came as near as possible to the front, even although [*sic*] the view of the platform was apt to be obscured by the heads of those before them."[2] While the lectures drew notable interest – "in anticipation of the lectures, "expectant audience members would talk amongst themselves, and then, when "a door [was] brusquely opened, the murmur cease[d], all eyes turn[ed] towards the master" – contemporary journalist X also noted that Charcot's voice was "dull."[3] Platel's comments were more critical: "He goes over his descriptions with his dull voice and drives the argument into the brain of his listeners, heavily and dully – as one drives in a nail with a large block of wood."[4]

The year of Charcot's death, Peugniez reflected on the physician's vocal style, and above all its clarity, remarking that it possessed, "neither the rounded tones, nor the sonority, nor the beautiful cadences, all of the attractive qualities which Lasègue and Trousseau possessed to such a high degree. But how many of them had his colour and above all such clarity!"[5] In his biographical novel, Guillain writes of Charcot's rhetorical style that the director had a "horror of 'exaggerated emphasis, just as he despised commonplaces. His language was slow, his diction impeccable; he did not use gestures and sat as much as he stood. His exposé was always remarkably clear.'"[6] X, too, noted that while his tone was dull, Charcot's speech was "clear."[7]

The importance of Charcot's manner of speaking in lecture is exemplified by the many reports about his diction. For some, the director seemed to lack prosodic variety, producing dull vocal tones verging on monotony. Some, of course, especially his admirers, felt that Charcot was rhetorically colourful. What appears to have repeatedly struck those who appreciated and those who criticized the doctor's vocal performance was that Charcot spoke clearly. Reports may vary on technical delivery, but Charcot's ability to convey a message, in these reports, is not questioned. People who listened, though they may have been bored, understood what he meant. Charcot's clear delivery of easily graspable content seats him comfortably in the language style of the sciences.

Positivism, which romanced doctors, among others, in the nineteenth century, relied on empirical evidence expressed in true statements, or the idea that "knowledge describe[d] reality."[8] Words, by extension, conveyed knowledge of material truth. Quasi-objectivist assumptions about language haunt us still.[9] Psychoanalyst and feminist cultural theorist Luce Irigaray has examined the language of contemporary patients diagnosed with hysteria, an illness distinct from its nineteenth century stylistic embodiment, but revelatory for its earlier form when read against the current hysteric's modes of language production. *To Speak Is Never Neutral*, a chronological collection of Luce Irigaray's published essays, begins with an introduction in which she pokes fun at the objective voice she must use in her work when she recognizes the falsehoods of the "objective" writerly position: "Rereading these texts affected me, and several comments, or ideas, came to mind. In particular, I felt irritated and amused by the language of science. I have for several years been confronting the reality of scientific requirements, those norms or criteria of a so-called rigorous process. I stand before them as if I had to answer to them, to submit to being judged. A kind of tribunal of discourse, deciding what good thinking, good exposition, and valid truth and research are. Supposedly, they are impossible outside of already existing scientific and epistemological frameworks. Off the beaten path, there is only poetry, politics, demagogic fantasy."[10] The scientific discourse one is required to speak in order to appear to be rigorous is supposed to be "divested of all *pathos*,"[11] is purported to lack emotion, personal conviction, subjectivity and doubt. Charcot, if he was aiming to speak scientifically, was, according to many of his reviewers who noted the wooden quality of his speech, on the right track. Irigaray continues, "The most exact science is supposed to be simultaneously atemporal and chameleonesque, versatile enough to change colour in order to blend into the background. The writing subject, perhaps especially she who writes in the field of science, "has become a machine, with no becoming – finished."[12] Or, deciding to say *I* in science class, Irigaray recounts, got her bad grades.[13] To deter from "scientific" discourse is to veer away from truth and into the mire of poetry or the indeterminable questions of politics. Convention so often insists that there is no truth in either. The language of science that privileges the removal of subjectivity, assuming this were possible or desirable, is, as Irigaray says, "supposedly a translator, or a perfect translation, an adequate copy of the universe."[14] At this site of perfect mimesis, we have lost any of the Platonic doubt about representation, and have instead a mistaken assumption that language – or the right language – can give us the thing itself.

Assuming an objective voice in language is a misrepresentation of what authorship actually entails.[15] There may be no truly objective language or, at least, feigning objectivity when one writes is disingenuous – accepted, required, often, but amounting to the continuation of what Irigaray calls an "unavowed imperialism."[16] Irigaray's phrase indicates both that positivist language is always already misleading and also that the stakes of its claim to authority are high.

To contemporize, very briefly, assertions of power through language, here is a recent and local example: the Canadian Psychiatry Association, for instance, claims on its website, in ways that sound rather proprietary if not defensive, that psychiatric disorders are rightly understood only via psychiatry. The CPA pamphlet on schizophrenia, designed for family members of or people diagnosed with the illness, an illness about which very little is known, states that, "This booklet is designed to help you, your family or a friend with schizophrenia to understand how schizophrenia can best be treated and managed. Everything will feel pretty chaotic and unpredictable at first"[17] But psychiatrists are here to help you through. Thank goodness. What can they offer? Off the top: "You will learn the meaning of new and important medical and technical terms. People in health care have their own words. You need to know them, understand them and be able to use them … The information here will help you gain some feeling of control. This will give you some very important peace of mind on the journey to recovery"[18] Peace of mind is a generous promise, and a state that the CPA believes can be achieved through knowing the right words, being able to speak the language of the mental health system, knowing what they know about schizophrenia. These recommendations for becoming a discursive chameleon are likely essential once one is engaged in a mental health system that demands a person speak its language in order to be understood or recognized as knowledgeable – even well – enough to be taken seriously. The instruction to learn the key terms, given first thing in the manual, reads like a survival guide, but for whom? The relationship between schizophrenics and language is incredibly tenuous.[19] Many studies have been done that attempt to unearth the polysemy, sideways code, and fragmentary speech associated with people diagnosed with schizophrenia. As a culture, we are only just beginning to understand the alternative ways people with schizophrenia make use of language. In a system wherein patients must speak the specialized jargon of physicians, the schizophrenic patient seems doomed to fail, despite the helpful literature. Still, we see that very material authority is given to the person who can speak well, who can speak in the rarefied style of medical professionals. The CPA pamphlet prescriptively teaches the performative strength of its rhetoric. Speaking its words can make or break a person's experience, and release from, of a labyrinthine mental health system. Speaking one's own way, even if this may be a trait of one's illness, is cautioned against.

The descriptions of Charcot's students halting their murmurings upon his entrance and clamouring to the front of the room to huddle about the teacher situate Charcot as an authorial presence. His monologue about neurology is the feature of the analyses of his vocal performance, while the patients who so often accompanied him on stage are underrepresented in accounts of the rhetorical style of the lectures. At the same time, emphasis is given to Charcot's exposé, and even for Platel, the most famous of Charcot's critics, to his argument. It was understood that whatever the material elements of the argument's delivery, Charcot made use of speech in order to transmit a series of facts that reflected the empirical reality of the nervous system; the ovaries; the body segmented, demonstrable and discoverable. Charcot, as well as his listeners, was nestled in a confidence in the sciences and in the straightforward purposes and logocentric thrust of language in their service. Despite their theatrical appearance, the lectures were conceived by many as pedagogical and explanatory ventures primarily.[20]

Medical positivism made use of language in part by occluding the possibility for reflection. As Habermas indicates, "By making a dogma of the sciences' belief in themselves, positivism assumes the prohibitive function of protecting scientific inquiry from epistemological self-reflection."[21] Science, and its so-called objective, instrumental use of language, is assuredly valuable, and its efficacy is a closed book. Charcot, who said, "I state what I see – nothing more," would never have admitted to what Irigaray concludes, which is that "*science is a question of style*."[22] Scientific language, gaining force in the nineteenth century through its production in medical spectacles like Charcot's, makes the assertion that words describe reality, transmit it, in an unquestionable pairing of material reality and signification. But the positivist ability to describe and its singular empirical reality were both unexplored assumptions. To state is always to do both more and less than this. Uttering statements with faith in their ability to accurately convey a material reality covertly performs presumption, reproducing the hegemonic value of articulacy's relationship to truth and disguising this as innocent, constative utterance devoid of performative force. This is the "unavowed imperialism" that Irigaray struggles against.

But, to quote Andrew Wernick, "why dig up Positivism only (presumably) to bury it again?"[23] Because the power of the medical institution over the hysteric, and reason over unreason was achieved through language, through reason's (Charcot's) monologue, it is important to note that language itself is often perceived as an instrument, as a means to an end. If one glances through the Diagnostic and Statistical Manual of Mental Disorders, for instance, one reads that language pathologies can be diagnosed by recognizing when people fail to use language for communicative purposes. The listed language disorders are: "language disorder"; "speech sound disorder"; (a wonderfully revealing) "social (pragmatic) communication disorder" (new to the DSM V); and (a hilariously paradoxical –

incommunicable?) "unspecified communication disorder."[24] That the purpose of language is communication, that communication can simply be used effectively or incorrectly and that language is a self-evidently effective tool are taken for granted by the authors of the DSM, which has, incidentally, been heavily criticized for its arrogant claims to authority and truth.[25] They are not alone in assuming that language is a communicative instrument.

About Charcot's rhetorical style, X wrote: "His voice is somewhat dull [sourde]; the speech is clear, precise, not meticulously arranged, sometimes slightly hesitant. But the master delays little in choosing words, he speaks simply, the elevation always comes from the subject. With a few very short phrases, he poses the problem to be resolved, the question to be studied, and immediately introduced the living examples … one listens only to his voice, monotonous like that of a puppeteer of wax figures."[26] Charcot may have had a tendency to hesitate slightly when choosing his words, but not for long, and his voice was clear and his speech efficient. Notably, in X's description, Charcot raises a problem to be resolved, a question that he promises to answer, and then immediately begins to work with the hysterics on stage, the bodies through which knowledge will be mobilized and questions will be resolved in answers. The hysterics' speech is not even alluded to by X, their words not taken to be purposeful or integral to the lecture. What the patients offer is a body that functions as an example, a malleable figure for demonstration of the doctor's monotonous, but still useful, communicative utterances. The prominence of the hysteric's body, and its subordinate place next to Charcot's voice, is indicated in X's final sentence: "One listens only to his voice, monotonous like that of a puppeteer of wax figures."

Charcot's scientific use of language gained force through its exemplary use of the female patient's body. As Scarry writes about the spectacle of public torture, we remember, "ultimate domination requires that the prisoner's ground become increasingly physical and the torturer's increasingly verbal, that the prisoner become a colossal body with no voice and the torturer a colossal voice."[27] In the medical spectacle too, wherein scientific reason demonstrated its power over the unreasonable female patient, at this site of discursive power, language acts as an instrument, and so does the patient – especially, so does the patient's embodied silence.

For so many observers of the lecture series, the hysteric appeared to be like a puppet or doll, a mute body-object Charcot could articulate at will.[28] For Binet and Féré, the hysteric seemed "comme une grande poupée dont

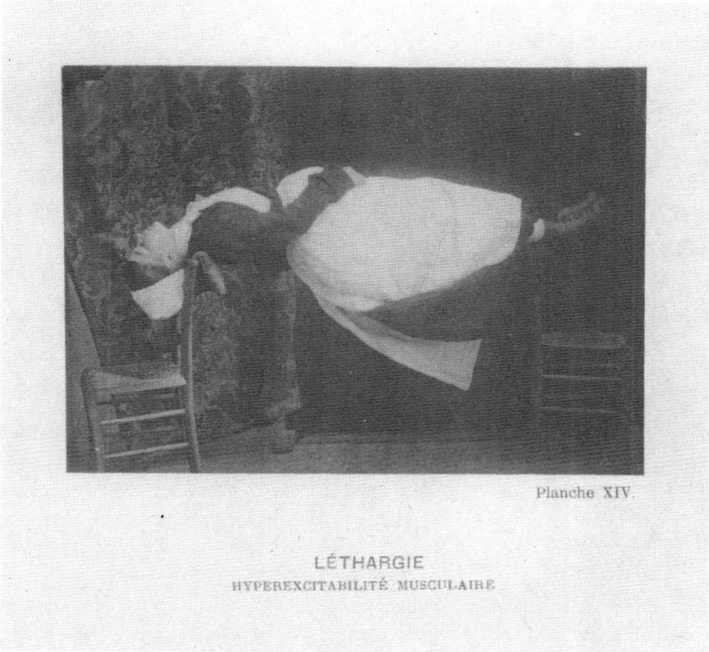

3.1 Augustine, *Lethargy: Muscular Hyperexcitability*. Plate XIV, *Iconographie photographique de la Salpêtrière* 3, 1879.

les articulations sont absolument souples"[29] (like a giant doll whose articulations are totally malleable) and her body parts had "la flexibilité de la cire"[30] (the flexibility of wax).

Delboeuf wrote of the hysteric that, "C'est un mannequin d'une intelligence sans égale"[31] (she is like a mannequin with unequalled intelligence). For Léon Daudet, "C'est le mannequin de l'atelier, plus docile encore et plus souple"[32] (it is a mannequin from the workshop, even more docile and more supple." For Claretie, "l'être humain semblait réduit ainsi à l'état de 'maquette' de bois dont se servent les sculpteurs en faisant jouer à leur fantaisie les articulations de ces mannequins"[33] (the human being seems reduced to the wooden 'maquette' sculptors use to articulate the body according to their desire).

A few notions advance themselves in these analogies. One is that the hysteric's body can be articulated at will, that it is susceptible to configuration. The Salpêtrière's experiments with electrically charged metal wands to alter

3.2 *Catalepsy Provoked by the Sound of a Drum*. Paul Régnard, *Les maladies épidémiques de l'esprit*, 1887.

patients' facial expressions after Duchenne de Boulogne, the theatrical use of a gong to throw hysterics into sudden poses fixed in catalepsy and the demonstration of the hysteric's rigid body propped across chairs in a back bend exemplify the continual onstage production of a manipulable body.

Another integral component of the description of the hysteric as a doll of one kind or another is the idea of the patient reduced, as Claretie rightly points out, to a body. The hysteric, bodily present, but vocally suppressed, is muted while the doctor speaks. Janet Beizer's book that topically addresses the French hysteric is tellingly titled *Ventriloquized Bodies*. Elaine Scarry also depicts theatres of pain as sites where power is achieved by the dissolution of the victim's language, especially when the person in pain screams, leaving them crying out at the level of the body, as their pain becomes translated into the regime's power. Likewise, in the Salpêtrière's hysteria shows, the patient was often spectacularly gestural, while the hospital director engaged in verbose explanation. The patient amounted to a prop in the service of the demonstrative doctor. Doctor Féré's remark that the hysteric could be played "like a piano"[34] is a revelatory one, for what his simile evokes is a double impression of instrumentality. The patient is like a musical instrument played by the doctor. The hysteric is made to move and sound according to the director's technical interventions. She is also a passive object made use of, used to another end, her value not immediate but deferred to other purposes.

Indeed, the hysteric's apparent muteness serves not only to ensure a smooth and effective spectacle of power, but also to prop up reasonable discourse (and therefore medical reason) itself. In *Madness and Civilization*, Michel Foucault writes about the discourse of reason which lives covertly predicated upon the silence of madness. He notes that:

> In the serene world of mental illness, modern man no longer communicates with the madman, on the one hand, the man of reason delegates the physician to madness, thereby authorizing a relation only through the abstract universality of disease … As for a common language, there is no such thing; or rather, there is no such thing any longer; the constitution of madness as a mental illness, at the end of the eighteenth century, affords the evidence of a broken dialogue, posits the separation as already effected, and thrusts into oblivion all those stammered, imperfect words without fixed syntax in which the exchange between madness and reason was made. The language of psychiatry, which is a monologue of reason about madness, has been established only on the basis of such a silence.[35]

According to Foucault, madness lives in a dual relation to reason. The rational discourse about madness can only speak on behalf of madness by silencing it. Reason requires the silence of unreason in order to carry on its covertly contingent monologue. Contrarily, madness lives grafted onto reason, comes to light only via its own silencing. Charcot's iconographic project consisting of hundreds of photographs, and the Tuesday lecture series in which he commented on hysteria while the female starlet's body in pain gained only the most brief and superficial recognition, presents a case of speech that relies on a certain muteness. And yet, Foucault writes that the separation between reason and madness is posited, insisted upon as though it has already happened, as an irrevocable inevitability. This means that the distinctive break between reason and unreason is a false one, not natural at all. Like positivist language's disavowal of the speaking or writing subject, whose "I" cleaves guiltily to the background trying dubiously to efface it/herself, a disingenuous opposition between the languages of reason and unreason has been treated as already effected.

Foucault's text, an analysis of the dynamics of discursive power as they operate in the asylum, presents a troubling account of the expulsion of mad people from the social realm and their confinement in institutions as the ultimate conceptual removal of unreason from dialogue with reason. Relegating unreason to the status of a disease ensured that the speaking of those diagnosed as mad could be dismissed; no longer would the mad person be considered an interlocutor. What falls aside are the beautiful stammerings between reason and unreason caught in a dialogic tangle of misunderstanding. In breaking off the dialogue, as Charcot aims to do, reason effectively says, "There is no need to speak. I already understand you. That is, I already understand that there is nothing worth understanding, nothing to understand. You have nothing to say." The former dialogic ambiguity, along with its implicit impossibilities for resolution or stark clarity, is replaced by a silencing of what appears to reasonable medical elites to be madness.

Foucault's description of discursive power and powerlessness echoes the many observations made about the hysteric appearing like a puppet, or an instrument to be played and spoken by the reasonable doctor. Indeed, the hysteric was not considered to be an equal discursive counterpart. She was deprived of the possibility for speech in many ways. When she was alive, she spoke a language without authority, not only a language of madness, which rarely receives credit for being valuable because it lacks something of the sensible, but also a language of *female* madness. Further, the surviving documents of her voice are those recorded by doctors, were selected and transcribed by the men who hurt her most. She is no longer here to tell her story, presuming she wanted to. There are holes in the archive. What to do about this voice full of gaps and its stuttered delivery?

HYSTERICAL GRAMMAR

Who may speak and who may not is a question of ethics. As Lyotard writes: "This is what a wrong [tort] would be: a damage [dommage] accompanied by the loss of the means to prove the damage. This would be the case if the victim is deprived of life, or of all his or her liberties, or of the freedom to make his or her ideas or opinions public, or simply of the right to testify to the damage, or even more simply if the testifying phrase is itself deprived of authority."[36] Augustine is one of Charcot's most written about hysterics. And yet little attention has been paid to her words. The pages of the *Iconographie* dedicated to Augustine's case feature a nearly equal volume of the patient's words and the doctor's, but weighed against the medium and its context within the popularity and authority of science in the nineteenth century the document begins to look like a battleground, where two distinct styles of utterance compete for attention. Language is the space where Augustine and the doctors wrestle for agency and possession of the patient's own speech.

The notes that accompany the hysteric's utterances and movements in the *Iconographie* record many wrongs committed against the patient. In Augustine's case, the most obvious violations include physical restraint, drug induced pacification, mechanical compression of her ovarian area over several days, induced seizure of her throat, and tongue. The patient is deprived of her liberties of movement – bound in a straitjacket, coerced into attacks for the purposes of photographing her, or alternately confined to her bed – and of speech. Once, for no known reason, while she deliriously carries on with her invisible interlocutors, the doctors bind Augustine in a straitjacket. The content of her hallucinations immediately swings into violent recurrences of her being raped.[37] The action triggers memories of restraint and cuts off her dialogue, altering the discursive experience of fantasy. On 24 November 1878, Charcot induced in Augustine a painful series of muscular contractions in the mouth, throat, and tongue, amounting to an aphonia that lasted days. Nothing could relieve her painful silence. Doctors tried hypnosis, amyl nitrate, ovarian compression for 36 hours – and it was more than a week later, on 2 December, that amyl nitrate inexplicably, finally lifted the aphonia.[38] It is instances like these that render the importance of agency and potentiality around sounding so palpable.

Being able to speak freely and being able not to speak if she chooses are integral potentialities for any living subject. As Lyotard writes, "Not to speak is part of the ability to speak, since ability is a possibility and possibility implies something and its opposite."[39] In the rare moments Augustine refuses to give details of her delirious visions or history,[40] maintaining her own silence, she exercises a right to maintain her privacy. The potential to choose what is uttered and when is important given Augustine's tendency toward what physicians describe as "involuntary confidences" and especially given the imposition of muteness that the doctors burden her with, while she rests in bed, and while she appears on stage.[41]

Augustine's silence is often involuntary; so too, sometimes, is her communication. She says, once, in hallucination, as though in a private encounter with her lover Émile, that she will keep their secrets – even as she utters them to the physician at her bedside. Because her speech is a jumble of the other side of half-heard dialogue, it is difficult to tell, but her secret may be that Émile has promised to heal her, releasing her from medical care. She says: "Compte sur moi, j'ai ton amitié … Tu m'as dit que tu me guérirais … Moi, je n'ai rien dit à la Salpêtrière"[42] (Count on me, you have my friendship … You said that you would heal me … Me, I didn't say a thing in the Salpêtrière). At another time, in a hallucinated fight with Georges, she recants his name several times, even as she denies it: "Georges! … Moi, j'ai dit ton nom à la Salpêtrière! Ce n'ai pas vrai, ayant eu une crise ou non"[43] (Georges! … Me, I said your name in the Salpêtrière! It's not true, whether I was having an attack or not). Sometimes Augustine is constrained to have the involuntarily communicated details of her life inscribed for publication. The medical institution publishes her words, but simultaneously undermines her vocal authority. Her words are absorbed into the intellectual property of the hospital's *Iconographie*, publicized, but not on her terms. Already diminished in value, the patient's utterances as they appear in the *Iconographie*, act as supports for Charcot's demonstration of hysteria. She is never asked to give her opinion of her experiences in the hospital, although some of her feelings about the Salpêtrière and its doctors do wind through her delirious babbling. Bourneville's transcriptions of Augustine's words are not substitutes for listening or proof of understanding.

Reading her words in the *Iconographie*, one does come to appreciate Augustine's *style*. When Augustine described the sensations in her body, she plunged into evocative simile. She said she had a spider in the ear.[44] She complained that she felt as though she was being pulled from toe to thigh with a giant needle. She hallucinated rats inside of her.[45] She had begun to menstruate in the night and recounted her dreams to the doctor – this time, slaughterhouses running with blood.[46] Her language veered into the poetic, and when she was given the chance to speak, her lexicon offered relief from the repetitive, explicative monologue that comprised Charcot's lectures.

At the same time, the hysteric's words lacked authority partly because of the way in which she spoke. Her manner of utterance, a poetic careening through signification, could be recognized only as part of her hysterical pathology by those who spoke primarily an unreflective scientific discourse.

Among the symptoms of hysteria as listed by Wilfred Abse, in his preface to the translation of Philip Wegener's *The Life of Speech*, are: semantic plentitude, paradox, and plurisignation.[47] Augustine's words are plentiful and rational clarity is not the most interesting or important feature of her speech. In her hallucinations, the hysteric's language performs according to the unconscious forces of condensation and displacement, singular material reality slips into a plenitude of signs, shifting size and proportion, weight and meaning. The hysteric defies communicative expectations. If one lingers with her words, one finds a whole body in language, a lexicon steeped in gesture, and a performance of language that points to the ethical spaces that can be made by speaking hysterically.

Augustine speaks often, but not often clearly. Her attacks blossom into dialogic scenarios in which she indulges in talking, becoming absolutely verbose. Bourneville calls her loquacious[48] and remarks that as she converses with her lover or her "*invisibles*," she will chatter without ceasing, in a "véritable *délire de paroles*"[49] (veritable *delirium of words*). How does she sound?

Giving attention to how Augustine appears to make use of language in the records, one inevitably also finds oneself tracking the movements of her mouth. Muscular openings for sound, and her mouth's closure pry apart our expectations around the communicative purposes of speech. Sometimes, Augustine is silent. Sometimes, in an attack, her tongue cleaves to the roof of her mouth and she cannot speak.[50] Sometimes her mouth is open in a wide rictus, though she makes no sound. Or her lips are "fortement serrées"[51] (sealed shut). She vomits. She screams loudly, defiantly, angrily. She screams a lot. For most of her stay in the hospital, half of Augustine's mouth was numb, and half was full of sensation. This was also true of her eyes and her vulva.[52] The active and passive physiology of her mouth resounds in her relationship to utterance. Sometimes she cries out, but her screams are stifled.[53] Sometimes the cry marks a sounded release from suffocation – "Avant le cri, on note parfois des secousses, du hoquet, de la suffocation"[54] (before the cry, we sometimes note tremors, hiccups, suffocation). Sometimes, she wants to make noise, but the doctors choose to sedate her and she is rendered quiet. If she cries out too much in an attack, they impose silence on her with any number of medical tricks.[55]

The number of references to the body in medical observations of Augustine's attacks is astounding. Bourneville's attention to Augustine's gestures and facial expressions that run outside the italicized components of the traditional attack may demonstrate the way the hysteric draws attention to the body's intimate relationship to language. As well, Bourneville may turn to bodily cues to flesh out the obscure content of her speech. While Augustine speaks enough to be described as chatty, and while the content of her delirium is certainly rich with meaningful experiences, understanding, for her audience, is sparse. Signification is plentiful, but content is nearly impossible to grasp with any exactitude.

> (*10 avril.* – Attacks – *Delirious Period*: frightened cries: "Oh la! La! *(ter)* [*sic*] … Pig! I'll tell papa! Rascal! Oh! La! La! … Papa! Help me!" Breathing is rapid, loud; then L … unleashes shrill cries, struggles, twists as though she is trying to escape someone's hold. In an attack, after the *period of large movements*, she comes to rest, for a few moments, her *arms in cruciform*. Then, *delirium*: "What do you want?" (*Repeated*) … Nothing? Nothing?" (Smiling physiognomy). "At the right time." (Looks to the left, lifts herself up part way, makes a sign of the hand, gives kisses). "Non! No! I don't want it." (New kisses … She smiles, executes movements of the torso, the legs). "You are starting again … That's not it! That is not all! (*Repeated*)." (She complains, then laughs). "You are leaving!" Physiognomy expresses regret; X … cries.)[56]

This transcription layers what appear to be embodied experiences of fear, struggle, sexual assault, and desire that uncomfortably connect and discordantly clash with one another. Reading these words, for me, produces a visceral discomfort with looking at moments too private and too painful to appear in a medical journal. I would love to leave this moment to Augustine, to let it rest in the vaults of unread histories, guarding this woman's privacy. And yet, these words were and are public, circulating in print and now in digital realms. And I do believe that attending to this passage, and passages like it, might offer a gesture of obfuscation. Words and movements inscribe themselves in the scene from the *Iconographie* above, and Bourneville seems to give comparable attention to each. He seems to struggle against the invisible content of Augustine's attack, gleaning only superficial clues from her cries, quotidian utterances, and gestures. For instance, it is unclear who the recipient of Augustine's words may be, and if it is only one person. She calls to her father for help. Augustine's medical history indicates that she took a lover, one of her brother's friends. She used to trade kisses with older men for candy. In the convent, she was punished for masturbating in her dormitory. She was raped by her stepfather at knife point. Once, she escaped the hospital to spend time with male friends. Because Augustine's sexuality and sexual history is complex, and because the delirious encounter features resistance and invitation, its conditions are unknowable. The rapid and fractured movement between enjoyment and pain might be a staccato combination of both Augustine's sexual agency and experiences of sexual assault. Her "no" is clear, her struggle as well. So is, "I don't want it." Let us not be ambiguous about that. Also, she kisses, smiles, regrets the parting of her sexual partner. Her tears may connote either disappointment that the encounter is over, which is Bourneville's interpretation, or they may express a response to the coercive undercurrent of the encounters experienced in this hallucination. Whether two or more separate sexual events take place in sequence or at once, or whether Augustine works through her fraught relationship to sexual play and assault in a single delirious collage, is also impossible to determine. The nature of the transcript medium, its being a medically biased account and a written document tracing a noisy gestural phenomenon that cannot be conveyed in writing, jumbles our impressions. So does, I think, Augustine's language. Further, what can a contemporary researcher make of the steady insertion of the ellipsis into Augustine's dialogue of one? What occurs in the space in which something is happening, or being said, but without clear articulation? Bourneville's ellipses indicate something not captured, or something too fast or too strange or too Augustine's to be written. In short, the … of the Augustine archive indicates an inexpressibility. Augustine's utterances are far from denotative in the fashion of language in the service of empiricism.

The force of Augustine's cries, laughter, and utterances is that they both sound, and sound against, legible content. In combination with her loquaciousness, Augustine's cries indicate an indulgence in making noise. It is no wonder that when she has "revenue à elle" (come to herself), the doctors describe her as "reasonable."[57] It is when she uses speech and gesture conventionally that she appears to them to be most herself; it is when she nears communicative comprehension that the physicians feel that she speaks closest to their language. Often, she does not. Readers are left in the mire of poetry and hysterical rhetoric.

Bourneville methodically transcribed many of Augustine's sounds. The *Iconographie* hosts hundreds of pages of patient utterances, cries, and gestures. Strikingly, while Charcot's stage manner has to be culled from second-hand reports on his theatrical style, the hysteric's style of speaking is depicted in great detail by Bourneville as he listens. What are recorded are fragments, exclamations, responses. These layer with thrashing, turning, protesting, gossiping, crying, screaming, and wooing in a compendium of speech and movement, sound and bodily expression. Augustine's lexicon is corporeal and linguistic. What Allen Weiss writes about glossolalia can equally be said about Augustine's hysterical grammar: "Glossolalia is language where the relation between sound and meaning breaks down; it is the realm of pure sound, the manifestation of language in the realm of its pure materiality. But this is not to say that glossolalic pronunciations are meaningless; rather their meaning is a result of non-linguistic functions … As such, they are manifestations of pure expression, language made body and gesture."[58]

In the hysterical attack, the materiality of sound and the expressive power of gesture collude to dismember impressions of the hysteric as mute and doll-like. As Augustine's body and inarticulacy foreground themselves, they present a challenge to the interpretive strength of reason. Rather than propping up assumptions about the discursive impotence of the hysteric and the discursive hegemony of medical positivism, the documents of Augustine's utterances pose threatening questions for the scientific appropriation of language. Her words are personal, carrying the weight of intimate subjective experience. Her vocabulary winds about the same invisible interlocutors though its repetition does not produce clarity. Her sounds are both animal and womanly. Her corporeal linguistics are erratic, acrobatic, precariously related to language, yet still recognizable by Bourneville, as part of the human gestural lexicon. The nature of language itself becomes impossible to take for granted. And the pervasive style of Augustine's lexicon comparatively points to the fact that objectivity is a style. Augustine's speech lacks authority, clarity, obvious function. The irreducible quality of her voice resists appropriation and translation. Perhaps this is why Charcot preferred not to indulge in dialogue with the hysteric on stage. What use could he make of her words if they did not make use of sense? And what challenge to empirical rhetoric might they perform?

Augustine's verbose inarticulacy may not have posed a pragmatic threat to Charcot's "reasonable" monologue about hysteria. The director's work

3.3. Augustine. *Attitudes passionnelles : Appel.* Plate XIX, *Iconographie photographique de la Salpêtrière* 2, 1878.

on the topic continued until his death. And yet, Augustine's words persist in the archive, injecting it with the force of her hysterical language. Hers may be vain vocal gestures, not useful or particularly descriptive, but they are forceful in their vanity. The hysteric's poetics are, as Bataille writes, in his treatise against instrumentality, "unstable, dangerous, and not completely intelligible," threatening to "destroy the stable and operative forms."[59] Augustine's inarticulacy points not only to the limits of reason, its inefficacy, but perhaps also to its undesirability. Corporeal utterance, turbulent signification and speech rendered sound in screaming and babbling open an ethical dimension that is possible within reasonable discourse, but only if it engages with the uncertain terrain of the other, not simply admitting its relationship to but opening itself again to the unknowable.

Look at Augustine's relationship to speaking, as it unfolds in Bourneville's transcriptions. When she speaks, it is often in dialogue with her brother, her friends, or her lover, as though they are present. Bourneville records her words in her hallucinations in detail, and yet, the events of her delirium, and her feelings towards them, are not entirely clear. She makes use of inarticulate utterance for herself alone. Her process of communication is essentially private in purpose.

The conversations that occur in Augustine's attacks are communicative, but for whom? Whereas Charcot's monologue disguises that it rests on the silent participation of the patient, whose muteness is essential to the discourse remaining "scientific," Augustine's solitary voice shows continually that she is engaged in a dialogic relation to another, whether or not the identity of this interlocutor is determinable.

One of the traits that may be particular to hysterical ways of speaking is this dialogue without the possibility of reciprocation. Irigaray points to language as the terrain in which the hysterical subject enacts her disappearance, or at least her disguise. As she observes, hysterics use the architecture of language to perform a de-centering of themselves, generating personal *ekstasis* or phenomenological displacement. Technically, "from a text approximately 20 pages long produced by the hysteric, (Irigaray) extracted at random three fragments of 42 lines."[60] These, she broke down into the sentence parts: subject (noun phrase 1), verb, direct or indirect object (noun phrase 2), adverb, adjective, preposition, and adverbial phrase (noun phrase 3)[61]. Her findings are illuminating:

> (You), whether explicitly stated or masked as *it/she/he*, animate or inanimate, dominates as subject of the utterance … Action verbs are frequent, especially in cases where *you* is the subject of the utterance: *vous aimez; vous restez; vous faites faire; vous demandez; vous regardez* … In addition, incompleteness prevails over completion, which can be seen in the morphological procedures as well as in the choice of verbs; the present or the future are more common than the past, the active than the passive, action verbs than verbs of being. When a verb expresses a condition, it most often appears to be either in process – in the process of elaboration within *I*, brought about by the actions of *you*, rather than established, stable, or the result of a prior development – or presented as established without reference either to a development or to an agent … Even if they describe an event in the past tense,

> the hysteric's utterance "translates incompleteness: *vous racontiez; vous parliez; j'écoutais; vous mettiez* [you were telling; you were speaking; I was listening; you were putting], etc. The action is ongoing, not complete."[62]

Irigaray also notes that: "When *I* is the subject of the statement, the object is *you: je vous écoute* [I listen to you]; *j'ai rêvé de vous* [I dreamed about you] … The contemplative's subject is *you*, and it carries the message, the main clause being not really much more than a dictum introducing the subordinate – *je me dis que vous aimez les roses* [I say to myself that you like roses] "Among the non-animate direct and indirect objects in the analyzed discourse, 80 per cent refer to (you)."[63]

Even as the hysteric utters "I," she turns her *I*, using regular elements of discourse, to depend upon *you*, to displace the *I* so that it is contingent upon, subordinate to, or in process in relation to *you*.[64] Angling herself outward, opening toward possibility, flung into incompletion, the hysteric and her *I* resist the empirical, the whole, the trappings of conclusion. There is a compelling attentiveness that emerges in hysterical grammar, one that opposes the violence of Charcot's monologic stature, achieved through the female patient's "quiet" body in pain. Her body is not an object, but a "centre of perspective, insight, reflection, desire, agency."[65]

Others. Cixous and Clément, after more than forty years, still have much to offer on hysterical discourse and feminine writing:

> *Voice!* That, too, is launching forth and effusion without return. Exclamation, cry, breathlessness, yell, cough, vomit, music. Voice leaves. Loses. She leaves. She loses. And that is how she writes, as one throws a voice – forward, into the void. She goes away, she goes forward, doesn't turn back to look at her tracks. Pays no attention to herself. Running breakneck. Contrary to the self-absorbed, masculine narcissism, making sure of its image, one of being seen, of seeing itself, of assembling its glories, of pocketing itself again. The reductive look, the always divided look returning, the mirror economy; he needs to love himself. But she launches forth; she seeks to love.[66]

Irigaray asks: "Would the fundamental project of the hysteric, always concealed in ordinary discourse, be to get himself or herself recognized as valid subject of the utterance?"[67] One wants to answer yes, as the most obvious movement toward the ethical. One wants to agree that the hysteric should be able to seek out, if not wholeness, then at least her subjective value within the statement. The hysteric ought to be able to use language for herself, ought to be able to mobilize the *I* however she pleases. And on the other hand, the ethical dimension of making room for *you* appears in the hysteric's discourse toward the other. The hysteric is a master of making space for the unknown in language, and her subjective position poses an alternative to reductive monologic speech. She challenges dominant assumptions about discourse from within the scientific regime, and overflows Bourneville's capacity for transcription with a delirium of words, words that make room for the other. Augustine, in her hallucinations, was almost always "with" others. It is difficult not to read her waiting, in the garden, to which she escaped on several occasions, often naked and often in the rain, as an ek-static act in relation to another, a form of waiting that positioned her in a state of becoming, without completion. Sometimes she made space in the bed next to her, physically indicating the hysterical continuum of relationality in her delirious grammar.[68] In these relational gestures, she located herself.

Cixous and Clément write: "As for passivity, in excess, it is partly bound up with death. But there is a nonclosure that is not submission but confidence and comprehension; that is not an opportunity for destruction but for wonderful expansion."[69] The hysteric's discourse points to a subject whose relationship to becoming is intensified, generating a fluid subjectivity that manifests itself exactly through speaking, sounding, gesturing. Though the content of her words is transmissible only with a multiplicity of limitations, gaps, and contingencies, the hysterical patient, even as she experiences an induced aphonia, is still within language. Her thought does not necessarily appear in speech, and sometimes her utterances reveal a dynamic of her thought that unhinges the efficacy of rational utterance. In her poetic combination of bodily gesture, sound, and word, an inarticulacy bound to private experience as a turbulent subject gains force, overflows the medical text's confines, stubbornly refuses accurate description. In the effusive quality of Augustine's speech, there is room for the other and still room for herself. Hers is a hysterical grammar that contains an ethical provocation: make room for the unknown.

What could happen if we aimed to position ourselves more hysterically? In fact, when one tries to read or write the hysteric, one inevitably ends up in this hysterical position, destabilized and caught in a suspension of incompleteness, looking for the other but unable to find her. So then:

what made Charcot's speech so flimsy that he could not make space for the other? What made him try to assert impassive vocal authority over a dynamic hysteria, insisting on his control and knowledge even as the hysteric on stage pried apart his grasp with unwieldy alterity?

CRY

In a lecture in 1888, Charcot introduced a patient, a hysteric who had appeared the preceding Friday. He declared: "The patient will serve to show us what I am advancing" – a hysterical attack provoked by hysterogenic points on the patient's body. He noted that organic bodies are less predictable than machines, and that although the attack should produce itself, it may not.[70] His rhetorical gesture towards contingency seems to have been strategically deployed in order to make the attack more impressive when it did occur. Having done this before (for over a decade) Charcot could not seriously doubt the outcome of his "experiment." In fact, as he narrated his discovery of la grande hystérie, beginning with his acceptance of the Salpêtrière directorship twenty years prior, and breezing by a dramatic recantation of his "sort of intuition" that led him to the famous illness, Charcot made clear that what dawned on him was that "it was always the same thing."[71] The similarity of features of the hysterical attack – their repetition – indicated that he was dealing with a "real illness." A possibility of the unpredictable was built into the lecture, but Charcot's command over the hysterical body was not a question for the director. As he described the physiological articulations of the hysteric's attack, breaking the process into its nosological phases, he reiterated: "despite its apparent variety of phenomena, it [the attack] is always the same thing."[72] Then an intern applied pressure to the hysteric's left breast, at a "hysterogenic point" and the attack began afresh. The attack and the hysteric showed themselves to be push-button, and the declaration that followed was a testament to positivist discourse as recurring visible reality expressed in nosological language: "Voila la période épileptoïde."[73]

The intern pressed her pubic bone, "We will now see if the patient is *ovarienne*," and then again, "On vient de presser de nouveau sur un point hystérogène et voici l'attaque épileptique qui se reproduit"[74] (We have just now pressed again a hysterogenic point and here is the epileptic attack, being repeated). The patient began to bite her tongue, and Charcot remained aloof, never losing his objective tone, saying that the hysteric occasionally bites her tongue, but not very often. He proceeded quickly to the next opportunity for description: "Now here is the famous arc-de-cercle you find described everywhere."[75] But then, the patient began to cry out – "all of a sudden" – wrote the stenographer: "The patient suddenly cries: "Mama, I'm afraid!"" Charcot spoke over her, continuing to describe the regularity of the hysterical attack, in tones reportedly dull and clear, but she continued to cry out, "Ah! Maman!"[76] Charcot's response: "You can see how hysterics scream. One might say that it's a lot of noise for nothing. Epilepsy, which is much more severe, is much more silent."[77]

Though Charcot's response falls to the descriptive and dismissive, consistent defaults for the director, I read this moment as a temporary interruption into the lecture's monologic flow, wherein Charcot finds himself suddenly having to respond to the patient's off-script "noise." When the patient cried out, Charcot seemed to stumble in his otherwise smooth explanatory monologue. The patient wailed for her mother in a moment Didi-Huberman has called the "show-stopper."[78] Why showstopper? Charcot's cool-headed, aloof manner on a stage, his monologic grandeur, was rarely, if ever, interruptible, except this time, by the cry of the patient. Not only did Charcot not expect or script the cry, the patient's visceral sounding resisted reasonable explanation or medical categorization, exerting a force of inarticulacy that the doctor's eloquence could not attend to. Charcot's reply, that hysterics scream about nothing and that epileptics have much more to scream about but are quieter, can be read as a weak effort to dismiss the hysteric's scream with a betraying tone of resentment. The director's response, a rhetorical impotence, is potentially undergirded by several sentiments: frustration (at having been upstaged), anger, (at having been interrupted and undermined), and/or embarrassment (at being unable to give adequate reply, of losing face before an audience of peers, of surrendering discursive control). He effectively stammers his intervention.

These parenthetical cries have uncommon force.[79] Compared against the desirable silence of the Salpêtrière's epileptics, the patient's cries rattle their retroactively placed grammatical constraints. They pose a brief but potent disruption into the usual discursive structure of the lecture series, momentarily able to switch power from the reasonable medical institution to the hysteric and her manner of sounding, at the site of the inarticulate and prosodic voice.

Hysterics were documented on many occasions as crying out. Charcot frequently produced pain and its accompanying cries in his patients onstage. Bourneville's bedside notes in the *Iconographie* are flecked with notations that read, "Cris." In the *Démoniaques* text alone, Charcot and Richer describe many cries. Depicting the phases of the hysterical attack, they note "des cris de douleur déchirants"[80] (heart-wrenching screams of pain). They similarly record "des cris automatiques" (automatic cries) and "des cris sauvages"[81] (savage cries). They take interest in the physiognomic portrayals of cries in art, remarking, for instance, that it is difficult to cry out if the face is contracted as demonstrated in a painting of an early hysteric by Raphäel[82] and they compare these to the physiognomies of wailing hysterics in their hospital, which often express astonishment, horror, and disgust.[83] The involuntary cries of hysterics in response to pain, in the *Démoniaques* volume, are said to be pitiable.[84] None of these cited cries seems to have provoked the response this anonymous hysteric's did in the 1888 lecture. That doctors cited many cries, and that crying out seemed to occur with regularity amongst hysterics, makes this cry in particular, and its showstopping power, worth investigation.

What can be said about Charcot's stammered reply to the patient's cry, and the force of the wailed utterance? Why was this cry so powerful? What can be learned about the potential meanings and consequences of the "ah!" by listening to the patient's cry with curiosity?

THE BEAUTY OF USELESSNESS
Against Instrumentality

Charcot wrote that the hysteric's production of *involuntary* cries elicited pity.[85] This remark and its allowance for symptomatic cries, cries a patient cannot help or hold back, raises the possibility that the hysteric's scream onstage in 1888 could have been willful, far from the ventriloquized puppet doctors and critics described in reference to the women who performed these staged attacks.[86] Perhaps the agency at the heart of the cry is what caused Charcot to turn from the path of reasonable exposition in order to dismiss the patient's cry as noise, to chastise her for screaming when, according to him, epileptics had much more to scream about yet maintained a (much more desirable) silence.[87]

The catch in Charcot's monologue was not permanent. Following the detour from the usual naming and describing of his lectures, he picked up his dull, emotionless tone again, resuming a discursive method that was transparently self-aggrandizing but also conscientious about scientific detail. Following the moment under scrutiny, he continued to lecture on the regularity of hysteria and its dominant phases. The cry, and the temporary disruption it elicits, is, then, above all, symbolic as an act of resistance. What the cry signifies is truly disruptive, however. And what can be learned from the hysteric rather than about her in this instance produces a swell of ethical possibilities.

That February Tuesday, Charcot did not like the hysteric's cry. The cry's potential as resistance to the reductive violence of positivist discourse does not mean that the patient liked to scream, though she may have. The combination of pain and pleasure experienced by the patient in the moment of her unleashed cry was and is unsharable. What we make of the "ah!" now is largely conjecture. The hysteric's mobilization of language to appear and conceal herself, and her utterances' precarious representation in the medical literature presents instances of speech that are only incrementally legible. Aiming to attend to the trace of the scream in the transcript runs the risk of vocal appropriation or of indulging in the myth that one can retroactively "give voice." How, then, do we listen to the hysteric, without pretending to hear?[88] Perhaps by experiencing the limits of our listening and the impossibility of hearing evoked by her cry.

The patient Augustine, the hysteric in the 1888 lecture, and their fellow inmates certainly lived in a state of being wronged, according to Lyotard's description, wherein victims of violence are deprived of vocality and thus testimonial commentary on that violence. Cast as an onstage property rather than a dialogic co-star in Charcot's monologic demonstrations, the patient was supposed to be mute. Her cry in the 1888 lecture is astounding because it sounds out where there is supposed to be silence. The "ah!" was audible but illegible. It is not unlike John Cage's provocative utterance, "I have nothing to say, and I am saying it."[89] It is possible that the hysteric had so much to say, and said it, but such that nothing *in particular* could be made of it. The act of crying out signals and performs the end of the hysteric's instrumentality. And it is not simply its opposition to muteness or silence that gives the cry its force. The cry, of all manners of utterance, is particularly potent because of its inarticulacy. It sounds, without sounding anything in particular. It runs contrary to transmission of the empirical since it signals the potential for meaning(s) without completing the significative work of communication. The cry leaves us desiring more, depending upon the hysteric to give it; significative potential is assured – she has something to say – but communication is by no means guaranteed – she may continue to scream saying nothing locatable. She reserves her right to withhold facts. She is not muted or silent but loud, yet still, we are caught waiting to see what she may or may not choose to say. We make room for her. We have no choice.

In part, what the anonymous patient's cry affects is an ethical imposition. It is an undeniable assertion of her humanity. It reopens a dialogue that positivist medicine has tried to close. It reasserts the value of the hysteric as an interlocutor. Levinas writes that what happens at the level of the face, also happens in language. The ungraspable epiphany of the face and the uncontainable secrecy of the voice "hail me and signify to me, by [their] nakedness, by [their] destitution, an order." Their presence is not a locatable object to be possessed or explained, but a "summons to respond."[90]

Other than laughter, what sound is more human than the sound of crying out? Even patriarchal philosophers, storytellers, and theologians have written at length and often about the primordial quality of the cry and of its presence at the linguistic origins of personkind. Jewish philosopher Martin Buber suggests that the word YHVH began as a primal sound like "Yah" and was used to express an original mystical experience. Following Rudolph Otto, he writes that "Yah" is a "numinous and primal sound."[91] Dante writes, somewhat hyperbolically, in his unfinished treatise on language, *De vulgari eloquentia* that, "ever since the Fall, human speech has always begun with an exclamation of despair: 'Heu!'"[92] For Michel Seuphor, author of *Le style et le cri*, the cry marks the common foundation of humanity and is a response to both pain and pleasure. Seuphor says "Le cri que je pousse me proclame semblable aux autres, à la multitude des humains qui jouissent et souffrent"[93] (The cry that I unleash proclaims me to be like others, like the multitude of human beings who experience *jouissance* and who suffer). Further expressing how crying out is a condition of shared humanity, Seuphor declares, "Je crie, donc je suis"[94] (I cry therefore I am). Hegel's figurative animal turns into original, linguistic man (for Hegel, most certainly a man) in a groan.[95] Thinking about humanity so often points to thinking about screaming. Even a brief tangle with Western philosophy's mega narrative finds ready examples of the cry as an integral part of becoming human, situating inarticulate vocalization at our origins.

What's more, it is easy to forget that screaming is not prior to or outside of language, but part of language. And like the scream that sounds from within language, the break between reasonable and unreasonable discourse cannot be absolute, because language is a flexible morphology, both cultural and relational. Ferdinand de Saussure, among other linguists and philosophers of language, teaches that in speech the entirety of language is contained, so that when one speaks, one speaks the entire history of language and at the same time modifies it.[96] When one utters from the margins of conventional syntax or when one screams, one also partakes in the iterative creativity of language. To listen to a scream is to listen to a vital piece of the human lexicon. The communal phenomenon of screaming is rarely obvious and is even less frequently banal. Though screaming in common to all of us, a scream can still rattle, startle, jolt, and frighten.

The impression that the hysteric was a voiceless doll, a passive body to be articulated by the Salpêtrière doctors, falls apart when she begins to cry out. Autonomous sound, coming from a figure that ought to be passive, is more than uncanny. The cry is monstrous. As she roars, she uncovers that the hysteric, too, is at least part monster. For Allen Weiss, "Monsters symbolize alterity and difference in extremis."[97] In his theses on monstrosity, Weiss also writes: "Imagine a disembodied blood-curdling scream. This is my final thesis."[98] The patient's cry is significantly forceful because it is radically embodied. Her cry is not from elsewhere, is not radiophonic or phantasmatic. It is a human cry of monstrous proportions, more so since she and her body had been conceived as mere sculptural material. Here, what is least expected and most disruptive is the patient's humanity.

Charcot and his audience, as physicians, authors, artists, and police, but most of all as people, surely identified with the phenomenon of screaming though they also may have been surprised by the patient's sudden cries. Charcot, on that day in 1888, was not empathetically moved by them, but what about his peers? The ragged sound of the woman's voice, toppling the director's narrative flow, likely affected some members of the audience? Ideally, some were shocked, in the Artaudian sense. Is it possible that the patient's cries produced a "vibratory action upon the sensibility" of her audience?[99] When Artaud writes the following, one feels oneself in the churning realm of inarticulacy mobilized against the stagnant authority of positivist speech, and believes in the force of the broken utterance: "To make metaphysics out of a spoken language is to make language express what it usually does not express: this is to make use of it in a new, exceptional, and unaccustomed fashion; to reveal its possibilities of physical shock, to actively divide and distribute it in space; to handle intonations in an absolutely concrete manner, restoring their power to tear asunder and to really manifest something; to turn against language and its basely utilitarian, one could even say alimentary, sources."[100]

The unexpected intonation of the hysteric may have physically shocked the onlookers to the pedagogical spectacle. Maybe, they were not merely inconvenienced by an interruption in Charcot's show, but experienced a visceral resonance, a bodily response to the sound of the patient's scream. The cry's power to tear asunder is partly in the vibrations of its sound. What might the affective tear manifest? In part, the hysteric's cry, indicating her humanity at the universal level of the cry, also loudly sounded her human secrecy. Her cry was at once most public and most private. Loud, with no determinable content. Indexical of her pain and her right to speak, depriving her narrators of the possibility for possessive domination through explicative narration, the patient's cry was hers alone. Like the face, the hysteric's cry was at once universal, belonging to shared human experience, and the most particular, sounding her radical alterity. As the hysteric cried out, she sounded her humanity and railed against being perceived as a passive object to be used in the service of medical pedagogy. She turned her voice against the utility of language, made language express what it ordinarily does not. The ethical imposition of her cry occurred as it physically rattled its witnesses. The sound touched them, worked on their organs, and could never belong to them nor give them a translation of its meaning. An offensive force opened them and denied them closure. Charcot's attempted dismissal was a weak and insufficient bandage for this wounding.

The cry stops the show because reason can no longer affect a pure and simple translation from one voice to another. The script and its hierarchy are subverted. Charcot could not make the patient's body speak exactly according to his will because she herself was speaking – in a surprising manner. When madness is not silent, and when it does not attempt to explain itself, but rather offensively exhibits itself as precisely inexplicable, radically ulterior, inaccessible, it ruptures the possibility for reason to maintain its unquestioning power over the mad person. The content of the cry cannot be determined, measured against standards of reason, or debated. The cry is not "up for debate." It just *happens*. It may say: "You can hear me but you can't explain me. I'm in immeasurable pain and the pain is my own, unknowable to you. This body is mine and not yours – see how I can set it screaming. Fuck this hospital and fuck your lecture. Fuck you and fuck your script. I want my mother to take me out of here now." It also may say anything else. The beautiful volatility of the cry is that we can and will never know.

The cry's force may lie in its being the most personal assertion, an enigma that can't be reduced to or by exposition. To cry out is not to be understood. This is precisely its power. It disrupts the utilitarian, resists capture, and cannot be explained.

By crying out, the hysterical patient dissolved her own use value and subverted the usefulness of language in the same moment, rocking the foundations of medical positivism and the rhetorical structure of the hysteria show. Her cry was immediate, unscripted, unexpected. It was also from a linguistic order that Charcot could not speak to, communicate with, or talk about with any authority. Given the history of scientific language and its decisive deafness to unreason, Charcot was out of practice, unable to meet the raw poetics of his onstage counterpart. The patient's cry produced, out of the positivist spectacle, an ecstasy of listening, where new modes of attention deployed themselves, becoming necessary once explanation and dismissal were found to be impossible. The result recalls Cage's celebratory exclamation: "all we can do is suddenly listen."[101] The cry had, and still has, the power to destabilize. We cannot hear, but we can admire the patient's "*Voice-cry*. Agony – the spoken "word" exploded, blown to bits by suffering and anger, demolishing discourse."[102]

Because reasonable rhetoric was such a prominent feature of disempowering female hysterical patients in order to solidify the power of masculine medical elites, that the cry interferes into the spectacle at the level of language is pivotal. The discursive structure of the lectures as delineated in the book's first and second chapters and as exemplified by statements of Charcot's such as, "I state what I see, nothing more" shatter upon the patient's sounded intervention.[103] The nature of the interference and its effects can be gleaned by being attentive to Charcot's reply. When Charcot stammers in response to the patient's cry, the fallen scaffold of the discursive structure of the lecture series and of the implicit gnostic power that clung to particular modes of speaking shows itself. The phrase loses its drive. Vocabulary totters. The deterioration of language as it is commonly understood is the only response to the inarticulate cry.

The possibility for the cry to truly disrupt, to truly intervene in the spectacle of power is evidenced in Charcot's non-reply. His stammer – not his muteness, but his wanting to say and simultaneously being unable to do so – indicates that his discursive power has been temporarily undone. What becomes apparent in the director's inability to give adequate reply to the cry is that positivist discourse has shattered under pressure from the patient's scream. For a moment, the hysteric's vocal gesture infects the asylum director, translates his voice into her own, shows the inadequacy of language and its taking place without explicative power. When Charcot's language begins to falter, the wailing patient hears a voice call back in its own impeded way. Reason is overtaken by the "muteness" on which it relies for its unquestioned authority. The cry generates a momentary transfer of power. To be rendered speechless in the face of the human cry is to perform according to the cry's logic, is to speak the indeterminacy covertly underlying the language of reason. By stammering in response to the patient, Charcot, provoked by the force of her ungraspable utterance, spoke a similar language of inarticulacy. For a moment, he repeated the stammered dialogue of ambiguity that Foucault says used to take place between reason and unreason.

The hysteric did not interrupt Charcot's performance of medical authority and the facile use of language it relied upon with a diatribe against the medical institution or a speech on the violence and inadequacy of objectivity. She did not explain her life or her experience at the hospital as a way of becoming her own narrator. Instead, she wailed an "ah," both refusing to use language Charcot's way and making language express what it ordinarily doesn't, including its own limitations. The hysteric's cry was both part of language and a relief from language. What could she have said that would have challenged the theatrically constructed power of Charcot's voice over hers? By letting herself cry out inarticulately, she exerted a force over articulacy itself. Suddenly Charcot's means of describing her attack, and thus his relationship to language, was revealed as brittle, small, inadequate. Description was the tiniest intervention into the hysteric's life, barely touching the truth of her, barely grasping the potential truths of her condition.

While positivism relies on empirical evidence expressed in true statements, or the idea that "knowledge describes reality,"[104] language, always, is a play at lack. As Lyotard teaches, language is mimetic, not translative: "One ought to forbid mimesis, but one cannot. In fact, things themselves are not grasped, only their images. If things were grasped, there would be no need to phrase. Or else, if we didn't phrase, there would be no need to mime. Phrasing takes place in the lack of being of that about which there is to phrase. Language is the sign that one does not know the being of the existent … One can thus only compromise with mimesis."[105] If language is a mimetic compromise for a customary lack of knowledge, then positivist language is revealed as a hopeful but dull oversight. Most of all, language itself speaks the human condition of not knowing. The compromise of language points to the ethical dimension of human relationships. To speak about a person is never to catch them, and to speak about a person is always to speak their escape. The hysteric's oblique cry and its illumination of rhetorical inadequacy teach that within the voice, the other's spaciousness thrives.

As Weiss writes, "Monsters exist in margins. They are thus avatars of chance, impurity, heterodoxy, abomination, mutation, metamorphosis, prodigy, mystery, marvel. Monsters are indicators of epistemic shifts."[106] The hysteric, overthrowing her instrumentality and the instrumentality of language simultaneously, poses an epistemic shift. Within Charcot's positivist lesson about her symptomatic body, she teaches us about the force and inevitability of ambiguity by crying out. Part of her lesson: language is always a compromise, crying out says as much as language can often say. There is no need to classify this: "Ah!"

FOUR

Hysteria in/as Performance

While the lecture series were at their height of medical importance and popular fame, the claim arose, from several circles, that Charcot's hysteria was contrived and that the hysterics were faking their symptoms. When A. Baudouin asked Blanche Wittman – later in her life, when she no longer exhibited the symptoms of hysteria and worked in the radiology ward at the Salpêtrière – if she had been faking, Wittman's reply was tinted with outrage. Baudouin had asked many times about the hysteria Wittman used to have, and about its marked absence from her later life. She had previously refused to answer his interrogations. Indeed, one wonders how she felt about the mysterious disappearance of her own symptoms. As Baudouin recounts, the conversation unfolded as follows:

> Listen, Blanche, I know there are subjects that you don't like to talk about; but you know that I have never ridiculed anything since we have been acquainted. I would like you to explain something about the attacks you used to have. After hesitating for a second, she replied: "Well! What do you want to know? – They claim that all these attacks were faked, that the patients pretended to be asleep and

> that the whole thing was a joke on the doctors. What's the truth in all that? – None of it is true. It's all lies; if we fell asleep, if we had attacks, it was because we were helpless to do otherwise. What's more, it was very unpleasant." And she added: "Fakery! Do you think it would have been easy to fool M. Charcot? Yes, there were tricksters who tried; he used to glance at them and say: 'Be still.'"[1]

According to Wittman, there were hysterics who faked attacks for attention, but these were lame attempts given the expert scrutiny of Charcot, who saw through the ruse with prompt dismissal. What were the differences between real and fake performances of hysteria?

The question as to whether or not the Salpêtrière hysterics were merely performing their attacks continues to pry open the archive precisely because the hysterics performed so often. Their illness was steeped in spectacle and the result was that hysteria became difficult to distinguish from theatricality. For the camera, for doctors – for attention, for visibility – for the amphitheatre audience, for their larger French public who would see the Brouillet engraving and read about hysterics in the papers – to be a nineteenth century hysteric was to perform. With gestures connoting extreme emotional states, ragged cries, feats of physical strength and technically impressive hypnotic mimesis, hysteria lent itself easily to theatrical comparisons.

French filmmaker Alice Winocour, who treats Augustine's character with an impressive autonomy that counters the many portrayals of the patient as a passive victim, suggesting that her reading of the lecture series is attentive in ways other readings are not, includes a scene in her 2012 film, *Augustine*, in which the patient, accidentally cured of her hysteria, throws a fit on stage that she has performed countless times in earnest but is suddenly forced to produce.[2] Scheduled to perform on the amphitheatre stage, suddenly, she finds herself having to preserve the authentic appearance of the lectures and hysterical attacks precisely by giving a fraudulent demonstration of hysteria's codes, rhythms, and symptoms – stylistic embodiments with which she is familiar, and which she is able to reproduce without the audience catching on to her departure from the usual helplessness that seemed to accompany her former attacks. She fakes it. And rather well. Partly, the attack is an erotic performance for Charcot, whom she is seducing in this film. In the intimacy produced by their shared knowledge that her orgasmic throes are put on, and that the audience does not know it, Augustine demonstrates a sensual self-possession that appears to the audience to be a rendition of the usual uncontrollable hysterical symptoms. Winocour's treatment of the feigned attack is fictional, but nonetheless provocative for questions around authenticity and fraud that haunted the real Augustine, and her co-stars at the Salpêtrière theatre.

Once cured, how is Augustine's performance of hysteria distinct from her earlier performances, in which she truly experienced the hysterical attack as part of the lecture performances? In this pivotal moment in Winocour's film, Augustine plays to the audience more than usual, and especially to Charcot. He, who normally plays "out front" to the crowd, while the hysteric, under hypnosis or under attack, is more likely to perform within the enclosure of her experience of her illness' symptoms, is suddenly a spectator as much as he is an actor. The shuffle in reflexivity when Augustine performs "illness" in quotation marks provokes intriguing questions around the magnitudes of performance in hysterical attack in the real-life medical shows.[3]

Again: what is the difference between authentically ill and self-consciously willful performances of the hysterical attack? In Winocour's version, is the key distinction that Augustine is in control of her technical execution of the stylized mega-symptom of la grande hystérie as opposed to helplessly possessed by its force? How helpless does a patient have to be against her symptom of theatre-making for her to be performing truthfully? At what point does her illness totter into the terrain of fakery? Once her musculature heals and the taut rigidity of the arm and hand with no known morbid origin finds itself inexplicably loosened, is Augustine a hysteric any longer? Unable to separate the hysterical attack from performance, what are we to make of the terms real or fake, true or false?

Indeed, Winocour's representation of Augustine's performances at the Salpêtrière picks up on something that makes the authenticity of hysterics on stage so susceptible to interrogation. The difficulty the audience to the hysterical performance in Winocour's film and the nineteenth century audience has in parsing levels of "authentic" and "put on" hysteria has a great deal to do with the way theatre infects and complicates the Salpêtrière's theatricalization of an already theatrical illness. While the medical spectacle was, on the one hand, a pedagogical lecture, it was, on the other hand, marked by many theatrical signifiers that were bound to raise a demonstration of true facts and real phenomena to dramatic proportions. As a result, many wondered if the hysterics' performances were real at all, and even if hysteria itself was an illness or a cultural phenomenon. I suggest it was both illness and cultural product, both authentically experienced in performance and caught up in registers of simulation and indulgence in theatricality. The question as to whether or not Charcot's hysterics and, indeed, Charcot himself, were faking is an important one, and its answer not simple. Tracing the intersections of the hysteric's authentic experiences, theatrical embodiments and entrenchment in the strange performance culture of the Salpêtrière hospital leads to intriguing collusion between hysteria and performance.

DOUBTS

Hippolyte Bernheim, director of a competing research hospital at Nancy, took issue with Charcot's equation of hypnosis with hysteria, and voiced doubts that the director may be narrowing the phenomenon to his hysterics as a way to become more famous. Bernheim produced an article to this effect called "L'hypnotisme de la Salpêtrière est un produit artificiel, la conséquence d'une apprentissage"[4] (The Salpêtrière's hypnosis is an artificial product and a learned cultural product). While Bernheim, whose critique settled on hypnosis, could not have discounted the reality of hysterical illness from his position within the medical community where research on hysteria was thriving, others did contest the sincerity of Charcot's project and the patients' relationship to genuine pathology. Following their falling out with the Charcot family, the Goncourt brothers wrote that Charcot amounted to nothing but a huckster and that he paid his hysterics to perform their "symptoms." It became rumoured that patients would perform fits with increased theatricality for a few cents slipped to them by an intern.[5] Freud doubted the sincerity of the hysterical performances as well. As he reflected in *Ma Vie et la Psychanalyse*, "Il me paraît impossible que plusieurs entre eux n'aient pas eu de doute sur la sincérité des sujets, n'aient pas compris l'invraisemblance de certains faits. Pourquoi n'ont-ils pas mis en garde Charcot?"[6] (It seemed impossible to me that many of them (the doctors) hadn't any doubt about the sincerity of their subjects, hadn't known the implausibility of certain facts. Why didn't they alert Charcot?)

Performer and dancer Jane Avril's memoirs describe the way patients brought on their own attacks and stopped them, with the help of a fellow patient accomplice to press on their ovaries, in order to be noticed by the hospital doctors and thus able to speak to them. She writes rather wistfully about her temporary institutionalization, saying that she lived:

> on the great professor Charcot's service, with the stars of hysteria, an ailment which, at that time, was creating a sensation. The foremost medical men, the best known thinkers of the entire world came in droves to attend the courses presided over by the master and to witness the demonstrations and experiments on his most famous subjects … I lived for two years [in fact 18 months] in this "Eden" – which it was for me, so much in this world being relative … There were those deranged girls whose ailment named Hysteria consisted, above all, in simulation of it … How much trouble they used to go to in order to capture attention and gain stardom. That prize went to the one who would find something novel to overshadow the others when Charcot, followed by a large group of students, stood at the bedside and observed their wild contortions, "arcs de cercle," various acrobatics, and other gymnastics … These patients had nothing to hide from little me – I was of so little consequence! – thus they didn't hesitate to let me know about what they used to call "the secret." They gave me the following directions: "when you see one of them come in, be sure to come to my bed and press hard on my ovaries." It was understood that this simple maneuver would suffice to interrupt the attack immediately, permitting the "patient" – recovering her wits – to have a conversation with the special person of the moment. When they sensed that the time of Charcot's visit was approaching, several threw a fit and I, now that the time had arrived, cooperated by doing what they had requested of me … Often, in the big amphitheater filled to the top, in front of the chiefs of the medical profession from all countries, Charcot gave his course, presenting his strangest "cases" on whom he performed numerous experiments with suggestion. For me it was a comic show to see these crazies come away so proud and delighted to have been chosen and pointed to by the "master." In my tiny brain, I was astonished every time to see how such eminent savants could be duped in that way, when I, as insignificant as I was, saw through the farces. I have said to myself since that the great Charcot was aware of what was happening.[7]

Avril's account presents a series of observations that point to the curious relationship between doctors and patients, between patients and performance of their illnesses. As Avril notes, garnering attention for a hysterical attack when so many patients could produce them may have been difficult. And there is a possibility that patients found pleasure in being noticed by the director, found satisfaction in making it to the amphitheatre stage to be "pointed at" by Charcot. The hysteric may have brought on – or indeed – put on the more dramatic qualities of her hysteria in order to be noticed or chosen for the stage performance. Bonduelle and Gelfland suggest that Avril's account of her time in Salpêtrière may have taken up the question of patient simulation to participate in a debate already going on in France about the potential fakery of the lecture series.[8]

What did Charcot have to say about all this? The director addressed doubts about hysteria's authenticity in his lectures when he said, "They say hysteria only exists in France, and only at the Salpêtrière, as if I had forged it from the power of my will." He defended with the now famous statement, "but in truth, I am but a photographer."[9] He sometimes used lecture periods to address patient simulation by demonstrating his competence at distinguishing between real hysterical phenomena and patients' attempts at fakery. His demonstration of the efficacy of his methods for testing the difference between the two sought to allay doubts of his witnesses. For instance, he said, in real catalepsy induced by hysteria, a patient's limbs could remain in active resting states for hours without fatiguing the muscles in the least. In fake catalepsy, an extended arm would begin to tremble. The most minor of oscillations could be recorded by a pressure drum and the slightest increase in breath measured by a pneumograph.[10] As he stated, rather over-emphatically:

> It is useless to insist further. A hundred other examples might be invoked which would only show that the simulation, which is talked about so much when hysteria and allied affections are under consideration, is, in the actual state of our knowledge, only a bugbear, before which the fearful and novice alone are stopped. For the future it ought to be the province of the physician, well-informed in these matters, to dissipate chicanery whenever it occurs; and to sort out the symptoms which form a fundamental part of the malady, from those which are simulated, and added to it, by the artifice of the patient.[11]

By putting facts once again firmly in his possession, Charcot may have alleviated audience concern, but his need to do so indicates that doubts were brewing.

Charcot's statements, and the range of doubts expressed by Charcot's critics indicate some of the dynamics of hysteria and its transmission at the Salpêtrière that made truth and falsehood difficult to parse. Hysteria, as it occurred onstage, in photographs, and in the bodies of the hospital patients, was remarkably specific. The hysterical attack was a singular phenomenon with ultimately little variation: large and rapid movements, acrobatics, the arc-de-cercle, and the period of hallucination, often erotic or violent, before the attack resolved. Charcot's assertion that only hysterics were susceptible to hypnosis, alongside the formation of a visual type that bordered on artistic genre, led Bernheim and others to remark that hypnosis and hysteria, at the Salpêtrière, were cultural phenomena, learned and not spontaneous. They were, in some ways, correct. True, hysteria, according to the dominant histories, had existed since the Greeks or the early Egyptians, and, outside Paris, hysteria was being diagnosed in the Germany, Britain, America, and elsewhere contemporaneously.[12] But, after Charcot died, the swell of hysterical performance all but disappeared from the hospital in the form that the director had popularized. Charcot's most famous hysteric, Blanche Wittman, gave up her symptoms. Charcot's pupil Joseph Babinski aimed to dismantle the master's work.[13] Even the hysterics of Freud and Breuer, so often linked to their neurologically afflicted French counterparts, bore dreamlike somatic expression in common with Charcot's hysterics, but abandoned the four-phase attack altogether. Hysteria, as it existed in Charcot's theatrical enterprise, was uniquely executed.

Avril's memories of patients bringing on their attacks, taking advantage of their bodies' ability to produce symptoms on command, picks up on the hysteric's indulgence in the dramatic crisis of her illness, in her yearning to be noticed, on her vanity. Avril also picks up on hysteria's troubled proximity to simulation. The hysterics, in her account, seem less to fake their symptoms outright, and more to surrender to the predictable mimicry embedded in the illness itself. As for the intentional deception of the director by the patients, as indicated by Freud, or the propensity for the medical staff to bribe the patients into putting on their hysterical shows, these claims about the insidiousness of the performance of hysteria seem ill placed, though they do indicate just how difficult it became for witnesses to Charcot's project to believe what they saw, or to be certain of what they were seeing. Charcot's feigned objectivity in the face of such a blatantly theatrical project could not have helped to ease suspicions. Two obstacles to the audience's certainty of authenticity present themselves: the theatrical transmission of hysteria, and the hysteric's inherent – and diagnostically supported – theatricality.

CITATION, REPETITION

If the hysterical body gave rise to a range of visually arresting symptoms, it also gave rise to doubt in those who witnessed them. Muddling the opposition between being and acting, hysterics and their bodies were, diagnostically, masters of simulation. The ability to simulate somatic pathologies or to achieve physiological symptoms in the absence of the illnesses that usually create those effects is, incidentally, still a symptom of diagnosable hysteria and its related illnesses in the twenty-first century. The hysterical body could bleed with no known cause. The patient's back could contort into a taut series of compressions, for no known physical reason. A hand might contract and fall permanently asleep. A neck might stiffen or an eyeball roll limply. Coughs without respiratory conditions. Lumps in the throat. Dora's discharge. To put it simply: to be hysterical was to have a mimetic body.

The connections between the body that lies professionally in the theatre and the hysterical body that lies are intriguing. Particularly, imitation, in both cases, whatever the theatrical genre, aims to tell a peculiar kind of truth, but through a semiotic knot of symbolic association and citation. In the theatre, things stand in for other things, and are never the things themselves. On stage, a pipe is not simply a pipe, but an iteration. The hysterical symptom cuts across sign and referent relationships accordingly. In a psychoanalytic semiotics, a lie can tell the truth, and even language that tries to be honest is never straightforward. As Freud explains, we remember, every sign is a symptom open to a series of differing meanings: "The hysterical symptom does not carry this meaning with it, but the meaning is lent to it, welded on to it, as it were; and in every instance the meaning can be a different one, according to the nature of the suppressed thoughts which are struggling for expression."[14] The unconscious force at work in the psychoanalytic subject claims the body to demonstrate a symptom – a sign of itself – according to a peculiar, enigmatic and particular logic. The straightforward sign/referent relationship is askew since, as Freud notes, these symptoms don't point to their unconscious referents in the nature of direct signification. Meaning is welded onto the sign, shifting the forms of both and leaving a trace of the creative production of the unconscious. In his analysis of Dora, for example, Freud finds that Dora's aphonia has to do with the absence of Herr K, whom she loves (though contemporary readers recognize this is not the case) and for whom she speaks. Without his being present, there is no need for her to say anything since she cannot speak to *him* and this silence speaks her love for Herr K more loudly than anything she could utter.[15] This manifestation of repressed material (in this case, Dora's love/desire for Herr K),[16] Freud only intuited based on months of other fragmentary material encountered during analysis.[17] The way in which the sign applies to the referent or the symptom applies to its unconscious provocation is particular to Dora's psychological make-up and living history. It is only *poetically* logical that this unconscious material "seized upon *this* chance event and made use of it for an utterance of its own."[18] For Charcot too, the absence of visible lesions in the nerve tissues of patients presenting symptoms lead him to differentiate between physiological tearing and *dynamic* or *functional* lesions, that is, lesions that could not be seen but that behaved like their material counterparts.[19] The absence of neurological signs of symptomatic expression found in post-mortem examinations led Charcot to coin the term, "neuromimesis,"[20] and to describe hysteria as an "inextricable labyrinth."[21]

The turbulent signification of the symptomatic hysterical body becomes even more obscure when the symptom is brought on by hypnosis – simulated – and really experienced by the patient – therefore real – but also called forth citationally, as an example of the typical hysterical symptom it parallels – not entirely real but pointing to the real. Charcot's excitement about the hypnotizable hysteric as a living tableau points exactly to this ability for citation. The hysteric's appearance on stage exacerbates the mimesis. In hypnosis, any physical configuration particular to hysteria can be brought forth, held for lengthy observation, and then released upon command. The hysterical body performs yet another feat of representation. And then the plot thickens. For the body that holds positions seemingly mimetically sometimes indicates their really taking place in the patient's experience. "We can make it [the symptom] subsist once she wakes." Charcot reported.[22] The symptom suggested in hypnosis, one the patient would not produce naturally, one that was therefore foreign to it, written on it iteratively, could carry over into the waking world, holding fast. The patient's body physically adopted in real life what was suggested in hypnosis, that is, the symptom adopted on stage *as though* it were real persisted beyond the performance. Really.

The reality of the production of hysterical symptoms declares itself in other cases. Once, Charcot accidentally hurt a patient who has been de-anaesthetized by another doctor. He could not see the nature of the patient's hypnotic experience and, assuming that the patient could feel nothing, the doctor pierced her arm with a long needle, only to have her cry out for him to stop. The hysterical symptom could be too true, on stage or surviving after hypnosis. It could also totter into the territory of the false. The symptom's simulated or citational nature, already a potential cause for the doubt people began to experience around hysteria's authenticity, becomes compounded as soon as hypnosis is at play. Emily Apter rightly draws attention to Charcot's work on hysterical vision, or *scotomization*, writing that "Charcot's *scotome scintillant*, characterized as an *éblousissement de ténèbres* ("dazzle of shadow") clouding the eyes of his female hysterics … interfering with the visual field, was associated by Charcot with the first stages of hysteria, the "douleur" or irritation of the eye that commenced the *aura hysterica*."[23] The hysteria performances did not just demonstrate visual pathologies in patients, but relied on producing them in hypnosis experiments, where hallucination was an integral component of the medical theatre. Hysterics could not see clearly sometimes; their vision blurred as an attack gathered force. At the same time, they often saw more than their spectators, observing phenomena that were imperceptible to the reasoned eye. The hypnosis experiments sought to find how far doctors could push a lie or suggestion, how true the hysteric would find it, how big the gap between what the audience saw and what the hysteric saw could widen. This was their entertainment and their experiment. Kerchiefs caught fire, audience members became assassins who needed to be poisoned, water became champagne, body parts were rendered sick, blood appeared where there were no wounds. The hysteric who hated the feeling of velvet touched it and believed she loved it. She was made to believe she loved one of the doctors; she kissed the hospital statue of Gall. There was no end to the ruses created on stage.[24] In hypnosis, the hysteric regularly performed within the imaginary world of the dramatic suggestions made by doctors. She saw what they told her to, truly entranced and not at all in the doubled world of the naturalist actress, who might move on the stage and in the Gabler household at once, who watches herself perform and lives in the moment-by-moment imagined time of both the play world and technique. How could the audience itself help becoming entranced by the performance?

The unreal presentation of the morbid symptom, its lack of material cause, its production through hypnosis, through hypnosis' power to make a suggestion – a lie – into a truth, believed by the patient and borne materially in her body, play truth and falsehood dangerously close to one another. In hypnotically suggested symptomatology and perception, the citation comes to resemble the reality that it, in part, is. The mimetic layers dashed through by the real must have been thrilling and destabilizing for the audience and the hysteric to witness and experience.

Add in the empirical method of nosological distinction and, somewhat ironically, performance begins to fray the objective beyond repair. Using the hysterical body to reproduce the same symptoms over and over, always referring to the master hysterical type, doctors and lecture observers lauded the power of the hypnotizable hysteric to reproduce symptoms on command. But the continual reproduction, the transfer of the hysterical signs to emblems, began to raise suspicions. Speaking of the power of hypnosis to call forth physiological phenomena, Charcot said, "Pouvoir reproduire un état pathologique, c'est la perfection"[25] (to be able to reproduce a pathological state – this is perfection). However, if the hysterical body is made to appear like a precise puppet too often, she begins to look like – a puppet. What is most real – the experience of – bodily articulations and painful phenomena – begins to appear fake through precise repetition. While Charcot argued that hysteria's potential for typified distillation made it a perfect object for scientific study – it could reliably reproduce empirically observable traits again and again, making it an excellent diagnostic example – the trouble arises: the consistency of symptoms across hysterics, the patients' sequential gestures so similar that the hysterical attack could be reduced to a type that did not vary, does produce suspicions around how involuntary hysterical symptoms were. Hysteria, as mentioned above, in the form in which it appeared on the Salpêtrière stage and in the hospital literature, seemed to disappear after Charcot's death. Freud's studies on hysteria, while they worked with hypnoid states and physiological symptoms like paralysis, aphasia, and ticks, were already far removed from the *clownism* and gymnastic thrashing of hysterics like Augustine and Blanche Wittman. People more recently diagnosed with hysteria present a series of symptoms quite different than the ones these women presented.[26] Charcot's hysteria does appear to be a particular aesthetic trope that lived only under unique conditions at the Salpêtrière during his directorship. Whatever Charcot said, hysteria was stylized. It was also deeply iterative. Its repetition across bodies did more than link the illness to rehearsal – it made hysteria a genre. One can enact the plague too often. Fall on the floor and twist all you like, but eventually, if you stay at it too long, the audience is going to tire.[27] This reference to Artaud's enactment of the plague, made famous by Anaïs Nin, relates to the hysteric in other ways. Part of the debate surrounding the believability of the hysteric's attack had to do with her tendency toward the theatrical, her indulgence in emotional and physical crisis, her presentation as an actress.

THE HYSTERICAL STARLET

Charcot, recognizing the spectacular, if not hypnotic, appeal of the patient's illness, used language to describe the hysterical attack that was explicitly theatrical. As noted in the first chapter, Charcot referred to the hysteric's hallucinations in attitudes passionnelles as an unfolding drama, saying, "Il est facile de suivre toutes les péripéties du drame auquel il croit assister et où il joue le pincipal rôle"[28] (it is easy to follow all of the incidents in the drama (s)he believes to be witnessing or where (s)he plays the principal role). The patient's rests between acrobatics were referred to as "entre-actes"[29] (95). Where the act began and ceased is not as easy to identify as Charcot postulated.

Like Bernhardt, who had cultivated an image of herself such that she appeared to be "the incarnation of theatricality,"[30] the hysteric was too, an embodiment of the theatrical. As Claretie writes, "Je ne sais rien de plus extraordinaire vraiment que le spectacle de ces pauvres filles qui, d'ailleurs, sont enchantées qu'on les regarde, car la joie de l'hystérique, à l'hôpital comme dans le monde, est de *jouer un rôle*! … Il y a à la Salpêtrière une hystérique fameuse, Geneviève, qui dit volontiers fièrement: – Moi, j'aurais inventé l'hystérie si elle n'avait pas existé!" Son amour propre, à elle, est d'être plus hystérique que les autres[31] (I know nothing more extraordinary, really, than the spectacle of these poor girls who are enchanted that we look at them, since it is the primary joy of the hysteric, in the hospital, as in the world, to play a role! … There is, at the Salpêtrière, a famous hysteric, Geneviève, who readily says with pride: – Me, I would have invented hysteria if it had not existed already! She fancies herself as being more hysterical than the others). Here, the hysteric is pictured as vain, and as proudly identifying with her role as a performer. A diva. A star.

Bourneville and Régnard wrote that one could tell the difference between the beds of hysterics and epileptics because the sleeping spaces of the former were so often decorated with ribbons, mirrors, artificial flowers, and pictures with bright colours. They even described one patient who would ask for colourful ribbons to be attached to her straitjacket.[32] In their remarks, the hysteric appears as a diva out of context. Vanity is one of her symptoms. And the outward decorative expression of her self-perception is at odds with her position as a sick patient.

Reports were that the hysteric loved playing a role and that she loved attention. "Les hystériques ne désirent qu'une chose, c'est qu'on occupe d'elles, qu'on s'intéresse à leurs petites passions, qu'on prenne part à leurs affections ou à leurs colères, qu'on admire leur intelligence ou leur parure"[33] (Hysterics desire but one thing and that is that we occupy ourselves with them, that we take interest in their little passions, that we take part in their affections or their rages, that we admire their intelligence or their finery). Charcot, too, noted the "intentional simulation, voluntary, in which the patient exaggerates real symptoms, or again creates all at once an imaginary group of symptoms. In fact, we all know that the desire to deceive even without interest, by a kind of disinterested worship of art for its own sake [culte de l'art pour l'art], though sometimes with the idea of making a sensation, to excite pity, etc. is a common enough occurrence, particularly hysteria. Here is an element that we meet with at each step in the clinique of this neurosis and which throws (there is no use in denying it) a certain amount of disfavour on the studies which [*sic*] are connected with it."[34] The hysteric had a propensity to overreact, and to act out. Even the director recognized her artistic impulse, and its potential to produce unfavourable uncertainty. Her theatrical nature was a diagnostic fact. Her emotions were changeable and: "L'amour-propre est toujours extrêmement développé, tellement que la plus légère plaisanterie devient souvent un cruelle offense, subie avec indignation, et contre laquelle il n'y aura pas assez de larmes pour protester. Tout devient un sujet de drame. L'existence apparaît comme la scène d'un theater … elles ne comprennent pas la simplicité (says the hyperbolic physician). Terreur, jalousie, joie, colère, amour, tout est exagéré, hors de proportion avec les sentiments justes et mesurés qu'il est convenable d'éprouver[35] (Self-love is always extremely developed, so much so that the lightest pleasantry often becomes the cruellest offence, endured with indignation, and against which there aren't enough tears to protest. Everything becomes a subject of drama. Existence appears like a theatre scene … they do not understand simplicity. Terror, jealousy, joy, anger, love, everything is exaggerated, out of proportion with the justifiable and measured sentiments that would be appropriate).

Richet, who wrote the above chastisement about the hysteric's emotional and theatrical relationship to her life, also wrote that hysterics could be studied by any actor for any emotional technique, since the patients were so sensitive to emotion, portraying their sentiments with strong bodily support, their faces and bodies demonstrating hallucinogenic content, conveying an alternate reality in a manner easily legible to her audience.[36] The extent to which the hysteric's conveyance of secondary realities sounds like techniques for acting, especially in light of the social realism of the nineteenth century, is striking.

One must ask if the Salpêtrière hysteric indulged in the pleasure of embracing falsehood primarily out of an artistic impulse, or because she could not help it, lying being one of her symptoms, or if imagining to the point of deception was a phenomenon both habitual and alleviating. In experiments conducted upon Augustine in 1877, for instance, whereupon she inhaled amyl nitrate and began a night's worth of erotic hallucinations, she later recounted that when an intern visited her, she had to exercise great self-control because when he took her hand, she was electrified from head to toe, mistaking him for M and becoming swamped with desire.[37] In a life spent moving between attacks and sleep, nightmares and waking dreams, one easily grants that Augustine would have surrendered to the relief these all night caresses with her lover may have offered. The truth of the passionate, tactile experience of the delirium brought on by amyl nitrate was surely a balm to the body and mind of the patient, who was so often touched in ways that she did not like or want. It is difficult to insist that the reality of the hospital weighed more authentically for Augustine than fantasies bred out of her past life outside the hospital walls. Still, Charcot and Richet's equation of the hysteric with the artist who indulges in theatricality (for art's sake, nonetheless!) demonstrates a fluidity between understandings of actor and patient, a tendency to link the hysteric to the art of theatre.

For many reasons, some explored above and some likely unknown, the hysteric couldn't or didn't resist being dramatic or read as such. Strangely, theatricality became part of her hysterical diagnosis. The hysteric seemed unable to resist letting her body fall into attack, easily giving into the passionate narratives of her delirium. It was exactly this flair for drama that brought the question of her authenticity into question. The hysteric's agency, her potential to resist the attack or to give in to it as she liked, the imposed dichotomy between helplessness and indulgence, flagged the possibility for fraud. If the patient was a decontextualized diva, wasn't she deciding to amp up her performance, choosing to ratchet up her emotions and bodily expressions? If she loved acting so much, who was to say that her attacks weren't precisely this?

The actress Sarah Bernhardt, however, found the Salpêtrière's hysteria distinct from her acting practice and the theatre in which she made her career. In 1884, preparing for the brain fever poisoning scene in *Adrienne Lecouvreur*, Bernhardt visited the hysterics ward at the Salpêtrière, but found her research there unhelpful because the hysterics were, she said, "too dramatic."[38] Delboeuf wrote that Bernhardt could never accomplish what the virtuosic hysterics could anyhow.[39] The professional actress and theatre manager's interest in the hysteria ward was likely based on the reputation of the hysteric as a spectacular performer of her illness. Her critique of the scale of theatrics is telling.

Was the hysteric, so open to hypnotic suggestion, so able to sway from the present tense into an overwhelming fit of memory, so interested in style, uniquely in contact with her imagination? She did seem, as Diderot wrote,[40] to be capable of "singular, bizarre, eloquent and even poetic exaltations of the imagination."[41] Doctors seemed to fluctuate between celebrating the hysteric's talents for artistic expression and deriding them for the same creative practices.

It seems that hysterics sometimes pretended too lightheartedly, not in the interests of the medical show. If they could perform well, better than Bernhardt, with amazing technical execution of emotions and scenes suggested by the doctors in hypnosis, special note was made in lectures and medical publications. But when patients began to take pleasure in telling falsities, doctors took a derisive tone: "Nothing pleases them more than to tell utterly false stories, to enumerate all they haven't done, and all they have, with incredible excess of detail."[42] Lasègue, who was the police medical examiner in charge of diagnosing hysterics and prostitutes said that "the need to lie, to invent, to talk crap as they say in the staff waiting room, is one of the forms of hysteria."[43] Richet wrote that "elles sont toutes plus ou moins menteuses"[44] (they are all more or less liars) and, disapprovingly: "Ces gros mensonges sont dits audacieusement, crûment, avec un sang-froid qui déconcerte"[45] (These fat lies are told audaciously, crudely, with a disconcerting cold-bloodedness).

Indeed, one wonders how misogynists like Lasègue and Richet were able to judge truth from falsehood when their appraisal was so dismissive. Doctors seemed expert at ignoring patient's pleas and tears, which were more often than not relegated to indulgent hysterical symptoms rather than phenomenological realities. However, Richet's moral devaluation of the hysteric's love for tall tales reveals an interesting knot at the heart of his outrage: the patient took pleasure in being watched and in being heard. She took pleasure in narrative. She gave herself over to the enjoyment of being theatrical. Despite criticisms like Richet and Lasègue's, which seem to revolve around discomfort with autonomous acts of female creation, the hysteric's characterization as "drama queen" helped to popularize her and her illness.

Hysteria's indulgence in theatre reproduced itself, outside the Salpêtrière walls, to a deeply interested public. In a peculiar manner, even the French courthouse began to resemble the theatre and the asylum. On trial: the hysterical assassin. The late nineteenth century was an era featuring very real dramatic actions that bordered on the plot lines of melodrama – in this case, attempted murders by women. The female crime of passion was an unusual French trend that shared an intriguing relationship to hysterical diagnosis. According to historian Ruth Harris, "literally hundreds of murderesses, between 1880 and 1910, committed crimes of passion against erring, irresponsible, or brutal mates and were almost invariably exonerated by the court."[46] Likened to melodramatic characters by journalists because of their over-the-top actions but also their typified victimhood and emotional performances in court, women on trial for crimes of passion actually moved audiences of the legal proceedings to tears on many occasions.[47] The "crimes of passion, and the way in which they were regarded as rituals to be repeated by any number of disgruntled females, were condemned as infantile, hysterical and an eminently feminine means of attracting attention."[48]

Amidst what seems to have been an iconic rash of hysterical women armed with vitriol and bullets, the Salpêtrière produced its own hysterical crime. In one instance, a female patient shot Gilles de la Tourette in the head with a pistol, claiming he had hypnotized her from a distance (he was hurt, but not killed).[49] Even in moments where the experience of being a hysteric at the Salpêtrière seems unquestionably real, the certainty of the patient's position arises out of the most unbelievable conditions. Hypnotism, a real-life Svengali, crossing boundaries of time and space to manipulate the mind of a patient, a woman angry enough to find a pistol and use it on hospital grounds – this is the stuff of fiction. And yet, there is documentation enough to prove that the shooting, if not the hypnosis, happened.[50]

Celebration of the mad murderess' theatrical possibilities had already occurred in the scientific community in the figure of Lady Macbeth in Duchenne de Boulogne's *Mechanism of Human Facial Expression* in 1862. Duchenne's publication, much like Darwin's *Expression of Emotions*, worked exactly to find the science in emotional affect through precise electrical provocation. What is less expected amongst scientific portraiture of well-executed feeling, is the inclusion of Lady Macbeth, caught in moments of murderous plotting, in Duchenne's volume. Using electric excitement of the facial muscles of a female model, Duchenne made efforts to produce an ideal expression of "cruelty," one of Shakespearean proportions. Duchenne spent nearly thirty pages in analysis of Lady M's scenes, describing how he aimed to capture her key qualities and emotions with his technology.[51] As Didi-Huberman recounts: "Duchenne was not daunted by the complexity of the role; he proposed to 'show that Lady Macbeth's homicidal fury was moderated by the feeling of filial piety that swept through her mind, when she discovered a resemblance between Duncan and her sleeping father.'"[52]

The *Iconographie*, then, followed in a tradition of scientific visual dramaturgy. Doctors and photographers at the Salpêtrière were part of the legacy of trying to make sense of the body's expressive qualities and using theatre in the experimental processes to do so. Despite their claims that indulgence in theatrics was a hysterical symptom, doctors were already steeped in a theatrical tradition of their own.

Resentment against the hysteric's wilful enjoyment of simulation, when she could not help it in so many other circumstances, seems misplaced, then. Especially since it was not only the hysteric who indulged in theatrics. The hysteric's entanglement with theatre, the ease with which descriptions of her illness could slide into language of acting, her appearance in a theatrical domain, onstage at the Salpêtrière, and the confusing way in which she was both convincing and unbelievable at once, made her relationship to authenticity intriguing and tenuous. But also, Charcot's curatorial

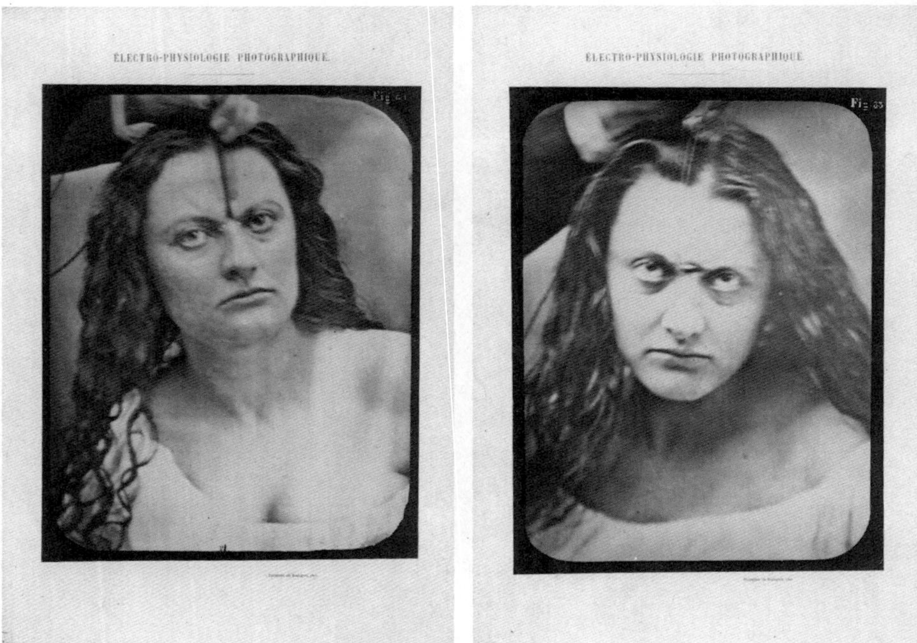

4.1 [a and b] *Figure 81: Lady Macbeth, moderate expression of cruelty* and *Figure 83: Lady Macbeth, ferocious cruelty*. Photographs by Guillaume-Benjamin-Amand Duchenne de Boulogne and Adrien Tournachon. Reproduced as part of a composite. Plate 9, Duchenne de Boulogne, *Méchanisme de la physionomie humaine, ou analyse* électrophysiologique *de l'expression des passions*, 1862.

influence in publicizing his medical findings invoked so many elements present in Western theatrical traditions that hysteria's reception could never escape equation with conventional forms of staging and acting.

Replication of the attack of grande hystérie was part of the Salpêtrière's project, but more than a little revelry in the hysteric's compliance in putting on a good show was taking place as well. Both modes of demonstration complicated medicine's relationship to accuracy. Why then, according to doctors, were hysterics burdened with the reputation of being highly impassioned, irrational producers of over-the-top narrative, prone to melodramatic crimes of passion? Why, especially in an age of empirical scrutiny, were they, over the physician producers of the spectacle, diagnosable liars?

THEATRICAL OVERLAPS, THEATRICAL APPEAL

There are basic features of the lecture series that link it to Western theatrical conventions. The amphitheatre and its stage, constructed under Charcot's directorship, featured focussed lighting of the two primary stage figures on display. Mme Bottard, the matron of the hysteria ward, coiffed the patients before they went on stage, dressing them in costume – "caracos" or "robes de fine toile" for photographs.[53] And what of the use of a feather on the patient's head to publicly embellish and measure bodily vibrations and tics? In his 1893 eulogy, Charles Féré, former student of Charcot, chose an unlikely exemplary feature of the lectures to describe the director's commitments to both knowledge and spectacle. He wrote that Charcot "did not pass over the opportunity to decorate the head gear of his patients with long feathers which excited above all the gaiety of the audience, but soon achieved by the diversity of their oscillations to make known the differences [between forms of diseases] which he set himself the task of demonstrating."[54]

Journalist Alexander Hepp wrote, of Charcot, that "the piercing gaze and staged drama of the lessons make the man more than a doctor: 'Monsieur Charcot is, in the world of science, a Parisian personality, and almost part of our theatre scene.'"[55] In early biographies and more recent historical work on Charcot's hysteria project, authors have pointed to Charcot's love for the theatre as an integral component of his lecture style. He admired the works of William Shakespeare, Jean Racine, and Molière, and cited their works in his lectures.[56] His love for the circus is also well known.[57] He even kept a trained monkey who shared a place at the Charcot dinner table. Charcot had a box reserved for him at the Théâtre de l'Odéon, where he could regularly take in the performances of Bernhardt, whom his wife adored.[58] Hugo and Dumas, then, were also part of Charcot's palette. When he visited France, Mme Charcot recommended that Freud take in one of Yvette Gilbert's excellent cabaret shows.[59] The weekly dinners hosted by the Charcot's often featured plays put on by the Charcot children, sometimes joined by interns from the hospital.[60] Charcot was a man passionate about theatre and, perhaps by extension, his mode of transmitting hysteria was overtly theatrical.

Indeed, Charcot directed the lectures in such a way that they were media for the transmission of scientific content and truly entertaining in form. Their spectacular appeal, which reaches far beyond the above list of hard theatrical signifiers, caused both congratulatory and suspicious reactions.

4.2 [a and b] Albert Londe, *Suggestions by Senses in the Cataleptic Period of "Le grand hypnotisme."* Plate VI, *Nouvelle iconographie de la Salpêtrière*, 1891.

The generic overlaps are numerous. Experimental hypnosis was not unlike the fairground somnambulist sideshow. The audience that witnessed the phase of the hysterical attack that featured codified poses, identifiable by descriptive terms like religious ecstasy, supplication, combat, and passion would have seen theatre bills and news clippings featuring actresses posed in similar fashion. The "living tableau" of the backbend or the amorous pantomime brought on by suggestion, without necessarily bearing a concrete genealogical link to earlier and/or current modes of conventional performance, certainly would have resonated with the more traditional theatrical forms. The dance pantomimes popular in the French boulevards, the mute statuesque assemblages in melodrama, the visually and kinetically strong acting styles of Sarah Bernhardt and Eleonora Duse, the emerging frenetic dance styles at the café-concert, even Ibsen's Nora dancing the tarantella – these theatrical experiences marking the nineteenth century would have contributed to the Salpêtrière audience experiencing the medical spectacle as theatre. Charcot and his photographic

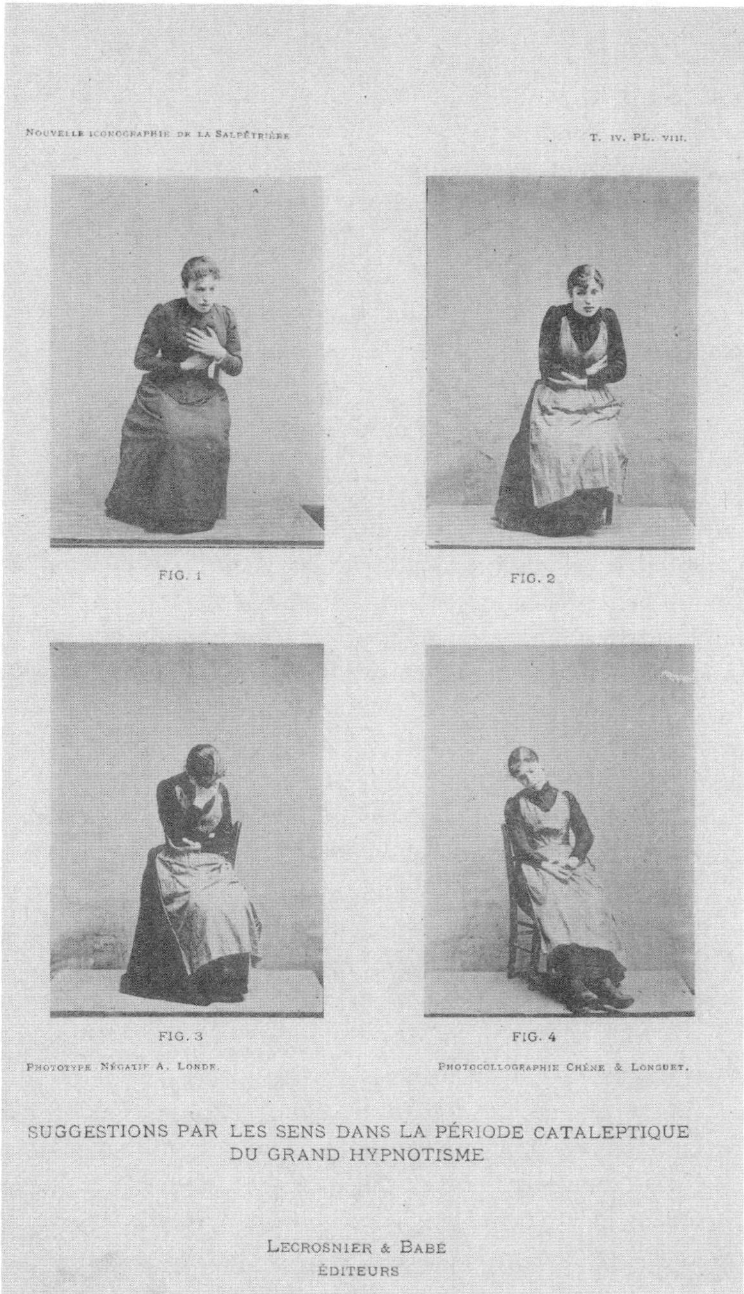

4.3 Albert Londe, *Suggestions by Senses in the Cataleptic Period of "Du grand hypnotisme."* Plate VIII, *Nouvelle iconographie de la Salpêtrière*, 1891.

team did their best, it seems, to artistically arrange the transmission of medical information, drawing on the theatrical traditions of the time.

The aesthetic dimensions of the *Iconographie* images are undeniable. In poses apparently struck in cataleptic response to the sounds of tuning fork, gong, or coloured glass (fig. 4.3), the patient's body is gesturally alive, communicative. The dramatic articulations of limbs, the sense in which contraction and release in the muscle groups is evident, the evocative emotional facial expressions (which resist any of the easily typified feelings from Darwin's volume) – all transmit a theatricality inherent in the corporeal print document and the body it shows. The patient here clenches her legs and buttocks, rising slightly from her chair, arms tight, aloft, with gentle fists that seemingly pull her upwards. She falls to one knee, attentively listening, with palms poised in prayer position, elbows thrust out. She leans into her hands with her breastbone, pushing hands back against her sternum, expression aghast. She retreats into her torso, as though cold, wrapping her arms about herself, collapsing her abdomen, drawing her knees back and to the side. Compare these photographs to the most famous image of Elizabeth Robins as Ibsen's hysteric, Hedda Gabler (fig. 4.5), or to Sarah Bernhardt playing Phèdre (fig. 4.6), and lines of genre blur again. A crouched Robins perches intensely, alert and capricious, arms taught, hunched over the manuscript she tears. Bernhardt – whose performance of "dolorous martyrdom" won her the review accolade "What a wonderful crucifixion!"[61] – appears, in the play's publicity photographs, stretching her arms outward in a manner bordering on religious, appealing to Minos with throat and breastbone open, actively kneeling in entreaty. The proximity to Augustine's crucifixion pose bears noting.

Dramatic stills of women playing at hysteria, whether the photographer's lens was professedly medical or formally artistic, activate a kinetic attention in the viewer. The dynamism of the poses provokes a desire to read for emotional and physiological clues that point to the character's inner life, or to the alternate reality she perceives, to interpret the visual markers of muscular articulation, gestural position, and facial expression to unfold the possible meanings of the moment and of the woman pictured.

What was to prevent the Salpêtrière audience from associating the rehearsal of these hysterical bodies in theatrics with the pretending, sanctioned lying, and showing off that went on in conventional performance spaces? The visuals of the attack were so resplendent that the illness was indivisible from the theatrical. Charcot and Londe in collaboration, made

4.4 Elizabeth Robins as Hedda Gabler, 1891. Photograph: Elliott and Fry.

4.5 Publicity photograph of Bernhardt in Racine's *Phèdre*. Originally published in *La Revue Illustrée*, 1 July 1895.

sure that the *Iconographie* closely resembled photography of the era's most alluring starlets in performance. Whether or not they employed a tactic of theatrical likeness consciously, to marry science and the arts, as Charcot did with consideration in other projects like *Les Démoniaques dans l'art*, or more accidentally out of their shared passions for the artistic media of photography and theatre, or as an inevitable reflection of the cultural atmosphere of their time, the effect is the same: the hysteric in photography begs for comparison with the *vedettes* of the late nineteenth century, bearing remarkable differences of stature and context, but undeniable similarities in terms of imagery.

The female hysterical character, it should be noted, found her way into high and low works of (dramatic) literature and live performance often. From Flaubert's Madame Bovary to the terrorized hysteric in the Grand Guignol horror play co-authored by physician and former Salpêtrière intern Alfred Binet and André Lorde, from Zola's Thérèse Raquin to the Goncourt's Germinie Lacerteux, the hysteric was a figure popularly deployed.[62] Ibsen, as an example, wrote, in his notes, that all of the women in *Hedda Gabler* were hysterics. Hedda's "hysteria motivates everything she does,"[63] whereas Mrs Rising is "the nervous-hysterical modern individual," and Thea Elvsted "is the conventional, sentimental, hysterical Philistine."[64] It is also pivotal to note that, while the hysterics at the Salpêtrière did enter into popularity, igniting interest in the aesthetic possibilities of hysteria (Janet Beizer describes the Salpêtrière's hysteria project as a "media event"[65]), the term became used broadly and diversely in France, to connote a number of unstable states encountered in modernity. As Micale writes: "The sheer accumulation of meanings of hysteria is nothing short of extraordinary. During the later 1800s alone, hysteria was employed as a metaphor for artistic experimentation, collective political violence, radical social reformism, foreign nationalism, and a host of other new and unsettling developments. It became shorthand for the irrational, the will-less, the incomprehensible, the erratic, the convulsive, the sexual, the female, 'the Other.' It was a synonym for everything that seemed extreme or frivolous or excessive or absurd about the age."[66]

While hysteria was a term used to connote a variety of irregularities in society and the arts, the term was not used so diffusely as to escape meaning. Hysteria at the Salpêtrière, as transmitted through photographs, the quasi-medical description of Bourneville's *Iconographie* and Charcot's lectures, advanced several performance tropes that resonated with contemporary theatre practices. The hysteric indulged in theatricality, giving herself over to the playing out of imaginary scenes in a manner that technically produced grand gestures and highly emotional vocal and facial expressions. She foregrounded her body, using it in unconventional ways, unafraid to make it contort or bear traces of ugliness. These figurations of the performing body also bore likeness to acting styles of the era.

What made hysteria so theatrically appealing? Likely, it was partly the hysteric's combination of the codes of performance of several popular nineteenth century theatrical traditions. Charcot's hysteria project occurred in a cultural moment where the overwrought techniques of melodrama were transitioning to more "natural" styles of acting and staging.[67] Grand gesture from earlier in the century was gradually being supplanted by acting that conveyed the inner life of the character. Bernhardt, though she rejected the comparison, is an especially good example of hysterical modes of performance as the performance of generic overlap because she has been described as straddling stylistic paradigms. She was also, as mentioned, a favorite of Charcot's and so doubly worth a moment of interested study. English reviewers of Bernhardt's performance of Doña Sol in Hugo's *Hernani*, for example, describe the actress' movement from "ostentatiously languorous poses" to fractured, rushed, passionate, and "spasmodic" performance in the final act:

> Then begins the torrent of impetuous force that bursts out like a waterfall, and overflows the barriers of restraint. Doña Sol has declared herself to be fiercer than the tigress robbed of her young, and has hurled her defiance at the head of Don Ruy Gomez. She has flung herself before Hernani, and pointed to the dagger as her last protector, and then, with sudden impulse, she changes to a despairing cry for mercy. This new key of passion was more startling than the first. The words, "Pitié! Vous me tuez, mon oncle, en le touchant! Pitié! Je l'aime tant! echo with a sharp and resonant thrill, until, in a transport of baffled love, and with an access of extreme tenderness, she bends down to the head of her lover and sobs out the words, "Non! Non! Je ne veux pas, mon amour, que tu meures."[68]

In a performance the *Telegraph* critic called delirious, John Stokes suggests the token mannerisms of Bernhardt's style are all present: "the sudden shifts in mood, the *ostinato* of her delivery, and the equally spasmodic movements of the body."[69] Bernhardt played these highly stylized traits across romantic works, the well-made play, and even her own rumoured nervous exhaustion and persona – for, according to Sardou, Bernhardt exaggerated all emotional aspects of her life, living at breakneck speed, resulting in an episode of "violent over-excitement, writhing, rolling on and gnawing at the carpet, weeping in sheer exasperation."[70] Melodrama? Epileptic cabaret or expressionist dance? Hysteria? Everyday life? Bernhardt stood out against even the most opulent stage settings and the most destructive business outcomes, her production of highly passionate and impressive gestures lending her a reputation of theatrical grandeur.

Likewise, Eleonora Duse, another of the era's most celebrated actresses, was lauded for the use of older, less subtle performance tropes in her role as la Demente in d'Annunzio's *Il Sogno*, in which "grand gesture, the frozen moment of extreme emotion, the tableau" – came out to play once again onstage.[71] Duse also, however, famously played several of Ibsen's strong, emotionally fraught heroines, including Nora in *A Doll's House*, tipping her into the performance modes of social realism. Hysteria, too, sat at the strange juncture of codified, over the top gesture and a complex inner life made of conflicting emotions and palpable memories playing itself out through the voice and body. Elin Diamond picks up on this stylistic dichotomy when she writes about the Freudian hysteric of Ibsen's social realism, the realist hysteric of Freud's little theatre of the analysis office and the juiced-up performances of Charcot, which she says sit closer to melodrama.[72]

Hysteria, for Diamond, is inextricably linked to realism – both access hidden inner life that motivates and complicates the character's external actions.[73] Richet, likewise, for instance, wrote of the Salpêtrière hysteric, that she "will hallucinate a real episode of her life, in particular the one that seems to have brought on her illness."[74] Richet's note about the hysteric's keen inclination to reproduce intense moments from her past runs closely to Freud's notions of trauma, repression, and abreaction. The realist play and the realist actress also present a woman with a past, behaving accordingly in the present, open to being interpreted by the audience in the role of the analyst.[75]

Diamond depicts the analytic situation with emphasis on the patient's confession and Freud's interpretation of her utterance, saying that, in analysis, the hysteric "lay(s) out the secret of her past."[76] Freud's psychoanalysis amounts, for her, to the "translation of the anarchic body."[77] For Freud's psychoanalysis, as for realism, the crux of the performance was "the problem or enigma that had to be solved."[78] Diamond compares Charcot's lecture series, described as "juiced up demonstrations," to Freud's cathartic method, stating that one was as far from the other as the "exciting but human scale dialogues of realism were from the constant teeth-gnashing, swooning, gesturing and shrieking of melodrama."[79] The comparison is clear. In the analogy, Freud's method of speaking, uncovering the past of the patient through dialogue and finally helping the hysteric to achieve catharsis via knowledge of the events that came to be expressed in her body relates to realism, whereas Charcot's dramatically indulgent demonstrations of hysteria connect him to melodrama.

One does want to ask how melodrama generically superimposes over the Salpêtrière hysteria show. Peter Brooks, following Eric Bentley, writes, after all, that "melodrama at heart represents the theatrical impulse itself: the impulse toward dramatization, heightening expression, acting out."[80] A description of genre reads, here, quite like hysterical diagnosis. However, in the theatrical pairing of Charcot and the hysteric, both presences on stage seem to "juice it up." The excesses of the hysteric's voice and body are theatrically expressive, but not as blatant as Charcot's, whose relationship to melodrama lies at the level of excessively explaining, without reserved subtext. His performance shares with melodrama a generic commitment to "rhetorical excess" and a propensity for predictability.[81]

Charcot received varying performance reviews for his lectures but he was, certainly, in touch with emotional tableaux and predictable forms. He speckled his lectures with gestural demonstrations of pathological corporeal states and vocal intonations that were said to shift the amphitheatre atmosphere. Medical biographer A. Lubimoff, an admirer of Charcot's manner, wrote that Charcot had a "singular aptitude" for "reproducing" illnesses through "gestures and general appearance [allure]." Furthermore, the doctor became grave at precise moments in the lectures, perhaps appealing to the audience's emotional investment in the hysterical attack. Lubimoff also wrote that, "In the pathetic moments, his voice had a timbre as attractive as a baritone making grave intonations."[82] As Marshall writes, "Other commentators went so far as to describe the neuropathologist as a 'skilled scientific actor' on the basis of his ability 'to show the gait characteristic of various nervous disorders, or describe with his hands different forms of choreiform movements.'"[83] Charcot's pedagogical style, described as dull by some, seems to have also, at times, presented nuanced techniques that exceeded mere description: modulation of the voice, theatrical references, bodily articulation, gestural presence. Some, like Felix Platel, gave him scathing performance reviews. Under the pseudonym, Ignotus, Platel famously criticized the director in Paris' *Le Figaro*, saying, "He monopolized hysteria. He astonished men. He frightened women. He practised in sum scientific ham-acting [*cabotinage*]. His success has been enormous. Oh the great allure of hamming it up! It has profited Charcot, but science also. He advanced science in the manner of Wagner, the great musical ham. Charcot and Wagner seem to me to be of the same race."[84] Not only is Charcot described, here, as rendering a scientific lecture theatrical, but he is accused of acting in a manner altogether hammy, over the top. Whatever Charcot said about being a photographer, he was an actor, and whatever he said about simply stating the truth, itself a theatrical incantation, after Molière: "I state what I see, nothing more,"[85] his contribution to medical positivism was highly stylized – comparable to Wagner, even. It was Charcot's theatrical grand-standing that the avant-garde artists the *Incoherents* decided to satirize in their mockery cafe performances of the medical spectacle. In the appropriate form of comedic monologue, Coquelin Cadet, as Dr Béni-Barde, fused therapy and entertainment, inviting "dear, delicate nervous ones" to partake in the festivities of the Hydropathes to be cured.[86]

The hysteric's performance was imbued with the subtextual subtleties of her real life, bearing traces of inexpressible elements of her perceptions and experiences, though these went unrecognized in the doctor's onstage descriptions, which explained the most obvious of the patient's movements, and postures, and which brought from the inside out even the hidden secrets of her anatomy. The uterus, the nervous system, the brain, the bodies sinews and tissues – these found their way into utterances both clear and repetitive and marked by just a touch of melodramatic villainy. Charcot never said "Tremble, all of you!" but he did say, "What you have before you is a living tableau!" The exclamation is declarative, and revels in the show about to take place. It juices up the spectacle. Melodrama does nip the heels in the hospital spectacles.

To follow Diamond's realist trajectory, contemporary historians and theorists have become almost obsessively intrigued by Augustine's past. But how significant was it to the Salpêtrière physicians? For a team of doctors who were interested in tracing hereditary transmission of hysteria, the patient's case history was recorded in brief. In the *Iconographie*, it fills only a couple of pages. It lacks the nuances that appeared through Freud's case histories of psychoanalytic dialogue, but did note events that may have coincided with, if not instigated, the outbreak of hysterical symptoms. The contemporary researcher, steeped in the language of psychoanalysis, or in social models of disability and mental illness, can easily be alarmed by the propensity for doctors to overlook these pivotal events, which were often repeated in the delirium that accompanied a hysterical fit, and which were shown, by their embodied repetition, to be meaningful moments of intensity in the patient's life. But the gnostic goals and labours of the Salpêtrière doctors rested elsewhere, namely, in the popularization of the typified hysterical attack via, as Diamond suggests, over the top demonstration. To Diamond, among others, Freud deserves to be criticized for his proprietary role as interpreter, for his wanting to discover the hysteric's secrets.[87] But compared to Charcot, who did not seem to be listening at all, Freud can almost be viewed as an attentive interlocutor, asking the hysteric questions about her life and her thoughts. His pursuit of knowledge, at least, was purposefully curative.

Diamond's connection of Freud's work on hysteria to readers and performers of social realism is based, in part, on the creation of complex characters by playwrights like Ibsen, characters whose motives and actions required a process of attentive reading, so that actresses like Elizabeth Robins are described as closely engaging with the play text, as though it offered forensic traces.[88] Robins, Diamond writes, was relieved to be able to play a woman so thoroughly complicated as Hedda Gabler after her performances in traditional melodramas where characters were typified and iconic, rather than riddled with subtleties and contradictions. Known for her detailed, precise, and, according to Shaw, "intensely self-conscious" acting, Robins translated the textual Hedda, enabling the critic/spectator to take on the role of spectator/analyst, gathering clues (the pistols, the portrait, the thinning hair) and tracing the outline of a "mental pathology."[89]

Freud's work on the unconscious never offered any easy map of the human psyche. Rather, the territory he discovered showed itself to be a shadowy terrain of false monuments, faulty signposts, and irretrievable sediments.[90] Whereas Charcot pointed continually to the neurological lesion in which hysteria was embedded, without proof, articulating a stable, solid solution to the enigma of hysteria, Freud sought hysteria's depths, and found himself ever revising his former work on the topic.[91] Hysteria did present its series of puzzles, and while Charcot claimed that he could produce the illness, exactly and repeatedly, he never did find the exact lesion he sought. Likewise, Ibsen never did allow the audience to "solve for Hedda."

Despite Charcot's connections to the scientific in naturalism, his and Zola's mutual investment in one another's work, or his certainty that his scientific research on heredity would become a marker of the naturalist genre, Charcot had little concern for the inner life of the patient, preferring instead to frame her as a series of dramatic postures and categorical gestures. Likely, he was a poor reader of Ibsen. The hysteric, though, through her own intervention into the theatrical transmission of her illness, appeared to merge the spectacular with the secretive. Her body signified in a matter verging on the melodramatic and certainly grand. She is described as being too passionate, too willing to indulge in artistry, making even unimportant events grandiose with meaning. And yet, images of the hysteric, transcriptions of her dramatic outpourings – these connote a real person, a woman sincere, vulnerable, suffering, often caught between temporalities and always performing. Nineteenth century actresses are consistently credited with straddling the genres of melodrama and realism as Western Europe experienced a stylistic shift in theatre. The hysteric did so as well.

The similarities were not lost on doctors or audiences of the medical show. Repeatedly, people used the language of hysteria to describe acting techniques and effects, and vice versa – the hysteric was depicted and described as being like the actress. The hysteric's performance was a combination of artistry, meaningful and visually stunning bodily signification, and a dose of the sensational interiority that accompanies madness. The illness seems to have acted as inspiration for many stage performers. If the actress did not conscientiously employ attributes of the medicalized hysteric, for many of their critics, the medical genre created a foil for interpretation.

For instance, Duse's performing style was, apparently, one in which she transformed herself into a true woman of modern times – the woman with hysteria.[92] Colleague Luigi Rasi located Duse's distorted face, of the kind often associated with mental illness, as the anchor of her acting style. He also remarked that her full-body communication of restlessness and emotionally fraught instability made her a perfect performer of hysterical characters: "Her eyes were agitated by imperceptible quivering, they flickered rapidly from side to side; her cheeks went from blush to pallor with incredible rapidity; nostrils and lips in motion … Then her body, to round off the portrayal of this type of person, had serpentine shifts of weight or profoundly languorous gestures and moved in perfect accord with the action and counterbalancing of her arms, hands, fingers, torso and counterpart activity of her face. And so, perhaps, the great actress was able to outclass everyone in her portrayal of characters with hysterical temperaments."[93] In Rasi's description, Duse naturally makes hysterical use of her body, so that she is easily able to play the myriad of characters who playwrights, directors, and audiences diagnosed with hysteria.

Gay Cima and Diamond both describe an onstage moment wherein Elizabeth Robins, playing Ibsen's Hedda Gabler, stared off in the distance as Brack told her of Lövborg's death.[94] Diamond interprets the following moment as evidence of the hysterical doubling effect that characters of Ibsen's social realist plays present. Robins is described as conveying two realities, expressing Hedda's haunting by the past, which causes an internal thought process at odds with the outward mechanics of the scene, while she is also embedded in the present tense of the play. I think the moment supports other tropes of the hysteric's relationship to theatricality. As Diamond writes about Robins' notes on the script: "When Brack recounts the shabby scene of Lövborg's actual death, Robins, according to Archer, gazed out to the audience 'evidently not taking in what Brack was saying.' In her promptbook, next to the line 'Illusion?,' Robins wrote 'grave and absent' and next to the line 'Not voluntarily?,' she indicated 'sad, far-looking eyes and a smile that says softly how much better I know Eilert than you.'"[95] In this splendid document of emotional choreography, Robins has charted her body's presentation of subtextual inner states. Robins, a long way from Bernhardt perhaps, has been described as a natural and subtle actress, able to convey the complicated and often contradictory characters of Henrik Ibsen. And yet another marker for the hysteria, the pleasure of being observed, appears with equal poignancy in the above description of Robins' attention to the physical details in her performance of Hedda. The actress' visible cues for her character's processes are preoccupied with appearance as much as they are with a deep reading of the play text. The moment celebrated by Archer, Cima, and Diamond, alongside descriptions of Bernhardt and Duse in performance, indicates a pivotal intersection between hysteria and more conventional acting – that of the intentional foregrounding of the body and the precise use of visible gesture to draw in an audience. Hysteria, as it appeared in Charcot's hospital, continually overlaps generically with melodramatic and realist genres in ways that cement the hysterical starlet within theatrical tradition.

In popular music hall performance too, hysteria exerted influence and found itself referenced by performers and audiences who would have been making links between hysteria's theatrical potential on stage in and outside the hospital. It is on the frenetic use of the whole body in café-concert and cabaret style song and dance that Rae Beth Gordon bases her thesis that hysteria is a most integral component of the legacies of these popular performance types. In cabaret, Gordon says, the performer – and vicariously, the audience – experiences and expresses a liberation from the inhibitions and social conventions around the body. Hysteria, she notes, like cabaret performance, is defined by perpetual movement and repetition of gestures.[96] The movement lexicon of café-concert singers and dancers, as traced by Gordon, is convincingly linked to the tics, grimaces, jolts, and acrobatic maneuverings of the hysterics in Charcot's hospital. In form and in content, hysteria as it was curated and publicized at the Salpêtrière, amounted to a series of movements, a choreography of the body. This artistic framing, a theatrical embellishment and reduction of the experiences of women diagnosed with hysteria, is what makes comparison between genres so deceptively easy.

Gordon, who follows the popularized hysteria spectacle in modern France to its appearance, at least in mimetic gesture, in carnival hypnotist shows, the dances of cabaret and café concert performances, and eventually early film, writes that the hysterical attack had theatrical potential enough that some of the hysterical movements transplanted instantly to public performances of song and dance at the café-concerts of Paris. *Gommeuses* dancers and "epileptic singers" filled popular stages with erratic and acrobatic gestures and frenetic song from the eighteen-seventies until the first decade of the twentieth century.[97] Journalist Georges Montorgueil wrote that "A good half of today's hit songs [in 1893] … belong to the late Dr Charcot's home for the agitated. They jerk and tremble. They have gesticulatory hysteria."[98] Edmond de Goncourt compared a woman dancing at the Eldorado café-concert to a Salpêtrière hysteric, describing her "heated bestiality … wild mane … big mouth and the toothy laugh of a Bacchante."[99] *Gommeuse* Mlle Abdala, credited with turning the grimace into an art form, twisted about, hysteric-wise, "like an eel."[100] The gommeuse is elsewhere described as having "legs that frisk about with zest," "the contortions of a strangling chicken," dancing in a manner both unabashedly sexual and tottering on jovial madness.[101] Jean Lorrain described the most famous epileptic singer, Polaire, like this: "Polaire! The agitating and agitated Polaire … in a blouse tight enough to bring on a spasm (of orgasm) … What devilish mimicry, what a coffee grinder and what a belly dance! … Polaire hops around, trembles, quivers, dances with her hips, pelvis, and navel, mimes all forms of shocks and shaking, twists, leans backward in the form of an arc, becomes upright, twists her … rolls her eyes up into her head, meows in ecstasy and … swoons … and to what music and what lyrics!"[102]

The legacy of hysteria's movement lexicon seems, from these celebratory and derisive descriptions, quite convincing. The wriggling sexuality of Polaire calls to mind the scandalized commentary on hysteria in the *British Medical Journal*, in which the *Iconographie* is accused of publishing "long pages of the obscene ravings of delirious hysterical girls and descriptions of events in their sexual history," which were, "in the words of the law-courts, 'matter unfit for publication.'"[103]

The strange case of dancer Jane Avril, who wrote about the hysterics as fakers, draws a concrete link from patient to performer. The event occurs at the *Bal de Folles*, an occasion on which the invited public intermingled with select Salpêtrière patients at a formal party at the hospital that was held at least as late as 1890. Part public performance, part celebration, it was an event where hysterics danced freely. It was at such a ball that Jane Avril discovered her calling as a performer. She wore one of Jeanne Charcot's dresses, and found herself carried away by the music. Emerging from a sort of trance, she found that her dancing, according to her memory, resulted in congratulations, compliments, and kisses of admiration. The result was not only an assurance that she would work on the stage – in fact, she writes, "Je fus guérie!"[104] (I was healed).

It seems that hysteria translated almost effortlessly to the stage. "In its restructuring of the body, hysteria created a new form of expression in the arts," Gordon writes.[105] Expressing her own doubts about the boundary between illness and performance, she also asks a question about the direction of artistic influence: "Is the café-concert hysterical because hysteria is everywhere in the period or does it offer itself up as a model for potential hysterics who couldn't resist imitating the grimaces and convulsive movements that would characterize the *Nouvelle Iconographie*?"[106]

The following description is not from a performance review, but from the *Iconographie de la Salpêtrière*: "She suffers from a fit of manic agitation where she laughs without reason, gesticulates, jumps and dances. The patient also stamps, grimaces and sticks out her tongue."[107] As for Charcot's interpretation of hysteria's relationship to dance, his views are intriguing – utilitarian and, at points, curiously artistically attentive. For instance, describing varying categories of *rhythmical chorea*, Charcot distinguished between movements that imitated life and abstract movements with no apparent purpose, which he considered to be more akin to dance. In a lecture, he compared hammering motions against measured, rapid, side-to-side movements of the head, which "def[ied] interpretation" because they had no corresponding physiological actions from everyday life.[108] Then, as a patient moved from rhythmically miming hammering, whipping eggs, and posing like an orator to something more expressionistic, Charcot searched for comparisons to other dance forms, "jigs of the Tsiganes or the Zingari dances of Andalsia."[109] When the movement had no known correlative in everyday life, Charcot's description bore traces of sensitive observation: "But sometimes, under the influence of an emotion, the doctor's examinations, for example, or sometimes spontaneously, small jerks, more or less accentuated, become manifest in the upper extremity of the left side. The patient brings her hand abruptly to the side of her body, or making alternative movements of pronation and supination, rubs her hand against her thigh."[110] Charcot categorized *rhythmical chorea*, as he did everything else. Classifications of minor and major (St Guy), ordinary and *Sydenham* rolled out in the director's usual manor. What is distinctive, though, is that in *chorea*, dance and hysteria were being classified simultaneously. Charcot closely linked fits of dancing to the neurological condition of hysteria, stating that they could in fact be expressions of the same lesions.[111] At the same time as medical terminology from the Salpêtrière and hysterical gestures found their way into dance halls and bars, Charcot was giving lectures on the classifications of dancing bodies, as dancing bodies – pathological, but stylized and rhythmic.

How precarious is the boundary between hysteria and performance, between the performances of the Salpêtrière hysteric and the grand actress or gommeuse? Visible similarities do not necessarily indicate technical or experiential equation. Generic overlaps between nineteenth century theatre traditions and the hysterical attack present a nearly irresistible impulse to link the performances concretely, in a causal lineage or a mimetic heritage. Gordon's question about direction of influence points to how easily comparisons across genres produce such provocative intersections of technique and presentation. Across mainstream and avant-garde forms of theatre, from melodrama, through realism, to the hydrophaths and gommeuses, audiences to the medical hysteria show had plenty of theatrical comparisons to make. The weekly hospital lectures were infected with associations to other stages where hysteria and its echoes played out. Hysterics and Charcot, renowned and chastised for their theatricality, were publicly recognized as performers. It may have been difficult for this reason, and for those listed above, for spectators to avoid the question: what if it's all *just* a show?

Without negating the potential links between the hospital and more traditional stages, the urge to classify hysteria as a theatrical illness ought to be balanced by a look at the hysteric's relationship to performance as it may differ from theatre proper.

PERFORMANCE IN/OF CRISIS

The diary text by Anaïs Nin is as follows:

> But then, imperceptibly almost, he let go of the thread we were following and began to act out dying by plague. No one quite knew when it began … His face was contorted with anguish, one could see the perspiration dampening his hair. His eyes dilated, his muscles became cramped, his fingers struggled to retain their flexibility. He made one feel the parched and burning throat, the pains, the fear, the fire in the guts. He was in agony. He was screaming. He was delirious. He was enacting his own death, his own crucifixion. At first people gasped. And then they began to laugh. Everyone was laughing. they hissed. then one by one, they began to leave, noisily, talking, protesting. they banged the door as they left … More protestations. More jeering. But Artaud went on, until the last gasp. He stayed on the floor. Then when the hall had emptied of all but his small group of friends, he walked straight up to me and kissed my hand. He asked me to go the café … Artaud and I walked out in a fine mist. We walked, walked through the dark streets. He was hurt, wounded, baffled by the jeering. He spat out his anger. "They always want to hear about; they want to hear an objective conference on the theatre and the Plague, I want to give them the experience itself. The

> plague itself, so they will be terrified, and awaken. I want to awaken them. Because they do not realize they are dead. Their death is total, like deafness and blindness. This is agony I portrayed. Mine, yes, and everyone who is alive … I feel sometimes that I am not writing, but describing the struggles with writing, the struggles of birth.[112]

Artaud, though he was subject to his private agonies – he did end up at Rodez quite raving – did not have the plague when he enacted it. And while Nin's description of the event leads us to a sympathetic view of Artaud – who was bold enough to show the plague instead of speaking on its behalf, descriptively, he still only showed a plague in performance. It was put on. It did not, as Artaud says, give the audience the plague itself.

It is poignant that Allen Weiss begins his article on Artaud, "Radio, Death and the Devil," by citing the Nin account of Artaud's enactment of the plague and then turning immediately to Susan Sontag's *Illness as Metaphor*. In Sontag's introduction to the work, she advances a thesis in relation to the use of illness as metaphor. She says: "My point is that illness is *not* a metaphor, and that the most truthful way of regarding illness – and the healthiest way of being ill – is one most purified of, most resistant to, metaphoric thinking."[113] To speak about illness abstracted is not to be ill. To enact suffering is not to suffer.

Charcot, who saw Bernhardt perform often, did not take her for a hysteric, though the public might have drawn its comparisons. The phenomenological experience of the female asylum inmate-performer was fundamentally different from these cultural performers, especially in its connection to pain and power. Nonetheless, her enactment of the hysterical attack was closely knit to performance.

To say that the hysteric was not faking her symptoms is not to say that she was disengaged from performance. And to highlight the hysteric's entanglement with performance does not mean that she was merely putting her audience on or that she was not authentically engaging in the expression of real pain or real pleasure. To reiterate the most convincing arguments that the hysteric was faking: in photographs and onstage, ever the performer, she bore resemblance to some of the age's major theatrical tropes; she behaved like an actress in a context that did not befit such vanity; the hysterical attack as it occurred in the Salpêtrière hospital consisted of a series of codified movements, amounting to an aesthetic series, that was a cultural product, a learned mode of expressing crisis, almost too mimetic and ritualized to seem real; and the patient revelled in her "illness," surrendering to oncoming attacks with a relish that raised suspicions about her agency or, oppositely (and on the side of genuineness), her helplessness.

In the small Salentine peninsula of southern Italy, people who have been "bitten" by spiders dance in the company of family, friends, and strangers, for days on end, drawing out a cure for their condition. The bite that some dancers of the tarantella can recall feeling, and some can't, often coincides with a moment of emotional or psychic crisis in their lives. Dancing is said to satisfy the spider who bit them and many have found, though less so in recent years, that dancing the tarantella alleviates symptoms of emotional and physical distress. According to anthropologist Karen Lüdtke, who has recently researched the historic tarantella and the ritual's contemporary presentations in tourist and popular performances, the truth of the ritual's healing powers and the authenticity of its practitioners are continually debated in Italy. Doctors, musicologists, new age healers, and skeptics try to find what causes the dancing of the tarantella with varying answers: the symptoms of the dance resonate with symptoms of actual spider bites; twenty-first-century mental illness diagnostics explain the combinations of physical and emotional symptoms in a tarantata; the healing power of musical tones account for the dancer's catharsis through dance and music; the tarantatas are faking it, or copying cultural norms in order to be part of an old Italian tradition. These explanations, though not surprising, seem out of context. Still, "the tarantata of southern Italy have variously been branded as mad, hysterical, psychologically unstable, exhibitionistic; the connotations of 'not being credible' associated with these classificatory tags marked the lives of many."[114]

There are still living tarantate in Salento.[115] If you watch Carpitella's 1960 film, *La terapia coreutico-musicale del tarantismo*, what appears strangely resembles the hysterical fits of the Salpêtrière women. Head thrashing from side to side, tensile back-bending, frenetic movement of the feet and face, a seemingly catatonic slumber. Anthropologist Ernesto De Martino, in the summer months of 1959, observed domestic dance rituals and pilgrimages to the church of St Paul in Galatino, publishing his observations in *La terra del rimorso* (1961). In a rare collaboration of researcher and filmmaker, De Martino took notes while Carpitella filmed a domestic tarantella ritual explicitly not staged for the camera.[116] I quote at length:

4.6 Photograph of a re-enacted home therapy in Nardò. Franco Pinna, 1959.

The floor is cleared, except for a few chairs and benches on the edge, seating observers and the musicians, including recently deceased violinist Luigi Stifani, a guitarist and an accordion and tambourine player. A white sheet is spread across the ground, delineating the ritual perimeter. In one corner stands a basket with offerings of money and paper icons depicting St Peter and Paul. Within the sheet's contours a young woman lies prostrate. She must be in her late twenties. Her dress and belt are white, and her ruffled skirt reveals long, white underwear, frilled at the ends. She is barefoot and her hair falls over her face and shoulders in tousled strains. Underneath, her expression is harsh and immobile, punctuated by eyes that open and close in response to the pizzica beats reverberating through the room. Four men in light summer clothes and sandals play the violin, tambourine, guitar and accordion. Their faces are marked by fatigue, the effect of playing from dawn till dusk, with nothing but brief breaks. Their notes bombard the distraught-looking woman lying lethargically on the floor without reacting to the melodies proposed. Then, triggered by a new piece, she begins to move, taking up the rhythm. Her feet tap and her

> head moves rapidly from side to side. She shuffles across the floor on her shoulders, increasing the momentum. Knees arched, she propels herself backwards on alternate heels, circling the entire ritual perimeter with her arms stretched out or folded on her chest. At one point, she tries to thread her body through the legs of a wicker chair, which tumbles over. She follows, rolling over and over, moving across the floor. She wrenches herself forward on her stomach, seeking the proximity of the instruments, as if hungry to absorb, almost touch every note.
>
> The violinist kneels down in response to her approach. His bow moves close to her ear and propels her onto her knees with her hands crouched in front of her, chest tipping rhythmically from side to side, embodying mutual interactions of "call and response." Abruptly, the tarantata springs to her feet and runs in circles, never losing the rhythm. Her moves include those of the pizzica, some danced on the spot, while a handkerchief, clasped between both hands, marks others. Her feet hit the ground rapidly, over and over again: stomping, crushing, destroying … The next morning, the first musical chords stretch the tarantata's body into an arc: her spine flexes into a bridge resting on her strained neck and heels. Within a few seconds she drops onto her back and rolls off the bed onto the ground. Numerous dance cycles are repeated. A short break is taken at noon, and only in the afternoon, winks between experienced bystanders confirm the first signs that recovery is close. The afflicted has eaten a little earlier. She keeps on emitting short, shrill screams. Her dance phases are shorter now and show a greater variety of steps. Then, finally, she breaks off in mid-cycle, signals to the musicians to stop playing and steadfastly walks to her bed. Relief spreads through the room. Just to be sure this is for real, a last tune is played. It is dedicated to St Paul. The young tarantata remains insensitive to the music and, grateful for her recovery, everyone present kneels in prayer.[117]

Lüdtke cautions, "the temptation of continuity is highly seductive."[118] Her warning applies equally to the unlikelihood of a culturally specific phenomenon like tarantism to be repeated elsewhere, as to hysteria proper to infiltrate the theatre. So why include a discussion of the Italian tarantella given the wisdom of such a cautionary note, and given my reluctance to equate one ritual with the other? The tarantata offers several instructive clues about how the hysteric may have performed her illness.

The overlap of gestural repertoire between tarantata and hysteric is extraordinary. The movements described and filmed, from screaming to back bend, the movements these women cycle through are strikingly similar. In fact, a willingness to mobilize the body in such marginal, kinetic ways – thrashing, wriggling, arching, kneeling, rolling – is a marked shared trait. And yet, the tarantata performs ritual codes that are distinct from those in the Salpêtrière. The culturally specific ritual music, played in collaboration, the religious iconography, the tarantata's violent distaste for bright colours, the symbolic connection to the spider and, perhaps above all, the tarantata's social mobility – her not being in an institution and her not being medicalized – set her apart from the Salpêtrière hysteric. The codified cultural specificity of the tarantella, while it points to differences of content, presents a compelling analogy in form. The hysterical attack, as it occurred during Charcot's directorship, was equally codified. It suffered from repetition. But to perform an attack that had a clearly delineated structure did not necessarily make the hysterics hucksters. Were they not engaging in a ritualized performance, following mores and indulging in communally reproduced movement sequences, but still leaning into the next movement or impulse with curiosity? I propose that performing hysteria involved leaping in faith as much as, if not more than, exemplifying rote choreography.

Playing out a delirious scene with one's lover may, sometimes, for the hysteric, not have been a helpless surrender to an intrusive memory playing itself out in the present moment. Sometimes, the hysteric may have allowed the scene to unfold with just a little self-reflexivity, akin to the stomping, crushing, symbolic movements related to the tarantata's understanding of her crisis, her performing "with" a spider who was no longer there. What kind of mimesis is this? The hysteric's playing into the stylistic tropes of her illness was mimesis *in performance*. In this way, the hysteric likely did technically resemble the traditional actress or the cabaret dancer. A performing woman may, basically, know what comes next, but her experience in performing towards the next moment leaves her in the present tense and suspended precariously in relation to futurity. She always improvises to a degree. And so with the hysteric.

Irigaray's hysterical grammar lesson demonstrates that the hysteric is, already, a self-displacing subject, one who finds satisfaction in moving herself off kilter. The hysteric, if we follow Irigaray, prefers to be in a position of dependence on the deferred arrival of the other. Her imagination, as manifested in her use of language, revels in contingency. Ritualized performance of her attack seems a fitting extension of this contingent self-perspective. The attack, in the precarity of performance, becomes another "other" the hysteric can engage with in both present and future tenses, leaving her in the most habitual space of her crisis, open to what (and who) comes next.

The hysteric regularly followed an unfolding hallucination, its own drama, as a reciprocal participant and witness. She enacted her attacks, drawing from her repertoire of several movements, states of awareness, breathing, sounding, using the tools available to her in the hysteria wing at the Salpêtrière to express her crisis. And the hysteric's relationship to her body was likely one of mutual performance and spectatorship. She could give in to an oncoming attack easily, or if we believe Avril, she could launch into an attack of her own volition. But, still following Avril, once she began, the hysteric could not stop herself without the aid of ovarian compression. Her body had mechanisms quite outside her control. Likewise, her illness produced those symptoms that could not be explained, and that could come and go with seemingly little impetus or explanation. Her body parts and functions were often foreign to her, not unlike characters acting on their own. To have a hysterical body was to watch oneself, often with a sense of mystery. For instance, patients are reported to have become nervous when a symptom disappeared. As Daudet says, "I saw clients of Charcot who were quite embarrassed when a sign or reflex, which they knew to be particularly dear to Charcot, disappeared: 'What will he think of this? He won't be interested in my case anymore! How should I act now, at consultation?'"[119] The hysteric maintained the ability to stun her audience, and sometimes this included herself. The hysteric's bodily autonomy, displayed in moments where her symptoms disappeared and could no longer be reproduced in a tangle of mimetic reality, is what, in part, lead to the hysteric's being labelled deceitful. Shifting symptoms that simply went away were blamed on the caprice of the hysteric: "les hémianesthésies, après avoir duré très longtemps, quatre ou cinq ans par exemple, tout d'un coup, brusquement, sans cause appréciable, sans motif plausible, disparaissent et ne laissent pas de traces. Les hystériques, disons-nous plus haut, ont un caractère mobile et changeant: leurs maladies sont de même capricieuses et fantasques à ce point qu'elles surviennent sans cause connue et qu'elles s'en vont de même[120] (The hemianesthesia, after having endured four or five years, for example, all of a sudden, abruptly, without apparent cause, without plausible motive, disappear and leave no traces. Hysterics, we say above, have a shifting and changeable character: their illnesses are likewise capricious and fantastic in that they occur without any known cause, and then they leave just the same). When secretive causes led to effects all too visible, the hysteric enacted her "significative evasion"[121] yet again. Had the doctors and their observers hallucinated the hysteric's symptomatology? Surely not! As Richet complained, "Il suffit d'une émotion insignifiante, presque inaperçue, pour dissiper des paralysies qui datent de plusieurs années"[122] (An insignificant emotion suffices, nearly imperceivable, to dissipate paralyses that have been around for several years). The doctors were mystified. So too, surely, was the woman whose body moved in and out of illness and wellness most capriciously. And yet, the body entangled in symptoms that signified irregularly was just another symptom of hysteria. A tricky one, because it is difficult to codify caprice. And yet this is one of the most general definitions of the hysteric: capricious. Who could tell if she was lying or telling the truth? Despite her waywardly functioning body, at odds with what medicine understood about morbid anatomy, the hysteric continued to produce a similar, erratic performance of her illness. She played hysteria perfectly.

Hysteria's entanglement with theatre is what troubles the certainty of accurate vision most, resulting in what appears to be what Munthe described as "an impossible muddle of truth and cheating."[123] In part, the theatricality of hysteria itself was cause for indecision and doubt about authenticity. And, in part, so was the illness' theatrical transmission, its theatrical appeal. Hysteria was, in so many ways, performance. The spectator of so much confusion between truth and falsehood wants to blame the hysteric for putting her on, does not want to be taken in. It is sometimes humiliating, to not be able to find one's way in the theatre, to find one's "hermeneutic pleasure"[124] sabotaged, to find one's gaze under pressure. As Diamond points out, in what I take to be the most compelling part of her argument, taking pleasure in reading the hysterical character often does not equate with the hysteric's being legible.[125] Hysteria teaches that performance thrives against the obvious. The limits of sight and understanding produce their pleasures as well. Illegibility is what keeps theatre going – representational play is its ally. To find ourselves in a crisis of signification and meaning is to find ourselves in festival, the world topsy-turvy. Maenads in their wildernesses. Vision slightly askew. Aware of the power of performance to destabilize certainty.

Was the hysterical patient faking? Who can tell? Was she performing? Absolutely. The accusations of her fraudulence – simulation of symptoms, willful indulgence, vanity, a flair for drama, celebrity, reproduction of rote mannerisms – all of these were aspects of her performance of hysterical illness though not exactly proof of her outright deception. Frenetic bodies in true distress gesturing with visual splendour; symptoms forging their way onto unsuspecting bodies with no actual cause; female patients gossiping about their love affairs, drawing doctors into their tall tales; a doctor of Wagnerian proportions; photographs that looked like theatre stills; a little theatre one could mostly count on, with predictable outcomes and striking effects; hypnosis; acrobatics; inner turmoil cast into delirious murmurings; screaming; posing; dancing.

We seem to be a long way from medical empiricism.

The patient Augustine often tore off her clothes and climbed out of hospital windows to run into the garden in the rain.[126] On stage, in visual prominence, she similarly escaped from view and, likewise, the doctors and her audience were left scrambling to find her. They could claim that they had, but their expressions of propriety and understanding rang as false as Judge Brack's "People don't do such things."

Speaking of last words, this time in a performance of her own, the hysteric Augustine mobilized acting in order to shift her own reality. Theatrical illusion was powerful enough to allow the patient Augustine to retreat from view twice more. First, she donned the clothing of one of the Salpêtrière doctors and slipped through the clusters of medical staff, patients, and visitors in the halls, through the courtyards and to the hospital gates. And finally – and this is an ending neither Didi-Huberman nor Winocour can resist either – she slipped away into the city, never to be seen again.

FIVE

Hysterical Strategies in Contemporary Performance

THE HYSTERIC'S LEGACY

Contemporary Representations of Historical Hysteria

Disappearance. The ability for the hysteric to disappear from view, to resist representational capture, even as she has been exploited by spectacle, is a focal point for this work. In a series of dramaturgical analyses of facets of hysteria's transmission through medical spectacle, ambiguity figures as one of the hysteric's major maneuvers to overturn the power exercised against her through representation. Who is she? What does she mean? How does she mean? Doctors were left blundering. The emergence of the hysteric and Charcot as famous figures in the nineteenth century hysteria project was achieved via a theatre of pain and power. This was also a theatre where the hysteric made unconventional use of her appearance. While she was made to support the Salpêtrière's hysteria project, she undermined its tenets by her unique performance, continually forcing a reconfiguration of the values and certitudes of certainty itself.

Analyses of the photograph, the amphitheatre stage, and cultural iterations of Charcot's project reveal that the hysteric found ways to draw attention to the limits of the spectacle from within its framework. As well, often, the hysteric threw the conditions of the scientific spectacle into question by contrarily appearing against expectation. Despite the regularity of the hysterical attack of la grande hystérie, the hysteric possessed an exceptional power to surprise, and to reveal pieces of herself despite the attempted erasure of her personhood.

In the Salpêtrière documents, the gravity of institutional violence committed against female patients at the level of representation is undeniable. I have aimed, in this work, to express the overt and subtle damages done to hysterical women in Charcot's hospital: public and private bodily harm, sexual violation, dismissal, objectification, use, exposure, reduction. Simultaneously, the chapters have sought out the hysteric's resistance to these phenomena. So often, it is simply by being herself that the hysteric points to the inherent weaknesses in these systemic modes of violence. Photographers were forced to new levels of technical innovation and flexibility in order to capture the hysteric's fiercely mobile body. Terminology spun out an anxious series of words to try to negotiate her dynamism. The excessive exposure of her emotional, intellectual, and sexual life in the *Iconographie* and on stage, framed by equally excessive empirical constraints, under scrutiny, ultimately reveals the uncontainable remainder of the hysteric's personhood that slips from view, bringing the inadequacy of positivist and misogynist spectacle into relief.

At every site where Charcot attempts straightforward employment of the hysterical patient as an example of a diagnostic category, the hysteric's presence draws attention to unexpected forces at work in the medical performance. In the remaining documents of the Salpêtrière medical theatre, there is a lot to be learned about theatre itself. The hysteric is a mischievous dramaturg. Under the hysteric's influence, the nature of looking at bodies in pain becomes fraught with doubt and the discomfort of responsibility. The theatrical photograph exhibits invisible scenes from the patient's life, extraordinary dimensions of her thought and gesture that lie beyond medical framing. Duration undermines the certitude of the image; the nineteenth century scientific parades of pathologies via photographs become swamped with human life. Because of the hysteric's persistence, the medical lecture is shown to be a compensatory performance of pain and power when the clear relationship between seeing, knowing, and expressing is shown to be a ruse in a theatrical project that is more about symptoms and screens, nostalgia and modern panic. The hysteric draws attention to the performative force of the inarticulate utterance by overturning her use-value, making her body-as-prop into a body-that-sounds. She repeats her typified symptoms so often and so dramatically that performance itself becomes an illuminated field for an increasingly uncertain spectatorship.

The hysteric behaved unexpectedly. Heaving wrenches into the machinery of the spectacle; speaking out of turn; screaming; making oral poetry out of her memories; falling unapologetically into inexplicable dreams; activating a beastly aggression against the doctor who would rather portray her as a sleepy, nostalgic relic from the past who likely never really existed; turning on her witnesses like an angry woman instead of a puppet, obscuring their view via vain changeability and relentlessly sideways symptomatic associations – the hysteric exercised agency over her privacy and her creative contributions to the medical spectacle despite the relentlessness and demeaning nature of her exposure. She could make use of the confines of the Salpêtrière's theatrical transmission of her illness in order to drop from sight or to come into view, either way outshining Charcot, medical empiricism, the values of clarity and certainty. Historically, the hysteric made representation much more dynamic and dangerous than Charcot had likely hoped it would be. Once in a while, she made spectacle humane, made it reflexively communicate both its potential for harm and its potential to undo itself toward the other. She often made visible her potential to overflow its confines with her personhood.

Quite a performative legacy. This book has continually drifted into the figurative, even as it has attempted to preserve the singular and unknowable experiences of the women who were part of Charcot's hysteria project. At the same time, the particularity of the subject(s) extends to other moments in performance as I learn from women like Augustine and Blanche Wittman. In researching their defiant performances, their vulnerable acts, and their strong theatrical interventions, I have become a more attentive spectator, looking for less likely signs. Having spent time with the hysterics of the archive, learning from their modes of performance and performativity, I am more equipped to read contemporary acts of feminist performance. Hysterical performance strategies include: mobilizing the breakdown of language to inarticulately represent experiences that resist explanation and understanding; challenging the accuracy of representation by drawing attention to representation's failures; telling one's own story as though it has value, despite mainstream indications that it does not; inviting the intimacy of witnessing while maintaining privacy; making political spectacle and modes of media exposure express what they ordinarily do not; deploying the naked trans/gender-queer/disabled/female form to disrupt ignorance about subjugated or marginalized bodies; demonstrating the value of not knowing through the unique relational exchange of performance; and revelling in irrational or emotional expression to generate ethical encounters. As I lift my eyes out of the nineteenth century research I have been engaged in, and look around, I see so many echoes of hysterical performance. I also see the historical hysteric taken up by performers, playwrights, scholars, and activists, which makes me wonder why the hysteric continues to return, why we find her so compelling, why we need her right now, in a world of public trials where women who have experienced sexual assault endure flagrant scrutiny without recognition, where psychiatrists still act as gatekeepers to gender reassignment surgeries, where Indigenous women are disappearing and being murdered but are also creating works of resurgence and reclamation.

Hysteria is currently a popular topic. In literature, cultural histories of nineteenth century hysteria (Diamond, Did-Huberman, Finn, Gordon, Marquer, Micale), biographies of Charcot (Goetz, Thuillier), feminist critiques of the medical patriarchy and the derogatory use of the term hysteria (Beizer, Harris, Noel Evans, Showalter), an attempted biography of the Salpêtrière's most famous hysterics (Hustvedt), even a proposed popular biography of hysteria itself (Scull), are in academic and popular circulation. I have heard the term "hysteria studies" bandied about at conferences, indicating that the topic is coming to resemble a field. In fact, Mark Micale formally identified "new hysteria studies" as a research field in his *Approaching Hysteria* in 1995.[1]

In theatre and film as well, Charcot and his hysterical patients occupy the theatrical imagination from small stages to the big screen. In Toronto's 2013 Fringe Festival, Alexander Offord's *Hystericon* featured three young actresses playing the Salpêtrière's most famed starlets. The *Hysteria* festival, begun out of Moynan King's initiative at Buddies in Bad Times in 2003, ran programming that embraced woman's disobedience until 2009. Playwright Anna Furse, drawing heavily from Showalter, depicts Augustine alongside a violin substitute for her voice in the play, *Big Hysteria*. The play relies on citation of the *Iconographie* images. Daniel Keene subverts the audience's ability to see clearly in his play *Photographs of A*, with alienating lighting effects, repeated utterances from the character Augustine that perform an active analysis of her stature as both person and image, and a screaming actress. Keira Knightley is said to have studied the Salpêtrière hysterics for her performance of Sabina Spielrein, Freud's patient and eventual psychoanalyst colleague, in Cronenberg's *A Dangerous Method* (adapted from a screenplay that was adapted from a book). Alice Winocour's 2012 film creates romance between Charcot and Augustine, and its British contemporary, *Hysteria*, makes a comedic link between ovarian compression and the invention of the vibrator. While I was doing my PhD, where so much of the research for this project happened, Sarah Ruhl's *The Room Next Door or The Vibrator Play*, featuring an American physician of women's emotions and his hysterical wife, a domestic detective after her own orgasm, was showing at Toronto's Tarragon Theatre.

Solo performer Audrey Wollen has turned historical hysteria's influence into artistic protests that question sexism in forms where dismissal and disavowal ordinarily reign. Wollen's photographic portraits highlight the political power of so-called feminine emotional landscapes, girlish states of sadness and fragility. *Sad Girl Theory* is a photographic selfie project rolled out on Instagram in 2015, in which Wollen pictures herself in states of sadness. Snot, tears, red eyes, softened postures, and frank, sad looking into the computer lens or into the high school bathroom mirror, reflected to her phone, mark this work, which Wollen relates is an exploration of how, "girls are being set up: if we don't feel overjoyed about being a girl, we are failing at our own empowerment, when the voices that are demanding that joy are the same ones participating in our subordination." She continues, in an interview with Lucy Watson of Dazed Digital, "Global misogyny isn't the result of girls' lack of self-care or self-esteem. Sad Girl Theory is a permission slip: feminism doesn't need to advocate for how awesome and fun being a girl is. Feminism needs to acknowledge that being a girl in the world right now is one of the hardest things there is – it is unimaginably painful – and that our pain doesn't need to be discarded in the name of empowerment. It can be used as a material, a weight, a wedge, to jam that machinery and change those patterns."[2] Wollen is inspired by many sad and strong women – Persephone, Frida Kahlo, Hannah Wilke, and the Salpêtrière hysterics.

Susanna Hood, in *She's Gone Away*, a solo dance performance from 2006 in collaboration with sound composer Nilan Perera, unearths a woman's unconscious through animal movements – a rat scuttling through the walls, a deer/horse stepping gingerly – and through truly undomestic uses of a teapot (after turning and adjusting the teapot at intervals in the dance for some time, she pees all over the stage, clutching the pot like a phallus). As she releases more and more layers of her character's repression, uncovering a memory of catching her parents having sex, Hood ratchets out a fragmentary portrait of her past through her erratic body, which is always playing both woman and her id, and through digital voice manipulation in which words like "tail" become ragged shrieks or uncanny soundings from the margins of speech. She dances a psychic portrait of a both turbulent and self-possessed woman, unafraid of looking and sounding in registers of ugliness and beauty in stuttered sequences.

In a particularly mystifying project, artist Tejal Shah photographs herself in the iconic poses of the women of Charcot's hospital. In a work she calls *Reinvention of Hysteria*, coined after Didi-Huberman, Shah places herself in the positions of the women of the *Iconographie*, and photographs herself, an agent of gallery spaces like MOMA's Little Gallery, disseminating her image for public view. Why she wants to play the suffering hysteric is unclear. Reproducing herself in the photographic position(s) of the Salpêtrière patients, Shah appears to find thinking through by iteratively occupying the hysteric's place irresistible. Her repeated image across the archive shows a nearly obsessive interest. She has invaded the space of the punctum. Seemingly finding herself pierced by intrigue, she has moved into the photographic space that caused the puncture. The effect of the collection of citational self-portraits is that the historical content and context of the photographs appears once again as intriguing, theatrical, tragic, immoral, and … less expectedly, silly. Shah's repeated face and body across photographs, including one in which she plays both the hypnotically slumbering Augustine, cast into a limp backbend, and the matter-of-fact nurse (likely Mlle Bottard), quite close to Brouillet's painting, so that she is both patient and caregiver in one take, recasts the *Iconographie* with an impish tone that seems to hinge on mockery. It is difficult for the viewer to hold her balance between the obvious time and care taken to pose and to photograph so closely to the historical documents and the appearance of Shah's mischievously infiltrating and proliferating the hysteric's image, now her own. Is this work making light, or taking time? Is it appropriative? So much so that Shah can reinvent hysteria on her own as the title of her work implies, by placing herself at both ends of a camera lens set to capture the historical starlets original capture? Or is Shah's performance a critique of the hysteria project, artfully undertaken but complicated so difficult to pin down? While *Reinvention* troubles interpretation, it is a strangely obsessive example (perhaps not unlike this work!) of a desire to return to the hysteric, to bring her into the present, recast in light of one's own art making practices, via one's own body.

Why this collective interest in hysteria? What is, as Catherine Clément writes, quite personally, "this source of this passion for disorder, for madness, for all that stumbles?"[3] Why, a century later, do we want to revel in the hysteric's crisis? Or, to put it another way, why does the hysteric continue to return?

The answer to this question can be found in perhaps the most compelling celebration of the hysteric as a woman and as a figure, Cixous and Clément's 1975 work, *The Newly Born Woman*. The text, which Sandra Gilbert calls, "a tarantella of theory,"[4] is a literary fit of memory, embellished autobiography, and delirious style. In it, Clément writes that, "Somewhere, every culture has an imaginary zone for what it excludes, and it is that zone that we must try to remember today."[5] In her act of remembering, "a history arranged the way tale-telling women tell it," Clément purposefully returns to the figures of the hysteric, the witch, and the tarantata – women who were forced to the margins of the patriarchal spaces they inhabited and who were materially repressed – because they posed too big a threat to the overall system.[6] Clément's view, after Freud, is that women's continual reappearance in differing spatial and temporal contexts as the iconic figures of witch, hysteric, and tarantata constitutes a return of the repressed. Women are forced to the margins, not fully excluded so that they can still function as "signs" for the signifying agents of patriarchy, but never fully included in the process of signification.[7] Inevitably, as Freud teaches, when the repressed returns, it is of a magnitude and intensity that is truly disruptive.

For Clément, the hysteric and the witch point to irresolvable fault lines in the social structure. By being excluded precisely as threats, and by returning, as the repressed returns, in crisis, shaking up the falsely normalized social flow, the hysteric and the witch are figures of uncommon force. The witch's sabbath, the hysteric's attack, the tarantella, under Clément's hand, become events in which the possibilities of femininity become unleashed in the celebration of crisis. The hysterical attack is the festival brought into the body, a suspended moment wherein the patient signifies from the dangerous symbolic mobility of her marginalization, instead of merely functioning "as sign," and she speaks.[8] The crises of these womanly figures are unapologetically sites of female pleasure, events in which a feminine libidinal economy is deployed, overflowing with endless potential for expenditure.[9] The hysterical attack is also a festival. The body disobeys convention, makes itself available for radical configurations, wasteful gestures, excessive vocalizations, embellishment, turbulence.

For Freud, the hysteric embodies remembrance. Her body, more than others, demonstrates how recollection alters the physicality, and how the return of repressed memories and impulses throw the body backward into a disremembered history in a moment that it is exactly history making itself recognizable. Freud himself, Clément delineates, was in history's sway – looking for the cultural memory traces that all people bear on their psychic mapping: "Throughout the period in which he listened to hysteria, Freud was like a prisoner of the mythology of origins."[10] Hysteria, for Freud, is an illness that remembers guilty daughters and guilty mothers – guilt, above all. Hysteria as Clément reconfigures it, is a different kind of remembering, a remembering of "femininity" and its possibilities, an expression of the "cracks in the overall system," and a mobilization of the feminine worthy of celebration.

Other women who revel in crisis hysterically: Augustine. Blanche Wittman. The innumerable unnamed hysterics acting out their particular breed of hysteria at the Salpêtrière. Dora. Anna Von O. Nora, not closing the door on her dutiful domestic doll-play, but badly dancing the tarantella, acting out what Bergman called brutal aggression,[11] Hedda Gabler playing the piano, an incomplete song much too upbeat for the occasion of Lövborg's death, her sound-making making little sense for the moment shared by the collective, churning out "a wild dance melody."[12] Harriet Andersson's portrayal of the hysteric tuned too clearly to her imagination in the 1961 Bergman film, *Through a Glass Darkly*. Charlotte Perkins Gilman's literary indulgence in female madness in her gothic horror tale, *The Yellow Wallpaper*, wherein her post-partum depression takes the form of a sumptuous derailment – a wailing husband, wife crawling over his prone body.

The hysteric comes back. She continues to preoccupy our imaginations. True, the hysterics from Charcot's day are long departed. The smatterings of mass hysteria in New York cheerleaders in 2012 are distant cousins, but not the same.[13] But, there are performing women today who manifest the tropes that those nineteenth century hysterics advanced. The hysteric, read now nearly entirely as a figure, still appears in ways that have true potential to "shake up the group."

What is hysteria's legacy? I agree with Clément. The hysteric arrives, partly, as the repressed, to show the cracks in the system, to point out the violent practices of patriarchy (always about the family) – practices that continue but that are not working. She draws attention to the power to signify from unexpected places within the spectacle, to the entanglements of body and language, to the force of vulnerability and the necessity of human connection. The current hysterical performer appears signifying, stepping out of her function as sign and speaks her own way, outside the constrictions of idealized femininity. She presents a kind of self-possessed womanhood that frays the borders of the feminine, which we know to be a harmful binary. She complicates the function of the unknowable, so that it swerves away from an inevitable feature of the undiscovered "dark continent" of femininity and begins to be mobilized as a valuable component of witnessing the suffering and the experiences of others. She appears to make use of signification in festival, unafraid of distress, of ugliness, of the unknown, of the unconscious. Unafraid of blood, and skin, and sexual fluids, what Clément calls the witch's media.[14] As with the Salpêtrière hysteric, she mobilizes her body, makes it perform feats, advances sex-first, flesh in the foreground. Her gaze challenges. Her voice seeks out errant modulations. She uses the body for something other than what it is usually used for. She performs, indulges in over-the-top theatrics. She enters into an extraordinary relationship to language. She makes the conventional modes express what they do not ordinarily express.

The hysteric's dynamism comes from unusual use of her voice, her body, her selfhood. These, she mobilizes in ways that refigure her "femininity" and her relationship to language, to hegemonic structures, to performance. The hysteric makes use of excess, vocalizing at the edge of language, indulging in emotion, expressing in bodily gestures that are both wild and codified, animal and womanly. She plays with exposure and concealment, and challenges the spectator's relationship to sight and understanding. Her performance, read against genres of movement and dance, theatre and sound, is interdisciplinary. Her intimate performance is alienating, uncanny, and visually resplendent.

Are there hysterics today? Yes.

FEMINIST ACTIVISMS AND DEPLOYED BODIES
New Anatomical Performances

Freud loved to quote Charcot as saying that hysteria was always related to the genitals.

Any time a person spends with Freud's corpus takes them on a journey sharply sexed, even in the early work, before he begins to uncover his theories of early childhood sexual development and theatre's Oedipus in bodies rebelling against gender roles. Girls take care of their fathers but want to take care of their jewel boxes. Repressing desire makes young women sick, Freud notes, as he spends hours talking to them about their sexual histories, about dads becoming ill and requiring constant bedside ministration, or becoming hard, and needing their daughters to keep lovers' husbands busy. Then, Oedipus causes Freud to stumble. A hypothesis so seamless that even years later, Derrida psychoanalyses Yerushalmi aiming to debunk Freud precisely by catching him trying to throw off the burden of fathers once again (my work, too, is an act of throwing off yet another patriarch), the Oedipal complex as primordially implicated in the operative structures of our human psyches works well for Freud. Until he has to think about what women are after. Jocastas accidentally in bed with their sons? Less compelling than a primal horde tearing a father's body to pieces.

In his lecture "On Femininity," Freud confesses that the problem of female psychic becoming has presented a conundrum. All that he has to say about femininity is "incomplete and fragmentary."[15] He takes note of the limits of anatomical explanation for feminine nature[16] – sperm is active and ova passive by comparison – not nearly enough to compete with the social pressures (Freud calls them impositions) that cultivate female passivity.[17] At the end of his lecture about how young girls move from bisexuality to heteronormativity, Freud announces his uncertainty: all he has described is how sexual function might inform a woman's becoming woman, and her being an "individual" "human person" is territory that implies other forces. Ambiguous processes are on Freud's horizon and he offers alternatives to trying to understand the mystery of femininity until psychoanalysis can come up with something more cohesive: "If you want to know more about femininity, inquire your own experiences in life, or turn to the poets, or wait until science can give you deeper and more coherent explanation."[18] As Freud is called upon to answer to the feminine experience, surrounded as he is by all those young hysterics he thinks are making poor decisions (Herr K was so handsome. What was the big deal? Dora can't be telling the truth when she says she isn't interested), he tries his best. What is going on down there? Penis envy. The theory that young girls become women who long for the material obviousness and the symbolic mobility of the phallus, the notion that women's pleasure is evasive and ambiguous, relies on the assumption that girls can't find their sexual equipment, and that there is little to look at. Charcot's appraisal of the ovaries as pushbutton links to mechanical reproduction of his attack, his measurements of women's menses and wetness, his unmedical attention to their voluptuousness: these scientific intersections with female sex parts need a hysteric's attention. A hysterical intervention.

Toronto performing artist Jess Dobkin makes thoughtful work about women's parts. She is famous for her *Lactation Station*, a project in which she served women's breast milk in a clean and unlikely bar. In *Vagina Clown Car* (2008), Dobkin pulled many fabric clowns from her vagina, cheekily designed after a car. In what she calls "a novel interpretation the traditional circus clown car,"[19] I see a novel take on the vagina. Considered alongside Charcot and Freud, who actively tried to "solve for woman" by focusing on her sexual anatomy, Dobkin's vagina offers a series of surprises, whimsically chosen and created by the artist. In this particular iteration (because her vagina has also been Neil Diamond in a duet she sang with herself at Buddies in Bad Times in 2012 [*Flowers*]), Dobkin's vaginal canal is so spacious and versatile that there is no telling what might spill out, or who, or how much/many. Her reply to the question about what female sex organs might mean doesn't answer the question so much as say, "If it is so mysterious, it may as well be a clown car." Her vagina is a trick horse. It has stunning capacity. Just when one thinks one understands its measures, another clown pops out.

In 2015, Québecois FEMEN activist Neda Topaloski, topless, screamed "Mon utérus, ma priorité" in front of stunned Culture Minister Hélène David at a press conference before she was escorted away from view by a security guard. Wearing Dionysian wreaths of flowers, tactically using their topless female bodies and screaming, FEMEN activists disrupt political media performances that otherwise avoid demonstrating the real stakes of policy and law, law that involves real bodies belonging to real women. FEMEN report that they anticipate security interventions and that this is when they become more visible and scream louder. Topaloski was drawn to the FEMEN movement, which began in Ukraine, partly because of the inspiring act of young women screaming with such force. She said, in an interview with *Macleans*, "I'd never seen women, young women, who scream so much and who never stop and who are not scared of the system."[20]

FEMEN's understanding of the political force of the female cry and female bodily gesture results in an activism that transforms the banal political performance into a dynamic momentary (and memorable!) uncovering of power relations. Seemingly irrational, bacchanal, the semi-nude and noisy intervention makes activism out of a politics that excludes many voices and bodies. The most common critique of FEMEN's topless tactics is that boobs distract from the grit of the issues, that activists like Topaloski losing their shirts are asking to be objectified or even objectify themselves alongside other female bodies. Among those who criticize FEMEN for using tactics that are more indulgent theatrics than substance is women's rights activist and writer Toula Drimonis, whose aversion to FEMEN's ignorant protests of the hijab are incisive, but whose comments like, "No one ever remembers what they're protesting. All they remember are a bunch of bare-chested women being led off kicking and screaming while amused passersby whip out their iPhones to snap a few pictures … I can assure you, no one gets past the boobs"[21] deserve questioning. To such criticism, Topaloski replies,

> people talk about our breasts all the time. And then people ask us, "Well, why do we talk only about your breasts?" Well, it's up to you to talk about something else, you know. There's nothing wrong or special with our breasts, and there's nothing weird about that either. It's not my fault that they have only been used to sell products. Now I'm guilty for giving my message and speaking for myself? No. Femen started as a protest movement that protested with our clothes on. And then nobody listens to women, nobody listens to women's protests, it's always marginal, it's not really society, it's just women. At some point, you realize there's only one thing that the system and patriarchy is interested in: women's bodies. You see it all around, so we decided to use that, but speak for ourselves and take back our bodies and identities and make them subjects, not objects.[22]

Alongside the maenadic floral wreaths, FEMEN's activist appropriations of public spectacles are bacchanals in that they are theatrical interventions into hierarchical rules for performance and spectatorship. Those who ordinarily live at the margins of civic involvement (young

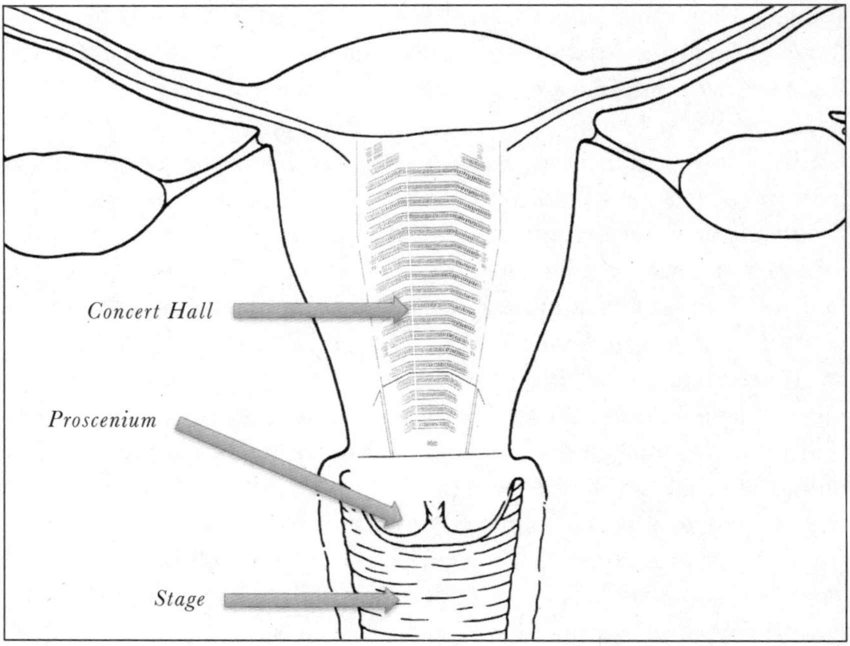

5.1 Dayna McLeod, Diagram of *Uterine Concert Hall*, 2016.

women) create momentary disruptions that force public speakers in suits to the background. Things get wild for a minute. Painted bodies, nipples bared, yelling from the guts, fighting the officers who try to quiet and remove them. If this is all that is remembered, it isn't a bad after-image. The hysteric has taught me that this moment in performance, with noise, breasts, rage, and combat, presents an alternate portrait of women that gives us a lot of chew on. Topaloski's use of theatrics to make her voice heard does not distract from her message in all ways. This explosive burst of a young woman appearing where she ought not to, in ways government officials would prefer she didn't, is a message that people held from meaningful political participation, pushed to the margins like repressed content crop up with the force of the id.

I joined Twitter to follow Dayna McLeod's *Uterine Concert Hall*. McLeod's "Vaginal New Media" project crosses up the medical and the personal, public spectacle and obscurity at the site of her uterus, which she has made into a concert hall.

The premise is quite simple: McLeod inserts a speaker – the Babypod, an instrument made for serenading fetuses/babies in utero – into the walls of her vagina and has DJs play shows for her uterus. Spectators who attend can see very little, but McLeod invites them to listen from outside the hall, with a stethoscope. Even with the most empirical and practical of technologies, the concert sounds very far away, not as audible as some audience members expect or would like. The iconic medical medium for listening to a person's organs acts as an imperfect transmitter of the sonic space of the uterine concert. Maybe this is important. Even as McLeod lies down and allows spectators to listen in with doctor's instruments, from doctor's viewpoints above her horizontal body, the medical ear can't hear a wild party set played just for a woman's parts, can't tune in to the sounds made for/next to a uterus being used extraordinarily.

Concerts for her uterus. Not for a baby inside. This alternate use of technology made for mothers, used for a uterus that McLeod has no desire to make home to any fetus, is a rejection of the instrument's heteronormative marketing plan. *Uterine Concert Hall* is a queering of the creepy hetero capitalist undertow that threatens new parents, where pressures to purchase in vitro speakers to soothe and cultivate early relationships between mothers and their fetuses accost potential parents whose algorithms lead to advertisements for breast pumps, bottles, and business chic maternity clothes. McLeod subverts the instrumentality the culture that generates and purchases Babypod products presumes that her uterus serves. This uterine concert hall is not purposed for childbearing, but exists, from time to time, in concert pop-ups, as a party space. The Bacchanal excesses of performance festivals sonically overflow the quotidian and the useful in McLeod's internal revelry. This uterus is for making sounds for. It soaks up a live DJ's rhythms and tones, resisting common expectations of purpose.

Outside these pop-up shows, McLeod gives *Uterine Concert Hall* a cheeky web performance. A Twitter feed, blog, and website function humorously, but also as critiques of discursive structures of objectivity and medicalization of the personal. Playing for the uterus is not playing for the baby-to-come. And McLeod's occupation of digital media, using the formal social media strategies of venue websites, indulges in communicating information to a spectator, but with emphasis on indulgence, rather than information.

In the "Tech Specs" section of the Uterine Concert Hall website, the hall's dimensions are given in approximations: the stage length is about 6.5 to 12.5 cm, diameter is 2.1 to 3.5 cm, and is flexible and expandable.

The proscenium measures about 2–3 cm in diameter. Unfortunately, there is no piano inside the venue and, the site quips, under "Lighting," "Currently, there is no fancy stage or effects lighting in the venue. *We also cannot accommodate pyrotechnics, regardless of your qualifications and expertise – sorry, it's a landlady issue." The landlady joked about in this list of prohibitions is the author, owner, and progenitor of the concert hall herself. This statement, a comedic tongue in cheek notice that ends in a typographic smile, performs a fierce questioning of the rhetorical structure it mimics: websites for venues often erase the person who runs the venue. They commonly perform objective tone. People who run concert venues are also often exactly not objective: they fundraise, they labour, they fret. Old performance venues are quirky and need the special attention of the people who manage them, people with their own quirks. But venue websites lay out tech specs, dimensions, photos of rooms – an anatomy of structure. Even with its humorous gesture, McLeod's lighting note and pyrotechnic prohibition use the style employed by venue contracts. They are explicative and the author assumes no personal responsibility for the conditions they describe. However, we know that the author of the website is so invested in the venue that it is biologically a part of her. As well, we know that she is only playing at objectivity. Making use of discourse to advance her artistic project. Her critical intelligence marks all aspects of *Concert Hall.* This makes McLeod's adoption of a venue site format, in which the living subject who toils and cares for the structure is effaced, another piece in the performative puzzle, and another play on medical framing as framing.

Likewise, on *Uterine Concert Hall*'s website, under the auspices of posting monthly "renovations" updates, McLeod publicly tracks her menstrual cycle. Sometimes McLeod's uterus is a space renovating itself according to its own rhythm, an agent setting its own schedule, despite McLeod's curatorial ownership. Nonetheless, she incorporates the monthly disruption into her discursive aesthetics, folding her periods into the venue website format. She writes, in May's update, "Ugh. Can't say May renovations were particularly fun. We tried to re-stage that scene from *The Shining*, but only managed to lay on the floor and moan." Here, menses is distinctively unmedical and personal. And while McLeod delivers her period news informationally, she also gives the reader plenty of vivid sensory reference. Her period has something of the spectacular blood flood from *The Shining* about it, and also the banal but visceral cramps and pressures that cause people who menstruate to lie around and moan every twenty-eight days or so. I can't help but think of the Salpêtrière doctors tracking hysterics' cycles, writing down any details that might fall under measurement, but also making special note that Augustine ran away from her room most often during these menstrual days, into the garden, into the night rain. They recorded her dreams at these times – slaughterhouses running with blood, red eyes. The private and visually poetic experiences of menstruation are casually and methodically relayed in each instance, though McLeod's communication is distinctly self-conscious in her deft use of tone.

Against instrumentality, against information, against medical gazes that suppose they know what a uterus can do, against the material factness of the physiological body, McLeod is both the instrument and the sonic event. She makes festival happen at the anatomical site of so much debate, disarming medical and moral discourses on the uterus, using hers so creatively that she confounds spectators and listeners, delightfully.

LEARNING FROM INDIGENOUS PERFORMANCE
Listening for Unexpected Sounds, Being Seen Seeing

As I contemporize and localize this research on nineteenth century French hysterical young women, and reflect on which young women and non-binary folks are most marginalized in Canadian contexts, thinking about who it is who is most fiercely resisting their erasure from or misogynist representation within dominant narratives, I of course think of Indigenous women and Two Spirit people, and Indigenous artists in particular. I cannot write about current and local acts of crying out and defiance by women against hegemonic violence and encoded hatred without writing about Indigenous performers.

Sam McKegney writes, citing an anonymous residential school survivor: "My story is a gift. If I give you a gift and you accept the gift, then you don't go and throw that gift in the waste basket. You do something with it."[23] In 2015, the Truth and Reconciliation Commission Report announced that Canada had been responsible for the deaths up to 6,000 Indigenous children in residential schools. The same report called for a national inquiry, in consultation with Aboriginal organizations, into "the causes of, and remedies for, the disproportionate victimization of Aboriginal women and girls," including an investigation into their murders, which completed in 2019.[24] In 2018, the federal government, following a legacy of environmental racism that disproportionately affects Indigenous women, purchased the Kinder Morgan pipeline that Indigenous communities, living on the land the pipeline proposes to occupy, oppose. The RCMP, at this moment, has explicit directives to use violence against women and children in Wet'suwet'en territory as it works to ensure the building of TransCanada fossil fuels infrastructure despite Supreme Court rulings.[25] Just short of one hundred Indigenous communities are without clean water with 137 drinking water advisories ongoing, despite Trudeau's promise to provide clean drinking water to all reserve communities by 2021.[26] These are affronts to human dignity, the kinds of violations of personhood and sovereignties that lead to youth suicide and mental health crisis. Ktunaxa poet Smokii Sumac calls this "the edge of the world too sharp."[27] These are some of the facts and stories we live amongst when we consider ourselves to be in a moment of reconciliation. These are facts and stories that require response.

Indigenous women are overrepresented in prison populations, more likely than white women and men to live on reserves without clean water or adequate housing, more likely to disappear, to be harmed by strangers, to be murdered without their perpetrators being caught or investigated. They have historically been institutionalized in large numbers and continue to be forcibly sterilized, the racist medical principles of who gets to count as a person still too prevalent. Indigenous women art-makers are also forerunners of cultural resurgence from the heart and from the guts, taking part in the work of nurturing stories, traditions, histories and contemporary, nation-specific, Indigenous becoming. They are producing "extraordinary growls, hums and whoops that seem to come from deeper within the human body than anyone else can reach," like Nunavut-born throat singer, Tanya Tagaq.[28] They dance and scream grief and defiance, like Anishinaabe ambassador Sarain Carson Fox dancing with mixed-ancestry Cree musician Chris Derksen in "The Missing," at Harbourfront Theatre or for the Basement Review.[29] They belt out vocables that rally us, like Buffy Sainte-Marie (Cree). They jingle dance for healing. They pow wow outside the fairground sideshow.

Working on training my ear to listen for sounds from the spectacle that shatter complacency, I hear Rebecca Belmore screaming; I hear Trina Qaqqa, from Baker Lake, standing in Parliament, asking for settlers to give their ears, saying that it is time to listen. I see Monique Mojica weaving powerful stories that undo colonial medical gazes. And I ask myself what it is to witness with responsibility.

Telling true things: Open the house. Take up space. On 8 March 2017, on the occasion of International Women's Day, 338 young women, including seventy Indigenous women, filled the seats of the Canadian Parliamentary House of Assembly and shared their views about Canada's future. Though the purpose of the event, as stated by its initiators, Equal Voice, was to encourage young women to become political leaders, listening to the delegates' brief speeches indicates that the women present needed very little encouragement to become political or to lead. Their words were often rousing and wise, commanding and tearful, and they indicated clear paths for an ethical future.[30]

Teanna Aygadim Majagalee of Skeena Bulkley Valley described acts of violence against the land and against Indigenous women and insisted that unless Canada's citizens and governments take steps to protect and stand up for both, we are doomed to continue to harm the lands and waters that support us and the women who create life. She also asked us to imagine the next hundred years as years of revolution lead by women. She then said, emphatically, that Canadians must listen to Indigenous voices: "We are not at reconciliation yet. We're at truth-telling."[31] Part of the truth communicated here is that there is no feminist or conciliatory future without decolonization. Part of the truth is that before the work of repairing relationships can take place, settler and settler-state listening is required. It is time to shift our attention to experts other than the ones who have until now, been most audible.

On the same day, Trina Qaqqa, from Baker Lake, Nunavut, speaking about suicide in her community, asked, "Where our non-Indigenous allies?" She called on Canadian citizens to work with her community members and, "Most importantly, to listen to us."[32] According to these two women, who turned a "mock" parliamentary performance for girls into a public summons to listen, listening is a political act and an urgent responsibility in a time of crisis.

Finding the complete recording of the Daughters of the Vote speeches was difficult. In my web searching, a few soundbites came up easily enough, but no link to a full video of the event. YouTube offered recommended links to footage of Trudeau speaking after each woman delegate's three-minute speech finished playing, disrupting the thread of truth-telling. I had to navigate ParlVu's unintuitive search engines for some time before I could see and hear every young woman speak in one stream. Listening, often, takes work. And in the fast-paced world of social media, we move on quickly. But as the months pass, I have continued to wonder about these appeals to listen and how to respond to a call to be available to listen to difficult truth-telling. How do we respond? How do we become the kinds of spectators who don't just watch the show and leave the work in the theatre or on the screen? How do I listen well, knowing there is so much I don't yet understand, or can't, and that the volume of all that is being said outweighs the possibilities of me attending to it all? How do I respond to a call to listen by activating my listening?

There are artists teaching about what it is to responsibly witness.

No one screams like Ojibwe Anishinaabe artist Rebecca Belmore. When Belmore washes the street in East Vancouver and lights candles, she carves out a space and time for a crisis of impossible return.[33] She washes for a long time. She lights close to a hundred candles. The ritualized pace of setting the space for *Vigil* turns taking time into making space – and one wants to ask how any amount of washing or any number of candles could be enough to mark the lives and deaths of Indigenous women from the lower east side. In a moment where individual interpersonal encounter comes to stand in for broader political relations, Belmore reaches out to a man who presents as a white settler and gestures for him to help her continue to light the candles. This is an act of commemoration and mourning we are all implicated in, whether we decide to engage or not. The man begins to help with lighting and a sense that there is so much work to be done that no one person can do it, and that settler men need to find ways to participate in the work of healing rather than in harmful legacies of genocide becomes palpable.

Belmore then screams the names of missing and murdered Indigenous women from the neighbourhood, listed on her arms, written on her body in marker. She cries out. Silence. Another name, silence. Her unanswered cries signal the absence of the women she calls, but also their having existed, their names written indelibly into a history of systemic racist violence and also on our collective memory. She re-remembers them. Does not let them be disappeared, but also draws attention to their inability to call back, their permanent disappearance. The deferral of the reply is endless. There is no closure. Belmore takes to the street where systemic oppression of Indigenous women plays out, and activates the space with hard work, with sounds that ring like questions, address, cries, and assertions. "Sarah," "Helen," "Andrea" are laden calls.

In the second half of *Vigil*, Belmore nails her dress to a telephone pole and tears it off with her own counter-movements. Wrestling and tearing, she becomes the agent of her own struggle and her own nakedness. Her physical labour – the struggle is athletic – reads as an analogy for sexual and physical violence, and also as a eulogistic effortful body work for missing friends, sisters, aunties, daughters.

Monique Mojica (Guna/Rappahannock) comes from a long line of Indigenous women performers, a continuum of four generations that, as mentioned above, includes founding members of Spiderwoman Theatre, Gloria and Muriel Miguel, as well as sideshow performers who "played Indian" at the Golden City Amusement Park, a competitor to Coney Island. In her most recent play, *Izzie M: The Alchemy of Enfreakment*, Mojica explores personal, "refracted" memories and intergenerational somatic traces of her mother having played an enfreaked other in racist spectacles. She says, in an interview:

> I started to look at sideshow and freakshow because I knew that my mother had been in a sideshow as a child, and my family had performed in the sideshow ... So, I started to look at some of the rage, resistance, shame, that my mother carried, and that she had passed on. And where I carry my mother's shame, where I carry my mother's rage. My mother uses that word, "freak." She still says, "They're lookin' at me. They're lookin' at me like I'm a freak." So I started to dig, I started to really dig. The early investigations for this work began with Turtle Gals Performance Ensemble as part of *The Only Good Indian* ... And one of the books that I went into was a book called *Freak Show* by a man named Robert Bogdan. And there was a quote in that that said that 'the freak show ... is the pornography of disability.' That's the quote. And that really, really resonated with me. Because I realized that the sideshows and the ethnographic congresses and all of those exhibitions that happened the past 150 years and have morphed over and over again ... Like, you know, the Paris exhibition where the Eiffel Tower is built, and the St Louis World's Fair and the Chicago Exhibition, the Buffalo Exhi... all those exhibitions that were designed to hold up ... white civilization and progress. Our purposes in those exhibitions where we were on exhibit was to

> provide the contrast and the savagery. So that those exhibitions and congresses of strange peoples were the pornography of othering. And that pornographic gaze on my body was still really, really active. That titillation for being as I am, fully clothed, was still porn. So, I started to dig around in that. It's really uncomfortable in there ... And the character I created is loosely based on my great grandmother, but she's a character who disappears herself. [Long pause.][34]

Izzie M., the play Mojica speaks about, features a character who stumbles out of a train wreck into a sideshow after having been incarcerated at the Hiawatha Asylum for Insane Indians, a real-life institution created in by the US federal government in Canton, South Dakota in 1899.[35] In both scenarios, Izzie is a performer, first modelling the good, demure "civilized" behaviour of a "recovered" rebellious Indigenous woman socialized into serving tea for asylum guests and then playing an invisible woman who mixes potions to disappear herself from harmful spectator gazes. Drawing attention to the sedimentary history of racialization in the freakshow and internment in institutions, one of Izzie's tricks is to wrestle free of a strait-jacket, Houdini-style.

In *Izzie M.*, Mojica intelligently harnesses the gaze. Chocolate Woman Collective's advertisement for the show is a cheeky ventriloquization of the sideshow's bravado:

> Step right up and pay your dues to witness a performance that transmutes time: a barbaric banquet boasting aberrant bodies and dusky denizens from exotic cultures – ALIVE!! Hurry! Hurry! Hurry!
>
> Behold the wonders of Injun rarities Monique Mojica (Guna and Rappahannock) and Barry Bilinsky (Metis/Cree), for a limited performance run. The spectacle will be held at the b current Performing Arts Co. in Wychwood Barns at 601 Christie Street for your amusement, July 13–22, 2018 at 8PM with blankaroo nights (PWYC) on July 15 and July 18 at 2PM.[36]

Audience members are invited into the theatre from the waiting area to gawk at the play by a fairground barker/talker (Barry Bilinsky) on stilts. Audience members are situated in the position of sideshow audience members and asked to grapple with what this means. As the press release for the play reads, "This juxtaposition between structure and story highlights the tension between Indigenous *hyper-visibility* – "Indians" marked as freaks and exotics – and our *invisibility*: a deliberate concealment and erasure of the evidence that marks our sustained presence on the landscape. Indigenous peoples, like the presence of the effigy mounds and earthworks, are 'hidden in plain sight.'"[37]

While we are promised a spectacle to satiate the hungriest of gazes, *Izzie M.* offers many moments where we find our viewing capacities destabilized, defamiliarized and open to critical reflection. The play is layered with spectres, Geronimo's ghost appearing in a pantry cupboard, the speaking land and a Metis giant, for instance, so that what is visible is not guaranteed. Seemingly domestic jars on display to the audience at all times, we find out, contain the materials needed for alchemy. Izzie might see the world from her childhood perspective, on all fours under the table at one moment, and then through the eyes of Corn Mother, from old, old stories, at another. Characters, materials, surfaces, and temporalities shift and weave continually in the performance. The masters of the spectacle of *Izzie M.* titillate and control the audience gaze at once.

In one scene that echoes memories held deep in the body, even generations later, Mojica lifts her apron to hold a projection of the Hiawatha asylum on her body while she half disappears under its image. I can't help but see this posture, where fists raise above Mojica's head, as strong, and the apron as a mirror held up to the audience to demonstrate a history in which we are all, as residents of Turtle Island, implicated. At the same time, Mojica is shielded from the violent architecture. She holds up the story, but is not subsumed by it, in this moment where the corporeal and the spectral blend to amplify Indigenous resilience in this all-too-real history of interned Indigenous people.

It is the final moment in the play in which the audience is asked to take responsibility for what it is that we see. In an unexpected temporal and technical flip, one that follows the language of ancestors in cupboards and the stuff of alchemy in pantry jars, Bilinsky and Mojica sit down to have a picnic. They open their turn-of-the-century picnic basket and take out movie popcorn, instantly recognizable by its red and white striped packaging. This familiar prop is anachronistically out of context and opens a critical moment of alienation. The houselights illuminate. The entire stage becomes a screen and contemporary footage of Indigenous land defenders

5.2 Monique Mojica in *The Strange Case of Izzie M.: The Alchemy of Enfreakment*, 2018. Mojica is holding up her apron like a screen and the "Indian Asylum" buildings are projected onto the apron and the backdrop on stage. The tea setting can be seen in the lower left of the photo.

from across the world plays like a looping news reel. Mojica and Bilinsky munch their popcorn and watch us watching powerful Indigenous resistance against land and resource extraction.

We are asked to evaluate how it is that we will respond, how it is that we will choose to watch this high-stakes spectacle playing out on the world stage. Under the gazes of the two performers, we could feel many things: judged, scolded, helpless, accused, withered. Instead, Bilinsky and Mojica begin to comment on the show we are giving them. "Beautiful, just beautiful," Mojica says. "Yes, look at that one," Bilinsky replies. While the performers watch us watching, they love us, audibly. They recognize our humanity and our potential to participate in this world meaningfully in a way that exactly opposes the othering stares of colonial hetero-patriarchal and psychiatric power. We are loved into responsibility. We experience, in this moment, what it is to be resourced by good faith in order to do the big, decolonizing, toppling work ahead. We experience a gaze that knows what it is to do harm and chooses to see differently.

To begin with hysteria and to end at love in an analysis of the history of gazes, after all, seems fitting. As I have followed the ethical possibilities of indeterminacy in performance, I have learned to lean into the contingency of not knowing because of who I am in relation. And giving space to the other while holding my own responsibility with great care – that is the kind of love I wish to see more of in world.

CONCLUSION

WHY I RETURN

Rosemarie Garland-Thomson writes, "Staring is a way of strongly reacting to another. It bespeaks involvement."[1] It is possible that I can't stop staring, that I have felt my gaze summoned and harnessed and have thus felt compelled to write this book. I return to engage and to be engaged by these women. I have, like artists sampling the *Iconographie* in performance, worked in the studio exploring how impossible it is to embody hysterical patients' experiences by replicating the *Iconographie* photographs in their poses, grimaces, and yawns. In 2011, I undertook a performance-based research project in which I tried to scream as closely as I could to Augustine's imagined scream. At the time, I was under the misconception that the anonymous show-stopping scream in 1888 came from Augustine. Why shouldn't the whole series of significant onstage moments be heaped upon the scaffolding of her figurative status? I thought I was screaming as proximately to Augustine's cry as possible while indicating the thickness of that space between us. I had the wrong girl. Performance thickens. I had promised myself to never make a performance iteration of a hysterical teenager's suffering because such a project seemed, at the time, exploitative and perverse, given the circumstances of her violation via spectacular dissemination. Presented with the task of researching through performance though, I determined to fail, and to revel in failing to represent Augustine's singular pain. I challenged the limits of my unknowing by mimicking, as precisely as possible, the still images of her photographed distresses and caresses. With a collection of photos from the *Iconographie*, including many of those in this book, I visited the dance studio and wrote foreign gestures into my tissues. The process was influential. After clenching, tightening, winding my body into postures of resistance, I let myself melt into one of Augustine's gentle self-embraces. The relief was palpable and infinitely far from the woman in the archive.

And here is this book. I am still not entirely comfortable with how this research and writing project slips between the figurative and the particular. My own interest is perplexing to me, and my feeling about the importance of not forgetting these young women, their experiences and their figurations also persists. Strategies I have found for writing through/against the paralysis that at times struck and maybe ought to occur with such an undertaking have been to try to write my own unknowing, and to demonstrate the personal nature of pain as well as the value of failing to grasp another's suffering or defiance while expressing– urgently – the importance of regarding the pain of others. One of the biggest motivations for continuing this work has been to overturn representations of the hysteric as solely a puppeted, voiceless object and violated subject. These narratives trouble me. This book is, in some ways, the product of following a hunch that teenage girls and young French women coming from conditions of poverty likely kicked up some resistance against that egomaniacal doctor, about whom enough historical biographies have been written. Also: I have leaned into the truths of theoretical and performance texts as much as more "conventional" forms of evidence. I have engaged in playful bricolage. Trusted bodies to contain valuable knowledge. Tried to listen backwards, and to offer some ideas – in the end, a series of dramaturgical renderings – as a cultural object in dialogue with the history of hysteria, steeped in its own field of academic interpretation. I have chosen to contribute to a collage of voices, rather than claiming identification or truth. In short, to not overestimate or underestimate the power and function of my own research. As an author, I believe in accountability, but I also agree with Barthes – that I am not the one who has the last word. The iterative force of the work, out in the small world of its readership, will shift its meanings. Hopefully its weak places will give and its contributions will replicate in reading. I wrote this when I was reading certain books, primary medical literature sources, and cultural histories of hysteria, and as I transitioned from what I now view as a colonial and paternalistic educational framework into the bright and necessary world of Indigenous Feminisms, with Disability and Queer Studies at my side. And so, there are contemporary voices that are missing here. Thinking of releasing this book into the world, part of me wants to holler: Just read Petra Kuppers! Listen to Derek Newman-Stille's poetry! Just look at James Luna performing! And then you will have what you need! But you wouldn't have this book. And so I send this out, saying also read Petra Kuppers and also study James Luna if you want more of the stuff that teaches us to be in relation with bodies and knowledges and one another.

Foucault had a whole crisis about authorship, at first wanting to efface himself to avoid perpetrating vanity, then – whoops! – realizing that unless he was personally accountable for his thoughts and his stakes in his study, he was actually practising a compromising evasion. I come to the study of hysteria with a set of hunches and ideas. Among them: there is often strength hidden in places conventionally perceived as weak. Performance is a site where expression and privacy can play along the edge of the ethical. People who think they know everything probably don't see anything very clearly. Dogmatism is both dangerous and incomplete. French teenagers had more going on than narratives of ventriloquism convey. We can get better at being in the world together.

How to look carefully at the archive but never claim to have avoided interpretation? The hysteric speaks to me partly because of what I hope to hear.

In spending time with the documented existence of the Salpêtrière hysterics, I have found so much that is worth attention. Photographic subterfuge, poetic language, layered temporalities, harmful misogynist and triumphant feminist fantasies, failed hypnosis experiments, theatrical indulgence, embellished and distended femininities. Hysterics have taught me a flush of modes of resistance, dramaturgical strategies. Researching the hysteric has made me a better feminist. Yet, the discomfort persists: is celebration at all an ethical response to attention to public coercion and harm?

Following my own admiration for the power of her story told in a lexicon that crosses up straightforward transmission, I come to believe in the power of interminable questions, inarticulate representation of the inexpressible, and troubled signification as a potent reflection of lived experience. Expressionistic gestures, the complicated nature of encounter, unexpected and interrupted intimacy, an ethics of personhood – these and outrage at positivist, misogynist violence, and interest in resilience glimmering from within suffering – have made writing this and responding to it something I have wanted to do.

Perhaps most of all, the hysteric, or the person I have imagined her to be, has moved me. I have continued to return to her because I am captivated by her in many ways. The nature of our encounter is complicated. Reciprocity is a difficult, and maybe an impossible word when dealing with an evasive historical subject, a person who is no longer here to respond. I presume, offer best guesses, read from my biased proclivities. But there is enough life in the historical documents that I assert that, in the archive, the hysteric is speaking too. I can't make out her meaning, can't get it right, but I keep going back to listen. I am really interested in *that*. In being summoned to respond.

MANIACAL LAUGHTER, BUTTONING UP THE BOOT, AND SENSATE FEMINISMS

In the middle of a lecture on hysteria and nineteenth century scientific discourses on femininity in a first-year gender studies class this year, I stepped out from behind the lectern to act out the scene written about in chapter 2 of this book, wherein the young woman, Valérie Durand, was arrested for buttoning her boot in public. As I stood up after miming this punishable act for emphasis, I found myself, as sometimes happens when mocking patriarchal perspectives from the past, unsettled by how steeped students, seminar leaders and I are, at our present moment, in a culture of sexual shame, harmful binaried perspectives, subjugating relationship structures, and gendered violence at the level of political policy, media, and lived daily relationships. Appalling in its "pastness," the nineteenth century is not so remote. I have said that studying hysteria has made me a better feminist. It is partly by spending so much time studying epistemologies of disenfranchisement in the past that I am able to attend to present instances of knowledge and power working against women, non-binary, trans, Two Spirit, and queer people, and people living with disabilities and mental health struggles. Studying medicine's entanglements with cultural production, hegemonic viewpoints and social change has made me a keen critic of those who claim authority and expertise. I also teach a course on how feminist psychiatrists have worked to overturn diagnoses in the DSM that were historically used to acquit men of rape, how ethnographic studies have shown that psychiatric institutions are dehumanizing spaces where the worst kinds of listening happen, and how women and genderqueer folks again and again assert that mental illness and psychological distress are results of classist, racist, sexist, transphobic societal systems that prevent them from living their lives well-resourced and within structures of care. In this course, we brainstorm how we might create more reciprocity and more open communication within caregiving professions and within the disciplines of medicine, psychiatry, and psychology. We study queer, feminist, anti-capitalist, and decolonial ideas that offer modes of relating that encourage ethics of respect and interdependency. We also study the histories of hysteria, looking for overlaps between antiquated but familiar systems of knowledge acquisition and professional, endlessly professing expertise, which is also, in the case of Charcot and his team of physicians, assault. Women diagnosed as hysterical in the past – Dora, Augustine, Blanche – teach us to question how we relate to one another in the academy, in medical and care professions and in the social world. With their help, we become more woke. We wake up. We attempt new kinds of listening. We get angry.

I live in a world where my perspective is illuminated by hystory.

As stand-up comedian Jenny Slate writes, deceptively simply, "I was born into a world where many men want to oppress all of the women with violence and laws and you or I can't say anything else anymore without also admitting that."[2] In Slate's stand-up comedy Netflix special, *Stage Fright*, she screams, screeches, lurches, enacts teenage orgasm, mimes youthful terror, and offers a physical performance that indulges in comedic over-the-top theatrics as she maintains honest dialogue about her anxieties and vulnerabilities. In the show, Slate moves between filmed footage of her childhood home and family, and her filmed live stand-up performance. Reflecting on growing up, being in therapy, and moving on from a recent divorce, Slate self-deprecatingly and self-lovingly gyrates the audience through youthful memories and impressions about adult sexuality. In her teenage bedroom, Slate takes us to her closet, where she unearths a box of scraps of paper. The underside of the box cover reads,

"This is a box of things that make me mad … I think it's ok if this box gets filled up. It's ok to be pissed off." Some slips say things like, "Bullshit" and "that I am horrified every other day." One reads, "Trevor."[3] Being angry at a boy who was her boyfriend, "for like a second" unfolds, in the stage performance, into a guttural, emotional, and corporeal reaction to misogynist sexual violence in 2019.[4] In the transcription below, I preserve the audio descriptions and closed captioning from the special as they contain valuable content without which there is an inadequate transmission of Slate's corporeal and tonal performance. I also include one observation of my own, in italics, a note on a revealingly garbled attempt to call this imaginary man "nice." The bit, which follows so many aesthetic tropes of hysteria with which we are by now familiar, is as follows:

> And I will say that for me it was very bizarre timing to, for the first time in my adulthood, like, literally to have a clear mind and be single, and lonely, and hoping for a new partner right when the #metoo movement dropped.
>
> Closed Captioning: [audience laughs]
>
> Just doesn't give you the best attitude about connecting with guys when you're just like, 'Wow, a lot of you have been *really* doing disgusting stuff and the rest of you were sort of complicit in this ancient, heinous thing.' And I would like, show up to like a 'coffee date' because I'm like afraid to meet anyone after dark and be like, 'Do you know?
>
> Audio description: [She gives an accusatory point]
>
> Do you get it?' Like, really, a guy would come up to me and be [*inarticulate, pressurized stammer*] nice and innocuous and say something like, 'Hey! I'm Trevor.' And you're just like, 'Hey Trevor. Do you think I'm a fucking sucker?
>
> Closed Captioning: [laughs maniacally]
>
> Audio Description: [Her fingers make a v-sign in front of her wagging tongue]
>
> Go sniff around someone else's stall, you bitch!'
>
> Closed captioning [audience laughs]
>
> Not great. Not great. Um …[5]

In the accusing pointing of her finger and the short but heavily posed questions, "do you know?" and "do you get it?" the legacies of misogynist entitlement groan and open like a chasm. The imaginary Trevor can't possibly account for it all and yet this is the context in which the encounter occurs. It is a deeply historied moment Trevor has entered. There is no moving outside it. Slate has written, in her book *Little Weirds*, that "Onstage and everywhere else, I know that there is so much that you could do to me. My vulnerability is natural and permissible and beautiful to me, and it should remind you of your responsibility to behave like a friend to me and the world."[6] Slate's description of dating in the midst of heightened suspicion and even fear of the structures, expectations, and possible breaches of consent involved in hetero-normative dating is powerful, delivered in the framework of live performance as a vulnerable summons to take responsibility for one another, and for Slate, specifically. She hyperbolically addresses the impossibility of assuming innocuousness in cis-gendered romantic encounters at a moment when sexual violence is foregrounded in popular discourse. So much of this violence has happened in professional domains. As theatre, performance, and film communities engage in discussions around sexual assault – *Canadian Theatre Review* just released its "Times Up" issue, featuring the documentary play by Ellie Moon about consent in the wake of the Ghomeshi trial – experiencing Slate's professional performance of rage at and defiance against the patriarchy, figured in the imagined (remembered, teenage?) Trevor expresses an intellectual, emotional, and sensorial terrain I inhabit as I try to live a feminist life in a paternalistic world that sits too uncomfortably close to the historical world I've studied.[7] I allow myself to ride Slate's rage and accusation because, as a woman, I already identify with her vulnerability. Her bewilderment about how to proceed in cis-hetero partnership in the midst of such a reckoning welcomes me, opens a place I already occupy and adds a chair for me to sit in, next to her, where many others are also sitting.

Sarah Ahmed describes feminism like this: "feminism: the releasing of a pressure valve."[8] As I complete this book and prepare to teach a course on sex, gender, and science, I read Ahmed, thinking through how arriving at feminism is data collection. Ahmed offers that to arrive to feminism is to reflect on the ways one has been affected by the world, the sensate and material experiences one has had that point to structures one finds oneself in with more awareness. As she says, "The personal is structural. I learned that you can be hit by a structure; you can be bruised by a structure. An individual man who violates you is given permission: that is structure."[9] Bodies gather knowledge about structures. Feminism puts us in the company of those who have gathered similar knowledges. And then, Ahmed writes, "Feminism can be empowering as a way of reinhabiting the past … Feminism, in giving you somewhere to go, allows you to revisit where you have been. We can become even more conscious of the world in this process of becoming conscious of injustices because we had been taught to overlook so much."[10]

We can do so much to and for one another. Our vulnerabilities are natural and permissible and beautiful. They remind us of our responsibilities to behave like friends to one another and the world. This is hystory.

Notes

INTRODUCTION

1 Silverman, *Art Nouveau in Fin-de-Siècle France*, 100.
2 Goetz, Bonduelle, and Gelfland, *Charcot*, 253.
3 Charcot, "Policlinique du Mardi 7 Février 1888," 75.
4 Sontag, *Illness as Metaphor*, 57.
5 Flanagan, "Hysteria and the Teenage Girl," 4.
6 Foucault, *Psychiatric Power*, 321.

CHAPTER ONE

1 See, for example, Richet, "Les démoniaques d'aujourd'hui," 340–72.
2 Didi-Huberman, *Invention of Hysteria*, 276.
3 Corbey, "Ethnographic Showcases," 338.
4 Clare, "Freaks and Queers," 150.
5 Corbey, "Ethnographic Showcases," 338.
6 Ibid., 341.
7 Ibid., 359.
8 Ibid., 345.
9 Mojica, *Manifesting Resistance*
10 Marquer, *Les romans de la Salpêtrière*, 48.
11 Kanani, "Race and Madness."
12 Qureshi, "Displaying Sara Baartman," 233.
13 Ibid., 234.
14 Moudileno, "Returning Remains," 202.
15 Ibid.
16 Clare, "Freaks and Queers," 150.
17 Kracauer, *From Caligari to Hitler*, 41.
18 In Kracauer's reading, *The Cabinet of Dr Caligari* was "a political parable of unchecked authoritarianism following the cataclysm of war." In the film, "Caligari stood for the state, while Cesare represented the sleepwalking masses who had been sent by the millions to kill and be killed" (Kracauer, *From Caligari to Hitler*, 41).
19 Charcot and Richer, *Les Démoniaques dans l'Art*, 61.
20 Guillain, *J.-M. Charcot*, 55.

21 Ibid.
22 Marquer, *Les romans de la Salpêtrière*, 121.
23 Michel Foucault, *Birth of the Clinic*, xii.
24 Ibid., vxiii–iv.
25 La grande hystérie is distinguishable from *petite hystérie* especially at the level of the convulsive and delirious attack with its distinct and regular phases. This attack is markedly absent from minor cases of hysteria, which may present other symptoms common to la grande hystérie, like contraction or paralysis of body parts, coughs, melancholia, etc. See Charcot, *Clinical Lectures*, 13.
26 Charcot and Richer, *Les Démoniaques dans l'Art*, 95.
27 Ibid.
28 Ibid., 97.
29 Thuillier, *Monsieur Charcot*, 29.
30 Charcot and Richer, *Les Démoniaques dans l'Art*, 97.
31 Ibid., 100.
32 Ibid.
33 Ibid., 102.
34 Ibid.
35 Ibid.
36 Ibid., 102–3.
37 Ibid., 105.
38 Ibid.
39 Axel Munthe, a bleeding-heart who broke from medicine to become a romantic author, tells a suspicious story of attempting to help a patient escape the hospital – by hypnotizing her. French historian Asti Hustvedt has investigated the credibility of his account, but can only verify its suspicious nature. See her *Medical Muses* for more on this, and read Munthe's account in *The Story of San Michel*.
40 Didi-Huberman, *Invention of Hysteria*, 8.
41 Bourneville and Régnard, *Iconographie photographique de la Salpêtrière*, 158.
42 Ibid., 133.
43 Ibid., 134.
44 Ibid., 146.
45 Didi-Huberman, *Invention of Hysteria*, 77.
46 Ibid., 18.
47 The grand rhetorical structure of Charcot's lectures can be read in most of the published materials on the topic and can be gleaned from the lectures themselves. I cite Didi-Huberman, using his summary description here, and stay close to him, citationally, because his *Invention of Hysteria* draws attention to the aesthetics of medical style, and it is there that I – and many scholars who published works after him, likely – first encountered any description of Charcot or the Salpêtrière hysterics. See Didi-Huberman, *Invention of Hysteria*, 8.
48 Didi-Huberman, *Invention of Hysteria*, 186.
49 Ibid., 192.
50 Ibid., 161.
51 Marquer, *Les romans de la Salpêtrière*, 128.

52 Didi-Huberman, *Invention of Hysteria*, 179.
53 Micale, *The Mind of Modernism*, 159.
54 For a history of modern works on faces, see Gunning's chapter in Micale's *The Mind of Modernism*.
55 Gunning, "In Your Face," 143.
56 Prodger, *Darwin's Camera*, 3.
57 Ibid., 13.
58 Ibid., 16.
59 Micale, *The Mind of Modernism*, 169.
60 Prodger, *Darwin's Camera*, 194–8.
61 Ibid., 147.
62 Simmel, *The Metropolis and Mental Life*, 89.
63 Ibid.
64 Ibid., 87–8.
65 Ibid., 88.
66 Didi-Huberman, *Invention of Hysteria*, 25.
67 Charcot, *Clinical Lectures*, 3.
68 Marquer, *Les romans de la Salpêtrière*, 122.
69 Londe, *La Photographie Médicale*, vii.
70 Ibid., vii–viii.
71 Ibid., 1–7.
72 Hiring Londe, a skilled experimental technician and artist, is evidence of the Salpêtrière's commitment to photography itself.
73 Londe, *La Photographie Médicale*, 447.
74 Charcot, *Clinical Lectures*, 5.
75 Silverman, *Art Nouveau*, 92.
76 Didi-Huberman, *Invention of Hysteria*, 22.
77 Ibid., 22.
78 Marquer, *Les romans de la Salpêtrière*, 82.
79 Freud, *Early Psychoanalytic Writings*, 14–15.
80 Charcot and Richer, *Les Démoniaques dans l'Art*, 117.
81 Thuillier, *Monsieur Charcot*, 55.
82 Dottin-Orsini, *Cette Femme qu'ils disent fatale*, 144.
83 Marquer, *Les romans de la Salpêtrière*, 41.
84 Thuillier, *Monsieur Charcot*, 124.
85 Didi-Huberman, *Invention of Hysteria*, 246.
86 Marquer, *Les romans de la Salpêtrière*, 115.
87 Ibid.
88 Ibid., 112.
89 Ibid., 87.
90 Bourneville and Régnard, *Iconographie photographique*, 87.
91 Ibid., 86.
92 Delboeuf, "Une Visite à la Salpêtrière," 139.
93 Charcot, *Clinical Lectures*, 7–8.
94 Ibid., 13.

95 Sontag, *Regarding the Pain of Others*, 81.
96 Marquer, *Les romans de la Salpêtrière*, 117.
97 Benjamin, "Work of Art," 220.
98 Londe, *La Photographie Médicale*, 90–4.
99 Barthes, *Camera Lucida*, 10–11.
100 Ibid., 6.
101 Ibid., 5–6.
102 Agamben, *Profanations*, 67.
103 Barthes, *Camera Lucida*, 5.
104 Ibid., 6.
105 Ibid., 28.
106 Ibid., 71.
107 Ibid., 65.
108 Ibid., 66.
109 Ibid.
110 Ibid., 26–7.
111 Ibid., 43–51.
112 Ibid., 43–5.
113 Weiss, *Phantasmic Radio*, 22.
114 Marquer, *Les romans de la Salpêtrière*, 112.
115 Ibid., 111.
116 Benjamin, "Work of Art," 223.
117 Freud, *Dora*, 57.
118 A discussion of hysterical symptomatology via Freud (and earlier, Janet) will be developed in later chapters.
119 For more on photography as evidence and the importance of photographic captions, see Benjamin, "Work of Art," 226.
120 Nancy, *Corpus*, 5. Nancy is writing specifically about the body of Christ, but also about all the bodies that make up the corpus of Western thought, including the body of the hysteric.
121 Rosenhan, "On Being Sane," 257.
122 Charcot and Richer, *Les Démoniaques dans l'Art*, 95.
123 Didi-Huberman, *Invention of Hysteria*, 106.
124 Ibid.
125 Barthes, *Camera Lucida*, 45.
126 Didi-Huberman, *Invention of Hysteria*, 160.
127 Ibid.
128 Benjamin, "Work of Art," 223.
129 Marquer, *Les romans de la Salpêtrière*, 114.
130 Didi-Huberman, *Invention of Hysteria*, 99.
131 Levinas, *Totality*, 194.
132 Ibid., 197.
133 Ibid., 198.
134 Levinas, *Humanism*, 32.

135 The face of the stranger summons me in its nakedness. The exposed face of the other is so vulnerable that I am at once capable of doing violence to it, even tempted to, and appealed to by the same face not to do so. And yet, even if I kill the other, Levinas says, I do not kill her otherness, I cannot kill the infinity that resists us in the face (Levinas, *Totality*, 199). Augustine's autonomy, despite the imagistic violence perpetrated against it, is relentless. The face of the other is not merely the face of a potential victim, but is the face that appeals to me *and* commands me, making me most vulnerable. In the appeal that can also be read as an imposition, my own dignity is at stake. "For Levinas, the dignity of the self arises in an unsurpassable moral responsibility to and for the other person" (Levinas, *Humanism*, xxviii).

136 Marquer, *Les romans de la Salpêtrière*, 118.

CHAPTER TWO

1 Didi-Huberman, *Invention of Hysteria*, 69.
2 Cixous and Clément, *The Newly Born Woman*, 7.
3 Freud and Breuer, "Charcot," 17–18.
4 Gilman, *Seeing the Insane*, 212.
5 Showalter, *The Female Malady*, 2.
6 Clark, *The Painting of Modern Life*, 133.
7 Didi-Huberman, *Invention of Hysteria*, 238.
8 Micale, *The Mind of Modernism*, 74.
9 Dottin-Orsini, *Cette femme qu'ils disent fatale*, 244.
10 Even though Showalter's *Female Malady* is on the topic of English Victorian representations of madness and femininity, she begins her text with a reading of the French painting by Pinel. The symbolic weight of this image floods national boundaries.
11 Aragon and Breton, "Le Cinquantenaire de l'hystérie," 1.
12 Dottin-Orsini, *Cette femme qu'ils disent fatale*, 243.
13 Clark, *The Painting of Modern Life*, 94.
14 Ibid., 132.
15 Ibid., 133.
16 Ibid., 85.
17 Ibid., 97.
18 Harris, "Melodrama," 58.
19 Homes and Tarr, *Belle Epoque*, 12.
20 Ibid., 12–13.
21 The Pancouke Medical Dictionary of the era describes woman's life as being constituted by the following stages: "Pre-puberty, puberty, post-intercourse, the state of pregnancy, the moment of giving birth, the post-natal period, the period of lactation, the end of menstruation, the post menopause." These phases of being all revolve, indicatively, around concepts of motherhood. By her very definition, woman was reproductive (Ripa 49). In Bruno's primer for children eleven to thirteen years old, the functions and the duties of women were explicit:

a woman's life was to be centred entirely on the household, where her role was to influence children, especially sons, to become morally exemplary adults (Offen, "Depopulation," 666). The potential for women's education to 'backfire,' despite its conservative aims, has been noted by Homes and Tarr in *Belle Epoque*: "The development of state education for women, designed to wean them away from the influence of the catholic church and to create a generation of good Republican mothers, also strengthened the social confidence and the intellectual armoury of women inclined to question the assumption of male supremacy" (Homes and Tarr, *Belle Epoque*, 12).

22 Harvey, *Paris*, 183.
23 Silverman, *Art Nouveau*, 71.
24 Offen, "Depopulation," 664.
25 Besnard, *Les prostitueés*, 79.
26 Offen, "Depopulation," 652.
27 Ibid., 652.
28 Ibid., 662.
29 Offen, "Liberty, Equality," 360.
30 Harvey, *Paris*, 183.
31 Ibid., 185.
32 Ibid.
33 Ibid., 183.
34 Ibid., 184–5.
35 Offen, "Depopulation," 669.
36 Harvey, *Paris*, 183.
37 Clark, *The Painting of Modern Life*, 35.
38 Schivelbusch, *The Railway Journey*, 191.
39 Homes and Tarr, *Belle Epoque*, 16.
40 Ibid., 85.
41 Harvey, *Paris*, 113.
42 For more on the micro-history of gaslighting, see Schivelbusch's *Disenchanted Night*.
43 Clark, *The Painting of Modern Life*, 212.
44 Ibid., 207–14.
45 Besnard, *Les prostitueés*, 108.
46 Schwartz, *Spectacular Realities*, 25.
47 Silverman, *Art Nouveau*, 63.
48 Offen, "Depopulation," 661.
49 Dottin-Orsini, *Cette femme qu'ils disent fatale*, 20.
50 Silverman, *Art Nouveau*, 70-1.
51 Thomas quoted in Harvey, *Paris*, 183.
52 Offen, "Depopulation," 657.
53 Besnard, *Les prostitueés*, 139.
54 Ibid., 108.
55 Ibid.
56 Ibid., 108–9.
57 Ripa, *Women and Madness*, 10.

58 Clark, *The Painting of Modern Life*, 105.
59 Besnard, *Les prostitueés*, 114.
60 Ibid.
61 Silverman, *Art Nouveau*, 63.
62 Besnard, *Les prostitueés*, 104–5.
63 Ibid., 105.
64 Ibid.
65 Many works have been written on the topic of what Dottin-Orsini calls "syphilophobie."
66 Apter, "The Garden of Scopic Perversion," 104.
67 Clark, *The Painting of Modern Life*, 104.
68 Besnard, *Les prostitueés*, 132.
69 Ibid.
70 Didi-Hubereman, *Invention of Hysteria*, 81.
71 Besnard, *Les prostitueés*, 66.
72 Ibid., 126-7.
73 Augustine herself may have been "traded" to her stepfather for sexual assault as well as domestic servitude in exchange for her mother's security. It was after her stepfather raped her that Augustine experienced hysterical symptoms of bleeding and paralysis. See Bourneville and Régnard, *Iconographie Photographique*, 124–8.
74 Besnard, *Les prostitueés*, 125.
75 Marquer, *Les romans de la Salpêtrière*, 266.
76 Dottin-Orsini, *Cette femme qu'ils disent fatale*, 29.
77 Ibid.
78 Ibid.
79 Silverman, *Art Nouveau*, 72.
80 Benjamin, *The Arcades Project*, 501.
81 Marquer, *Les romans de la Salpêtrière*, 27.
82 Ibid.
83 Thuillier, *Monsieur Charcot*, 155.
84 Claretie, *La vie à Paris*, 135.
85 Ripa, *Women and Madness*, 116.
86 Doerner, *Madmen and the Bourgeoisie*, 137.
87 Didi-Huberman, *Invention of Hysteria*, 91.
88 Scarry, *The Body in Pain*, 53.
89 Marquer, *Les romans de la Salpêtrière*, 143.
90 Richet, "Les démoniaques d'aujourd'hui," 353.
91 Ibid.
92 Ibid., 354.
93 "Les spectacles effrayants et tristes qu'offrent les patients pendant les crises" (the horrifying and sad spectacles that the patients offer during an attack) (Charcot and Richer, *Démoniaques dans l'Art*, vi).
94 Cixous and Clément, *The Newly Born Woman*, 8.
95 Didi-Huberman, *Invention of Hysteria*, 72.
96 Ibid., 68.

97 Ibid., 69.
98 Richet, "Les démoniaques d'aujourd'hui," 345.
99 Delboeuf, "Une Visite à la Salpêtrière," 125, 258.
100 Foucault, *Discipline and Punish*, 57.
101 Thuillier, *Monsieur Charcot*, 229.
102 Goetz, Bonduelle, and Gelfland, *Charcot*, 235.
103 See the transcripts of Charcot's lectures and Marquer (91) for more examples of inclusive language that links the audience to Charcot and not the patient.
104 Micale, *Approaching Hysteria*, 74.
105 Goetz, Bonduelle, and Gelfland, *Charcot*, 238.
106 Renooz, "Charcot Dévoilé," 245.
107 Charcot and Richer, *Les démoniaques dans l'art*, 55, 61, 63.
108 Ibid., 61.
109 Marquer, *Les romans de la Salpêtrière*, 99.
110 Richet, "Les démoniaques d'aujourd'hui," 345.
111 Dottin-Orsini, *Cette femme qu'ils disent fatale*, 234.
112 Restorative nostalgia, which tried to reconstruct the past without recognizing that the past has shifted, indicatively doesn't think of itself as nostalgia, but rather as "truth and tradition" (Boym, *The Future of Nostalgia*, xviii).
113 Scarry, *The Body in Pain*, 28.
114 Delboeuf, "Une Visite à la Salpêtrière," 270.
115 Ibid., 125.
116 Ibid., 121.
117 Richet, "Les démoniaques d'aujourd'hui," 152.
118 Offen, "Depopulation," 662.
119 Delboeuf, "Une Visite à la Salpêtrière," 135.
120 Scarry, *The Body in Pain*, 28.
121 For more on dreams as wish-fulfillment and the function of manifest content to carry latent content, which is always a wish, see Freud, *The Interpretation of Dreams*, especially chapters 3–5.
122 Delboeuf, "Une Visite à la Salpêtrière," 133.
123 Ibid., 134.
124 Comparisons of the hysteric to a doll, wax figure, automaton, and wooden artist's mannequin are cited at length in Marquer 147–8. The patient's reception as doll and puppet will be further explored in chapter 3.
125 Delboeuf, "Une Visite à la Salpêtrière," 264–5.
126 Ibid., 264.
127 Ibid., 265.
128 Scarry, *The Body in Pain*, 51.
129 Ibid., 58.
130 Richet complains of women hurting themselves and blaming the doctors. According to him, some women cut themselves with scissors and pretended that the doctors gave them cuts. Delboeuf's anger is about the women hurting themselves, in private, and blaming the doctors in a private theatre of their own. For he has

no complaint that doctors *actually hurt patients all the time*. In fact, the hysterics' self-harm can be read as an aim to control the pain they experience or as a way of "making sense" of their experiences of pain by giving themselves wounds and associating the doctors with the production of those wounds (Delboeuf, "Une Visite à la Salpêtrière," 355–6).

131 Delboeuf, "Une Visite à la Salpêtrière," 139.
132 Ibid.
133 Ibid., 130.
134 Richet, "Les démoniaques d'aujourd'hui," 348.
135 Ibid., 352.
136 Scarry, *The Body in Pain*, 27.
137 Richet, "Les démoniaques d'aujourd'hui," 347.
138 Richer cited in Richet, "Les démoniaques d'aujourd'hui," 352.
139 Delboeuf, "Une Visite à la Salpêtrière," 268.
140 Baudouin, "Quelques Souvenirs," x–xiii.
141 Boym, *The Future of Nostalgia*, xiii.
142 See, for instance, Freud's early work on hysteria with Breuer in *Studies on Hysteria* or in *Interpretation of Dreams* or in the case analysis of *Dora*.
143 Scarry, *The Body in Pain*, 18.
144 Cixous and Clément, *The Newly Born Woman*, 6.
145 Ibid., ix.
146 Ibid., 5.
147 Ibid., 7.
148 In 1983, Jean Louis Signoret, a former Salpêtrière neurologist, identified each audience member (Micale, *Approaching Hysteria*, 195).

CHAPTER THREE

1 Marshall, "Dynamic Medicine," 143.
2 Ibid., 144–5.
3 Ibid., 144.
4 Ibid., 145.
5 Ibid., 143.
6 Guillain, *J-M. Charcot*, 144.
7 Ibid.
8 Habermas, *Knowledge and Human Interests*, 69.
9 One need only look to Derrida's corpus, which intends to derail writing from its logocentric position. According to the work of Barthes, McRobbie, and many others, more than a century after positivism's heyday, writers of all kinds are still under its tyranny.
10 Irigaray, *To Speak*, 1.
11 Ibid.
12 Ibid.
13 Ibid., 2.

14 Ibid., 1.
15 It is also a misrepresentation of the pivotal spirit of scientific inquiry, wherein real people conduct real studies into real things. Accountability of the researcher is integral to research work.
16 Irigaray, *To Speak*, 2.
17 Canadian Psychiatric Association and the Schizophrenia Society of Canada, *Schizophrenia*, 1.
18 Ibid.
19 Irigaray especially has published valuable and attentive work on schizophrenia and language. Also see Abse and Wegener and Schreber.
20 This questionable assertion will be explored at length in chapter 4.
21 Habermas, *Knowledge*, 67.
22 Irigaray, *To Speak*, 2.
23 Wernick, *Auguste Comte*, 4.
24 American Psychiatric Association, *Diagnostic and Statistical Manual*, xiii.
25 See, for instance, Lafrance and McKenzie-Mohr, "The DSM and Its Lure of Legitimacy" in a special issue of *Feminism and Psychology*, "DSM and Beyond," and Dodd, "The Name Game" in *History of Psychology*. For an example of the Canadian Psychiatric Association's disturbing claims to language and discursive power, see, for instance, Canadian Psychiatric Association and the Schizophrenia Society of Canada's *Schizophrenia*.
26 Marshall, "Dynamic Medicine," 144.
27 Scarry, *The Body in Pain*, 58.
28 Modern France seems to have been immersed in cultural works around dolls. From mannequins in arcade shop windows to the display of "living dolls" with mechanical lungs to mimic human breath to depictions of dolls come to life or dangerous automatons in literature, French culture in the nineteenth century appears to have been teeming with dolls. For a closer look at the trope of the living doll in French modernism, see Dottin-Orsini.
29 Marquer, *Les romans de la Salpêtrière*, 141.
30 Ibid., 148.
31 Ibid., 141.
32 Ibid., 147.
33 Claretie, *La vie à Paris*, 148.
34 Delboeuf, "Une visite à la Salpêtrière," 133.
35 Foucault, *Madness and Civilization*, x–xi.
36 Lyotard, *The Differend*, 5.
37 Bourneville and Régnard, *Iconographie photographique*, 150.
38 Ibid., 195–6.
39 Lyotard, *The Differend*, 10.
40 Bourneville and Régnard, *Iconographie photographique*, 135.
41 Ibid., 158.
42 Ibid., 148.
43 Ibid., 150.
44 Ibid., 142.

45 Ibid., 138.
46 Ibid., 132.
47 Abse and Wegener, *Speech and Reason*, 25.
48 Bourneville and Régnard, *Iconographie photographique*, 158.
49 Ibid., 148.
50 Ibid., 138.
51 Ibid., 144.
52 Ibid., 128.
53 Ibid., 146.
54 Ibid.
55 Ibid., 127.
56 Ibid., 140.
57 Ibid., 154.
58 Weiss, *Aesthetics of Excess*, 118.
59 Bataille, *Theory of Religion*, 72.
60 Irigaray, *To Speak*, 44.
61 Irigaray's studies of how people with diagnosed mental pathologies make use of language may seem an ironic project, given her suspicion of objectivity – in some ways, such a project carries traces of Charcot's project of descriptive rationalism. However, Irigaray's attention to the particular grammar of the hysteric, as compared to, for example, that of schizophrenics or obsessives, while it applies a codified canonical system of marking grammatical structures to utterances one wants to leave open, is attentive and explorative in its use of grammar. Irigaray does not aim to wedge hysterical speech into grammar's structure. Rather, she measures hysterical speech against grammar, looking for the ways the hysterical subject makes use of grammar to express herself.
62 Irigaray, *To Speak*, 45.
63 Ibid.
64 "Adverbials of time most often express an attempt at orientation on the part of the subject with respect to the temporal co-ordinates of (you), notably the moment of his or her speech: quand vous me dites au revoir; avant de vous rencontrer; avant que vous me parliez [when you said goodbye to me; before knowing you; before you spoke to me]" (Irigaray, *To Speak*, 48–9).
65 Grosz, *Volatile Bodies*, xi.
66 The citation continues, "Moreover, this is what Valéry sensed, marking his Young Fate in search of herself with ambiguity, masculine in her jealousy of herself: 'seeing herself see herself,' the motto of all phallocentric speculation/specularization, the motto of every Teste; and feminine in the frantic descent deeper deeper to where a voice that doesn't know itself is lost in the sea's churning" (Cixous and Clément, *The Newly Born Woman*, 94).
67 Irigaray, *To Speak*, 47.
68 Bourneville and Régnard, *Iconographie photographique*, 162.
69 Cixous and Clément, *The Newly Born Woman*, 86.
70 Charcot, *Policlinique*, 174.
71 Ibid., 175.

72 Ibid.
73 Ibid.
74 Ibid., 176.
75 Ibid.
76 Ibid.
77 Ibid.
78 Didi-Huberman, *Invention of Hysteria*, 259.
79 Borrowing from Bataille, for whom stammering in response to the Intimate has "uncommon force" (*Theory of Religion*, 96).
80 Bourneville and Régnard, *Iconographie photographique*, 105.
81 Ibid., 100.
82 Ibid., 30.
83 Ibid., 17.
84 Ibid., 102.
85 Ibid.
86 Certain cries, especially involuntary cries in a hysterical attack, are permissible since they fall under the rubric of explanation; cries the physicians read as voluntary are equated with bad behaviour and the melodramatic tendencies of hysterics. The emotions communicated via cries in the hysterical attack have a neurological but not an experiential reason. Outside of an attack, the hysteric has no reason to scream.
87 Even if the cry was involuntary, and this is unknowable, its untimely occurrence provoked Charcot to annoyance. In fact, the voluntary/involuntary nature of the cry, given what we know about the entangled nature of performance and life, is nearly impossible to determine.
88 Even if we abandon the tempting vanity of being right, how do we learn from the hysteric, who was delivered to the public as the most familiar stranger, without performing the conditions of the original intrigue around her personality? My hope is that by aiming to read the patient's cry the limits of legibility will show themselves, making clarity, naming and conclusion impossible. Though I cannot make sense of the cry, I cannot help but sense its potential for rebellion.
89 Cage, *Silence*, 109.
90 Levinas, *Humanism*, 32.
91 Buber, *The Prophetic Faith*, 28. Buber maintains that at the origin of the name YHVH is not a word that meant once "of divine nature" or "inhabitant of the mountains," as is commonly conceived, but rather a primal sound, an old "tabu-word," "god-cry" or "stammer" (Ibid., 37). Like Otto, Buber believes that monotheistic prayer is a more evolved form of what was once a crude and unrefined early religious sentiment that was expressly tied to an inarticulate sound.
92 Heller-Roazen, *Echolalias*, 18.
93 Seuphor, *Le Style et le Cri*, 251.
94 Ibid., 245.
95 Interest in the force of the human cry caused Edvard Munch, famously, to paint *The Scream* – a painting so popular that it appears on twenty-first century coffee mugs. In somewhat less well-known examples, the aural potency of crying out was

the seed of Austrian and German Expressionism's *schrei* performances and moved World War I field hospital veteran Alfred Wolfsohn to develop a scream-singing style based on the cries of his injured comrades that is still studied in France today (For more on Alfred Wolfsohn, see Centre artistique international Roy Hart, "Alfred Wolfsohn," available at https://web.archive.org/web/20161017171632/http://www.roy-hart-theatre.com/site/alfred-wolfsohn. For more on schrei acting, see Kuhns's *German Expressionist Theatre: The Actor and the Stage*). The nineteenth and twentieth-century avant-garde is marked indelibly by the human cry. Canonical literature around the cry markedly absents women and gender non-conforming scholars and theorists, among whom I would place the French teenage hysterical performer, who understood what it meant to cry out, profoundly so.

96 Saussure, *Course in General Linguistics*, 14, 18–19.
97 Weiss, "Ten Theses on Monsters," 125.
98 Ibid.
99 Artaud, *The Theatre and Its Double*, 89.
100 Ibid., 46.
101 Cage, *Silence*, 46.
102 Cixous and Clément, *The Newly Born Woman*, 94.
103 Charcot and Richer, *La Foi qui Guérit*, 117.
104 Habermas, *Knowledge*, 69.
105 Lyotard, *The Differend*, 22.
106 Weiss, "Ten Theses on Monsters," 125.

CHAPTER FOUR

1 Goetz, Bonduelle, and Gelfland, *Charcot*, 40.
2 See Mirbeau, Furse, even Dottin-Orsini and Didi-Huberman for examples of the hysteric portrayed as an objectified victim.
3 "Magnitudes of Performance" is used here after Schechner in "Magnitudes of Performance" in *By Means of Performance*.
4 Showalter, *The Female Malady*, 274.
5 Thuillier, *Monsieur Charcot*, 218.
6 Marquer, *Les romans de la Salpêtrière*, 41.
7 Bonduelle and Gelfland. "Hysteria behind the Scenes," 37.
8 Ibid., 39.
9 Thuillier, *Monsieur Charcot*, 117.
10 Charcot, *Clinical Lectures*, 14–17.
11 Ibid., 18.
12 For an excellent analysis of American hysteria, see Smith-Rosenberg's "The Hysterical Woman."
13 Noel Evans, *Fits and Starts*, 6.
14 Freud, *Dora*, 57.
15 Ibid., 56.
16 And his wife, Frau K, and her father. And her aggressive ambivalences towards these figures as well, of course.

17 Freud wrote *Dora* staying true to the content of the analysis, but shifting the order of the emergence of information and interpretation. The unveiling of Dora's symptomatology was gradual and fragmentary – out of order (24).
18 Freud, *Dora*, 123. One of the rare connections between Charcot and Freud's understandings of hysteria is in the indirect presentation of the physical symptom. Charcot's diagnosis of this feature is much simpler than Freud's, but it is important to note that Charcot, too, was dealing with a "lying" body, that signified away from the neurological lesion that was at fault for the simulating body.
19 Charcot, *Clinical Lectures*, xli.
20 Ibid., 14.
21 Ibid., 13.
22 Marquer, *Les romans de la Salpêtrière*, 152.
23 Apter, "The Garden of Scopic Perversion," 92.
24 See Delboeuf for a full account of just a few days of experiments and their many tricks of sight.
25 Thuillier, *Monsieur Charcot*, 124.
26 Interestingly, theatricality carries over to contemporary diagnoses of hysteria, although the arc-de-cercle does not. Hysterical personality, has been defined by the DSM (II) as being "characterized by excitability, emotional instability, over-reactivity, and self-dramatization." Also in the DSM II, the hysteric is described as being "attention-seeking, seductive, immature, self-centered, vain and dependent" (Agras, Kimble, and Williams, "A Comparison," 1198).
27 Unless you are Anaïs Nin. Full transcription of this anecdote appears later in the chapter.
28 Charcot and Richer, *Les démoniaques dans l'art*, 102.
29 Ibid., 95.
30 Stokes, Booth, and Bassnett, *Bernhardt*, 2.
31 Marquer, *Les romans de la Salpêtrière*, 130.
32 Noel Evans, *Fits and Starts*, 31.
33 Richet, "Les démoniaques d'aujourd'hui," 354.
34 Charcot, *Clinical Lectures*, 14–15.
35 Richet, "Les démoniaques d'aujourd'hui," 343.
36 Ibid., 352.
37 Bourneville and Régnard, *Iconographie photographique*, 190.
38 Marquer, *Les romans de la Salpêtrière*, 129.
39 Goetz, Bonduelle, and Gelfland, *Charcot*, 266.
40 Diderot wrote the above not about hysterics but about women in *Sur les femmes* (1875). More work could be done on the relationship between women, imagination, and hysteria. For instance, Bourneville and Régnard wrote that if hysterics read novels, they were eminently more hypnotizable than those who did not (Noel Evans, *Fits and Starts*, 42). A hefty body of literature has emerged on the topic of feminist writing or feminist creativity and madness or hysteria already. See, for instance, Bernheimer and Kahane's *In Dora's Case*; Felman's *Writing and Madness*; Gilbert and Gubar's *Madwoman in the Attic*; and Hunter's "Hysteria, Psychoanalysis and Feminism."

41 Beizer, *Ventriloquized Bodies*, 72.
42 Richet cited in Beizer, *Ventriloquized Bodies*, 43.
43 Finn, *Hysteria, Hypnosis*, 79.
44 Richet, "Les démoniaques d'aujourd'hui," 344.
45 Ibid.
46 Harris, "Melodrama," 31.
47 Ibid., 45.
48 Ibid., 53.
49 Thuillier, *Monsieur Charcot*, 227.
50 Actually, Munthe, a kind of benevolent Svengali, recounts trying to spring the patient Geneviève from the hospital by hypnotically suggesting to her a series of (successful) test escapes. When Charcot caught him, he was fired (Munthe, *The Story of San Michele* 304–13).
51 Duchenne (de Boulogne), *Méchanisme*, 157–86.
52 Didi-Huberman, *Invention of Hysteria*, 227.
53 Thuillier, *Monsieur Charcot*, 230.
54 Marshall, "Nervous Dramaturgy," 1
55 Finn, *Hysteria, Hypnosis*, 72.
56 Thuillier, *Monsieur Charcot*, 155.
57 Ibid.
58 Marquer, *Les romans de la Salpêtrière*, 87.
59 Appignanesi, *The Cabaret*, 28.
60 Beizer, *Ventriloquized Bodies*, 31.
61 Stokes, Booth, and Bassnett, *Bernhardt*, 49.
62 For a literary history of the hysteric in late nineteenth-century France, see Marquer or Micale.
63 Diamond, "Realism and Hysteria," 75.
64 Henrik Ibsen in Cole, *Playwrights on Playwriting*, 157, 161.
65 Beizer, *Ventriloquized Bodies*, 3.
66 Micale, *Approaching Hysteria*, 218–19.
67 Between these historic standards and outside their margins fell other, cross-pollinated genres – romanticism, symbolism, the well-made play, the variety, and the avant-garde concert, among others.
68 Stokes, Booth, and Bassnett, *Bernhardt*, 35.
69 Ibid.
70 Ibid., 21.
71 Ibid., 158.
72 Diamond, "Realism and Hysteria," 66.
73 Ibid., 22.
74 Richet, "Les démoniaques d'aujourd'hui," 353.
75 According to Freud, to enjoy a realist play, the audience member must be neurotic. See Freud, "Psychopathic Characters on the Stage."
76 Diamond, "Realism and Hysteria," 70.
77 Ibid., 73.
78 Ibid., 68.

79 Ibid., 66.
80 Brooks, *Melodramatic Imagination*, xi.
81 Ibid., 36.
82 Marshall, "Dynamic Medicine," 144.
83 Ibid.
84 Ibid., 131.
85 Charcot and Richer, *Démoniaques dans l'art*, 117.
86 Gluck, *Popular Bohemia*, 135–6.
87 For especially convincing critiques of Freud's therapeutic process as problematically patriarchal, see Ritchie Robertson's introduction to Dora in the recent (2013) Oxford edition or Koffman's *The Enigma of Woman*.
88 Diamond, "Realism and Hysteria," 78–9.
89 Ibid., 78.
90 Even the theories most focussed on the object, on the penis, in the sexual development of children that constitutes the formation of their unconscious, hinge on mythopoetic time and events that are only partly true (the Oedipal event, the primordial murder by the band of brothers, etc.).
91 See nearly any of Freud's works for such self-conscious revision, but especially the second introduction to Freud and Breuer's *Studies on Hysteria*.
92 Via Adelaide Ristori (Stokes, Booth, and Bassnett, *Bernhardt*, 137).
93 Stokes, Booth, and Bassnett, *Bernhardt*, 141–2.
94 Charcot himself seems to have had an Elizabeth Robins/Hedda Gabler moment of fixed staring. One day, historian Silverman documents, "Daudet observed Charcot, who was unaware of his presence, in a state of fixity and contemplation in his library and described the doctor as riveted, immobile, staring rigidly ahead, embodying all the features of a hypnotic trance that proceeded undisturbed for almost an hour. Henri Meige offered another instance of Charcot's intense capacity for withdrawal. During a period when he was completing research on aphasia, Charcot worked successively through the nights. One night, completely absorbed by the figures he was drawing to illustrate various forms of aphasia, he mechanically wrapped some of his hair around his forefinger, turning it tighter and tighter in circles. Later, when he realized what he was doing, Charcot had to cut off the hair to release his finger. This automatic behaviour, carried on during a state of artistic concentration, contained all the features of the involuntary actions carried out during the hypnotic state, what Charcot identified in his patients as 'cerebral automatism'" (Silverman, *Art Nouveau*, 101).
95 Diamond, "Realism and Hysteria," 79.
96 Gordon, *Why the French Love Jerry Lewis*, 104, 107.
97 Gordon, *Dances with Darwin*, 11.
98 Ibid.
99 Ibid., 14.
100 Gordon, *Why the French Love Jerry Lewis*, 75.
101 Ibid.
102 Ibid., 77.
103 Goetz, Bonduelle, and Gelfland, *Charcot*, 186, 214.

104 Avril, *Mes Mémoires*, 30.
105 Gordon, *Why the French Love Jerry Lewis*, 62.
106 Ibid., 61.
107 Gordon, *Dances with Darwin*, 15.
108 Charcot, *Clinical Lectures*, 195–6.
109 Ibid.
110 Ibid., 188.
111 Ibid., 191.
112 Nin, *The Diary of Anaïs Nin*, 191–2.
113 Sontag, *Illness as Metaphor*, 3.
114 Lüdtke, *Dances with Spiders*, 11.
115 Ibid., 12.
116 Another of De Martino's descriptions, this time of a gathering of tarantatas at the Church of St Paul, is as follows:

A tarantata all dressed in white drags her feet to the chapel entrance, leaning heavily on two male supporters. Another is carried over the threshold. Her limbs drop loosely and heavily. Inside the chapel, the light is dim. Flames, brought here as signs of devotion, flicker through the red plastic of cylindrical wax containers. An old lady lies on the only available bench. Her fingers clasp the hand of a man sitting by her petrified face. A hooded figure squats on the altar step. A young girl in white kneels in front of St Paul's barricaded statue, while a relative supports her from behind. Another tarantata has climbed on top of the altar. Her head leans against St Paul's tapestry, as if listening attentively, hopefully. Voices and prayers ring through the air. Thet are melodic, desperate, grateful and occasionally punctured by the piercing cry of the tarantata: "A-hi!" Inquisitive faces, framed in sunlight, peer through the chapel's portal. The crowd outside is packed tightly. Some are there for the festival, many to witness the tarantata. The mass of onlookers splits open at the tarantata's command. Dressed in black, she approaches the chapel on her knees, cutting an aisle into the surrounding throng. She moves, at first, as if lame or injured. Then, suddenly, she is on her feet, galloping back and forth. The crowd retreats as her steps carve out a large circle. Her arm thrashes upwards threatening the film camera shooting from an overhead balcony. A policeman seeks to calm her male assistant, enraged by the film crew. The afflicted continues her reckless rounds. Her guardian stands motionless, hands on hips. She begins to swirl on the spot and he moves close, holding his arms around her body and skilfully catching it as she drops backwards, unconscious, it seems. With a slight gesture, he summons the policeman nearby to pass over a cushion lying ready, which he tucks under her tousled hair. Cited in Lüdtke, *Dances with Spiders*, 37.

117 Lüdtke, *Dances with Spiders*, 45–7.
118 Ibid., 14.
119 Didi-Huberman, *Invention of Hysteria*, 239.
120 Richet, "Les démoniaques d'aujourd'hui," 347.
121 Weiss, *Phantasmic Radio*, 22.
122 Richet, "Les démoniaques d'aujourd'hui," 347.

123 Munthe, *The Story of San Michel*, 203.
124 Diamond, "Realism and Hysteria," 71.
125 Realism is not the first theatrical tradition to teach us this. At the origins of Western drama, the Dionysiac vision that infected Pentheus and the delirium of the Bacchanals in Euripides' play show that in the theatrical festival of Dionysus, the audience's eyes, too, may not be seeing what they think they are.
126 Bourneville and Régnard, *Iconographie photographique*, 166.

CHAPTER FIVE

1 Micale, *Approaching Hysteria*, 5.
2 Watson, "How Sad Girls Are Finding Empowerment through Being Sad Online."
3 Cixous and Clément, *The Newly Born Woman*, 59.
4 Ibid., xi.
5 Ibid., 6.
6 Ibid.
7 Ibid., 7.
8 Ibid., 28.
9 Ibid., 21.
10 Ibid., 47.
11 Fredrick Marker in Bergman, *A Project for the Theatre*, 12.
12 Ibsen, *Hedda Gabler*, 303.
13 Flanagan, "Hysteria and the Teenage Girl," 4.
14 Cixous and Clément, *The Newly Born Woman*, 35–7.
15 Freud, "On Femininity," 169.
16 Ibid., 146.
17 Ibid., 149.
18 Ibid., 169.
19 Dobkin, "Vagina Clown Car."
20 Wherry, "Neda Topaloski Explains."
21 Drimonis, "I Am a Feminist."
22 Ibid.
23 Robinson and Martin, *Arts of Engagement*, 14.
24 Truth and Reconciliation Commission of Canada, 41.
25 Dhillon, "Exclusive: Canada Police Prepared to Shoot Indigenous Activists."
26 Corbey, "Reconciling Promises and Reality."
27 Sumac, "Poem after Reading Article on High Functioning CPTSD."
28 Doherty, "The Sides and Sounds of Tanya Tagaq."
29 Carson-Fox, "The Missing."
30 "Equal Voice Historic Daughters of the Vote."
31 Ibid.
32 Ibid.
33 Belmore, "Vigil."
34 Mojica, *Manifesting Resistance.*
35 Yellowbird, "Wild Indians," 3.

36 Chocolate Woman Collective, "Reclaim, Create, Perform!"
37 Chocolate Woman Collective, "Izzie M."

CONCLUSION

1 Garland-Thomson, "Staring at the Other," 9.
2 Slate, *Little Weirds*, 13.
3 Slate, *Stage Fright*.
4 Ibid.
5 Ibid.
6 Slate, *Little Weirds*, 8.
7 Alvarez et al., "Times Up," 1–104.
8 Ahmed, *Living a Feminist Life*, 30.
9 Ibid.
10 Ibid., 30–1.

Bibliography

Abse, D. Wilfred, and Philipp Wegener. *Speech and Reason: Language Disorder in Mental Disease with a Translation of* The Life of Speech. Charlottesville: University of Virginia Press, 1971.

Agamben, Georgio. *Profanations*. Translated by Jeff Fort. New York: Zone Books, 2007.

Agras, Stewart, Ray Kimble, and James G. Williams. "A Comparison of Two Methods of Diagnosing Hysteria." *American Journal of Psychiatry* 132, no. 11 (1975): 197–9.

Ahmed, Sarah. *Living a Feminist Life*. London: Duke University Press, 2017.

Alvarez, Natalie, Barry Freeman, Laura Levin, Kimberley McLeod, and Jenn Stephenson. "Time's Up." *Canadian Theatre Review* 180 (2019): 1–104.

American Psychiatric Association. *Diagnostic and Statistical Manual of Mental Disorders*, 5th ed. Arlington: American Psychological Association, 2013.

Appignanesi, Lisa. *The Cabaret*. London: Yale University Press, 1984.

Apter, Emily. "The Garden of Scopic Perversion from Monet to Mirbeau." *October* 47 (Winter 1988): 91–115.

Aragon, Louis, and André Breton. "Le Cinquantenaire de l'hystérie." *Art and Popular Culture*, 27 July 2014.

Artaud, Antonin. *The Theatre and Its Double*. Translated by Mary Caroline Richards. New York: Grove, 1958.

Augustine. DVD. Directed by Alice Winocour. France: ARP Sélection, 2012.

Avril, Jane. *Mes mémoires*. Paris: Phébus, 2005.

Barthes, Roland. *Camera Lucida: Reflections on Photography*. Translated by Richard Howard. New York: Hill and Wang, 1981.

Bataille, Georges. *Theory of Religion*. Translated by Robert Hurley. New York: Zone Books, 1992.

Baudouin, A. "Quelques souvenirs de la Salpêtrière." *Paris Médicale* 15, no. 1 (1925): x–xiii.

Beizer, Janet. *Ventriloquized Bodies: Narratives of Hysteria in Nineteenth-Century France*. Ithaca: Cornell University Press, 1994.

Belmore, Rebecca. "Vigil." *Rebecca Belmore*. Accessed 2 July 2017. http://www.rebeccabelmore.com/video/Vigil.html.

Benjamin, Walter. *The Arcades Project*. Translated by Howard Eilan and Kevin MacLaughlin. Boston: Harvard University Press, 1999, reprint 2004.

– "The Work of Art in the Age of Mechanical Reproduction." Translated by Harry Zohn. In *Illuminations*, edited by Hannah Arendt. New York: Schocken Books, 1988.

Bergman, Ingmar. *A Project for the Theatre*. Edited by Marker Fredrick and Lise-Lone Marker. New York: Frederick Ungar, 1983.

– *Through a Glass Darkly*. Sweden: Svensk Filmindustri, 1961.

Bernheimer, Charles, and Claire Kahane. *In Dora's Case: Freud–Hysteria–Feminism*. New York: Columbia University Press, 1985, reprint 1999.

Besnard, Tiphaine. *Les prostitueés à la Salpêtrière et dans le discours médical, 1850–1914 : Une folle débauche*. Paris: L'Harmattan, 2011.

Bonduelle, Michel, and Toby Gelfland. "Hysteria behind the Scenes: Jane Avril at the Salpêtrière." *Journal of the History of Neurosciences* 7, no. 1 (1998): 35–42.

Bourneville, Désiré Magloire, and Paul Régnard. *Iconographie photographique de la Salpêtrière*. Edited by Adrien Delahaye. Paris: Progrès médical, 1877–80. Bibliothèque Universitaire Pierre et Marie Curie: Les Collections de la bibliothèque Charcot. Web. 21 Feb 2012.

Boym, Svetlana. *The Future of Nostalgia*. New York: Basic Books, 2001.

Brooks, Peter. *The Melodramatic Imagination: Balzac, Henry James, Melodrama and the Mode of Excess*. New York: Columbia University Press, 1985.

Buber, Martin. *The Prophetic Faith*. New York: Macmillan Publishing, 1977.

The Cabinet of Dr Caligari. DVD. Directed by Robert Wiene. Germany: Decla-Bioscop, 1920.

Cage, John. *Silence*. Middletown: Wesleyan University Press, 1961.

Canadian Association for Theatre Research. *Performing the Anthropocene*. 2017.

Canadian Psychiatric Association and the Schizophrenia Society of Canada. *Schizophrenia: The Journey to Recovery. A Consumer and Family Guide to Assessment and Treatment*. 2007.

Carson-Fox, Sarain. "The Missing." *Basement Review*. YouTube. 2014/16. Accessed 18 January 2020. https://www.youtube.com/watch?v=nToJqgSdb6o.

Charcot, Jean-Martin. *Clinical Lectures on the Diseases of the Nervous System*. Edited by Ruth Harris. Translated by Thomas Savill. New York: Routledge, 1991.

– "Policlinique du Mardi 7 Février 1888." *Leçons Cliniques de la Salpêtrière 1888–1889*. Paris: Progrès Médicale, Bibliothèque Universitaire Pierre et Marie Curie: Les Collections de la bibliothèque Charcot. 2012.

Charcot, Jean-Martin and Paul Richer. *Les Démoniaques dans l'Art*. Paris: Delahaye et Lecrosnier, 1887.

– *La foi qui guérit*. Paris: Macula, 1897, reprint 1984.

Chocolate Woman Collective. "Reclaim, Create, Perform!" (2018). http://www.chocolatewomancollective.com.

– "Izzie M." (2018). http://www.chocolatewomancollective.com/izzym.

Cima, Gay. *Performing Women: Female Characters, Male Playwrights and the Modern Stage*. Ithaca: Cornell University Press, 1993.

Cixous, Hélène, and Catherine Clément. *The Newly Born Woman*. Translated by Betsy Wing. Minneapolis: University of Minnesota Press, 1986.

Clare, Eli. "Freaks and Queers." *Gender and Women's Studies in Canada*, edited by Marg Hobbs and Carla Rice, 149–62. Toronto: Women's Press, 2018.

Claretie, Jules. *La Vie à Paris : Vol II*. Edited by Victor Havard. 3rd ed. Paris: Motteroz, 1881.

Clark, T.J. *The Painting of Modern Life: Paris in the Painting of Manet and His Followers*. New Jersey: Princeton University Press, 1984.

Clément, Catherine. *The Weary Sons of Freud*. New York: Verso Books, 2015.

Cole, Toby. *Playwrights on Playwriting: From Ibsen to Ionesco*. New York: Cooper Square Press, 1960.

Corbey, Raymond. "Ethnographic Showcases, 1870–1930." *Cultural Anthropology* 29 (1993): 338–69.

– "Reconciling Promises and Reality: Clean Drinking Water for First Nations," David Suzuki Foundation, accessed 8 December 2019. https://davidsuzuki.org/wp-content/uploads/2018/02/reconciling-promises-reality-clean-drinking-water-first-nations-SUMMARY.pdf

Debord, Guy. *The Society of the Spectacle*. Translated by Donald Nicholson-Smith. New York: Zone Books, 1994.

Delboeuf, Joseph. "Une Visite à la Salpêtrière." *Revue Biologique* 54 (1896): 139–42, 258–78.

Dhillon, Jaskiran. "Exclusive: Canada Police Prepared to Shoot Indigenous Activists, documents show." *Guardian*. 20 Dec 2019. https://theguardian.com/world/2019/dec/20/canada-indigenous-land-defenders-police-documents.

Diamond, Elin. "Realism and Hysteria: Toward a Feminist Mimesis." *Discourse* 13, no. 1 (1990–91): 59–92.

Didi-Huberman, Georges. *Invention of Hysteria; Charcot and the Photographic Iconography of the Salpêtrière*. Translated by Alisa Hartz. Cambridge: MIT Press, 2003.

Dobkin, Jess. "Vagina Clown Car." *This Is My Work*. 2008. http://www.jessdobkin.com/jd_work/clown-car/.

Dodd, Jennifer. "'The Name Game': Feminist Protests of the DSM and Diagnostic Labels in the 1980s." *History of Psychology* 18, no. 3 (2015): 312–23.

Doerner, Klaus. *Madmen and the Bourgeoisie: A Social History of Insanity and Psychiatry*. Translated by Joachim Neugroschel and Jean Steinberg. Oxford: Basil Blackwell Publisher Limited, 1981.

Doherty, Mike. "The Surprising Sounds and Sides of Tanya Tagaq." *Macleans*. 12 November 2018. https://www.macleans.ca/culture/books/tanya-tagaq-on-her-desperate-attempt-to-alleviate-indigenous-suffering/.

Dottin-Orsini, Mireille. *Cette Femme qu'ils disent fatale*. Paris: Grasset, 1993.

Drimonis, Toula. "I Am a Feminist But I Will Never Identify with Sextremism." *Huffington Post*, 8 June 2014. http://www.huffingtonpost.ca/toula-foscolos/femen-group_b_5654376.html.

Duchenne (de Boulogne), Guillaume Benjamin Armand. *Méchanisme de la physionomie humaine*. Paris: Jules Renouard, 1862.

Equal Voice. "Daughters of the Vote." http://www.daughtersofthevote.ca.

"Equal Voice Historic Daughters of the Vote." Filmed 8 March 2017 at ParlVu. https://parlvu.parl.gc.ca/Harmony/en/PowerBrowser/PowerBrowserV2/20170308/-1/26891.

Felman, Shoshana. *Writing and Madness*. Translated by Martha Noel Evans. Ithaca: Cornell University Press, 1985.

Finn, Michael. *Hysteria, Hypnosis, the Spirits, and Pornography: Fin-de-Siècle Cultural Discourses in the Decadent Rachilde*. Newark: University of Delaware Press, 2009.
Flanagan, Caitlin. "Hysteria and the Teenage Girl." *New York Times*, 29 January 2012.
Foucault, Michel. *Birth of the Clinic: An Archaeology of Medical Perception*. Translated by A.M. Sheridan Smith. New York: Vintage Books, 1994.
– *Discipline and Punish: The Birth of the Prison*. Translated by Alan Sheridan. New York: Vintage, 1979.
– *Madness and Civilization: A History of Insanity in the Age of Reason*. Translated by Richard Howard. New York: Vintage Books, 1988.
– *Psychiatric Power*. Translated by Graham Burchell. New York: Picador, 2003.
Freud, Sigmund. *Dora: An Analysis of a Case of Hysteria*. Translated and edited by James Strachey. New York: Collier Books, 1963.
– *Early Psychoanalytic Writings*. Translated and edited by James Strachey. New York: Collier Books, 1963.
– *The Interpretation of Dreams*. Translated and edited by James Strachey. New York: Collier Books, 1963.
– *Ma vie et la psychanalyse*. Translated by Marie Bonaparte. Paris: Gallimard, 1950.
– "On Femininity." *New Introductory Lectures on Psychoanalysis*. Translated and edited by James Strachey. New York: Collier Books, 1963.
– "Psychopathic Characters on the Stage." *Tulane Drama Review* 4, no. 3 (1960): 144–8.
Freud, Sigmund, and Joseph Breuer. *Studies on Hysteria*. Translated and edited by James and Alix Strachey. Middlesex: Penguin Books, 1974.
Garland-Thomson, Rosemarie. "Staring at the Other." *Disability Studies Quarterly* 25, no.4 (2005): 9.
Gilbert, Sandra, and Susan Gubar. *The Madwoman in the Attic: The Woman Writer and the Nineteenth-Century Literary Imagination*. New Haven: Yale University Press, 1984.
Gilman, Charlotte Perkins. "The Yellow Wallpaper." *Herland and Selected Stories*. New York: Signet Classics, 1992.
Gilman, Sander. *Seeing the Insane. Dallas:* Lincoln Press, 1982.
Gluck, Mary. *Popular Bohemia: Modernism and Urban Culture in Nineteenth-Century Paris*. Cambridge: Harvard University Press, 2005.
Goetz, Christopher, Michel Bonduelle, and Toby Gelfland. *Charcot: Constructing Neurology*. Oxford: Oxford University Press: 1995.
Gordon, Rae Beth. *Dances with Darwin, 1875–1910: Vernacular Modernity in France*. New York: Routledge, 2009.
– *Why the French Love Jerry Lewis: From Cabaret to Early Cinema*. Stanford: Stanford University Press, 2001.
Grosz, Elizabeth. *Volatile Bodies: Toward Corporeal Feminism*. Bloomington: Indiana University Press, 1994.
Guillain, Georges. *J.-M. Charcot (1825–1893): Sa vie, son oeuvre*. Paris: Massib, 1955.
Gunning, Tom. "In Your Face: Physiognomy, Photography, and the Gnostic Mission of Early Film." In *The Mind of Modernism: Medicine, Psychology, and the Cultural Arts in Europe and America, 1880–1940*, edited by Mark Micale, 141–71. Stanford: Stanford University Press, 2003.

Habermas, Jürgen. *Knowledge and Human Interests.* Translated by Jeremy Shapiro. Boston: Beacon Press, 1971.

Harris, Ruth. "Melodrama, Hysteria and Crimes of Passion in the Fin-de-Siècle." *History Workshop Journal* 25, no. 1 (1988): 31–63. https://doi.org/10.1093/hwj/25.1.31.

Harvey, David. *Paris, Capital of Modernity.* New York: Routledge, 2003.

Heller-Roazen, Daniel. *Echolalias: On the Forgetting of Language.* New York: Zone Books, 2005.

Homes, Diana, and Carrie Tarr. *A 'Belle Epoque'?: Women in French Society and Culture 1890–1914.* New York: Berghahn Books, 2007.

Hunter, Diane. "Hysteria, Psychoanalysis and Feminism: The Case of Anna O." *Feminist Studies* 9, no. 3 (1983): 464–88.

Hustvedt, Asti. *Medical Muses: Hysteria in Nineteenth-Century Paris.* New York: W.W. Norton and Co., 2011.

Ibsen, Henrik. *Hedda Gabler, Four Major Plays.* Translated by Rolf Fjelde, 221–309. New York: New American Library, 1965.

Irigaray, Luce. *To Speak Is Never Neutral.* Translated by Gail Schwab. New York: Routledge, 2002.

Kanani, Nadia. "Race and Madness: The Experiences of Racialized People with Psychiatric Histories in Canada and the United States." *Critical Disability Discourses* 3: 2011.

Koffman, Sarah. *The Enigma of Woman: Woman in Freud's Writings.* Translated by Catherine Porter. Ithaca: Cornell University Press, 1985.

Kracauer, Siegfried. *From Caligari to Hitler: A Psychological History of the German Film.* Princeton: Princeton University Press, 1947.

Kuhns, David F. *German Expressionist Theatre: The Actor and the Stage.* Cambridge: Cambridge University Press, 1997.

Lafrance, Michelle N., and Suzanne McKenzie-Mohr. "The DSM and Its Lure of Legitimacy." *Feminism and Psychology* 23, no. 1 (2013): 119–40.

Levinas, Emmanuel. *Humanism of the Other.* Translated by Nidra Pollen. Chicago: University of Illinois Press, 2006.

– *Totality and Infinity.* The Hague, Boston, and London: Martinus Nijhoff Publishers & Duquesne University Press, 1979.

Londe, Albert. *La Photographie Médicale: Application aux sciences médicales et physiologiques.* Paris: Gauthier Villard et Fils, 1893.

– "La photographie dans les sciences médicales: Le nouveau laboratoire de la Salpêtrière." *La Nature.* Paris: 1893.

Lüdtke, Karen. *Dances with Spiders: Crisis, Celebrity and Celebration in Southern Italy.* New York: Berghahn Books, 2009.

Lyotard, Jean-François. *The Differend: Phrases in Dispute.* Translated by Georges Van Der Abbeele. Minnesota: Minnesota University Press, 1988.

Marquer, Bernard. *Les romans de la Salpêtrière: Réception d'une scénographie clinique: Jean Martin Charcot dans l'imaginaire fin-de-siècle.* Geneva: Librairie Droz, 2008.

Marshall, Jonathan. "Dynamic Medicine and Theatrical Form at the Fin de Siècle: A formal Analysis of Dr Jean-Martin Charcot's Pedagogy, 1862–1893." *Modernism/Modernity* 15, no. 1 (2008): 131–53.

– "Nervous Dramaturgy: Pain, Performance and Excess in the Work of Dr Jean-Martin Charcot, 1862–1893." *Double Dialogues* 4 (2003). http://www.doubledialogues.com/article/nervous-dramaturgy-pain-performance-and-excess-in-the-work-of-dr-jean-martin-charcot-1862-1893/.

McLeod, Dayna. "Uterine Concert Hall: An Intimate Concert Venue Based in Montreal." Accessed 1 July 2017. http://www.uterineconcerthall.com.

Micale, Mark. *Approaching Hysteria: Disease and Its Interpretations*. Princeton: Princeton University Press, 1995.

– *The Mind of Modernism: Medicine, Psychology, and the Cultural Arts in Europe and America, 1880–1940*. Stanford: Stanford University Press, 2003.

Mojica, Monique. *Manifesting Resistance: Intergenerational Conversations about Activist Memory Projects across 'the Americas.'* Nogojiwanong: Aging Activisms, 2018.

Moudileno, Lydie. "Returning Remains: "Saartjie Baartman, or the 'Hottentot Venus' as Transnational Postcolonial Icon." *Forum for Modern Languages* 45 (2009): 200–12.

Munthe, Axel. *The Story of San Michel*. 1929. Reprint, New York: E.P. Dutton and Co., 1945.

Nancy, Jean-Luc. *Corpus*. Translated by Richard A. Rand. New York: Fordham University Press, 2008.

Nin, Anaïs. *The Diary of Anaïs Nin. Volume 1 1931–1934*. Boston: Houghton Mifflin Harcourt, 1969.

Noel Evans, Martha. *Fits and Starts: A Genealogy of Hysteria in Modern France*. Ithaca and London: Cornell University Press, 1991.

Offen, Karen. "Depopulation, Nationalism, and Feminism in Fin-de-Siècle France." *American Historical Review* 89, no. 3 (1984): 648–76.

– "Liberty, Equality and Justice for Women: The Theory and Practice of Feminism in Nineteenth-Century Europe." In *Becoming Visible: Women in European History*. 2nd ed. Edited by Renate Bridenthal, Claudia Koonz, and Susan Stuard. Boston: Houghton Mifflin, 1987.

Prodger, Philipp. *Darwin's Camera: Art and Photography in the Theory of Evolution*. Oxford: Oxford University Press, 2009.

Qureshi, Sadiah. "Displaying Sara Baartman, the 'Hottentot Venus.'" *History of Science* 42 (2004): 233–57.

Rayner, Ben. "Uterine Concert Hall: The World's Most Intimate Concert Venue." *Toronto Star*, 4 September 2016. https://www.thestar.com/entertainment/music/2016/09/04/uterine-concert-hall-the-worlds-most-intimate-concert-venue.html.

Renooz, C. "Charcot dévoilé." *Revue Scientifique des Femmes* 6 (1888): 241–7.

Reynolds, Sîan. "Women's Mobility in Belle Epoque Paris." In *A 'Belle Epoque'?: Women in French Society and Culture 1890–1914*. Edited by Diana Homes and Carrie Tarr, 81–94. New York: Berghahn Books, 2007.

Richet, Charles. "Les démoniaques d'aujourd'hui." *Revue des deux mondes* 37 (1880): 340–72.

Ripa, Yannick. *Women and Madness*. Minnesota: University of Minnesota Press, 1990.

Robinson, Dylan, and Keavy Martin. *Arts of Engagement: Taking Aesthetic Action in and beyond Canada's Truth and Reconciliation Commission.* Waterloo: Wilfred Laurier University Press, 2016.

Rosenhan, D.L. "On Being Sane in Insane Places." *Science* 179, no. 4070 (1973): 250–8.

Saussure, Ferdinand de. *Course in General Linguistics.* Translated by Wade Baskin. Edited by Charles Bally and Albert Sechehaye. New York: McGraw-Hill, 1966.

Scarry, Elaine. *The Body in Pain.* New York: Oxford University Press, 1985.

Schechner, Richard. "Magnitudes of Performance." In *By Means of Performance,* edited by Richard Schechner and Willa Appel, 19–49. Cambridge: Cambridge University Press, 1990.

Schivelbusch, Wolfgang. *The Railway Journey.* Berkley: University of California Press, 1986.

– *Disenchanted Night: The Industrialization of Light in the Nineteenth Century.* Berkeley: University of California Press, 1995.

Schreber, Daniel Paul. *Memoirs of My Nervous Illness.* New York: New York Review of Books, 2000.

Schwartz, Vanessa. *Spectacular Realities: Early Mass Culture in Fin-de-Siècle Paris.* Berkeley: University of California Press, 1998.

Seuphor, Michel. *Le style et le cri.* Paris: Seuil, 1965.

Showalter, Elaine. *The Female Malady: Women, Madness and English Culture, 1830–1980.* New York: Penguin Books, 1985.

Silverman, Debora. *Art Nouveau in Fin-de-Siècle France: Politics, Pathology and Style.* Berkeley: University of California Press, 1989.

Simmel, Georg. *The Metropolis and Mental Life.* Chicago: University of Chicago Press, 1971.

Slate, Jenny. *Little Weirds.* New York: Little Brown and Company, 2019.

Slate, Jenny. *Stage Fright.* Netflix. 2019.

Smith-Rosenberg, Carroll. "The Hysterical Woman: Sex Roles and Role Conflict in 19th Century America." *Social Research* 39, no. 4 (1972): 652–78.

Sontag, Susan. *Illness as Metaphor.* New York: Vintage Books, 1979.

– *Regarding the Pain of Others.* New York: Picador, 2003.

Stokes, John, Michael Booth, and Susan Bassnett. *Bernhardt, Terry, Duse: The Actress in her Time.* Cambridge: Cambridge University Press, 1988.

Sumac, Smokii, "Poem after Reading Article on High Functioning CPTSD." YouTube. 2017. Accessed 18 January 2020. https://www.youtube.com/watch?v=9BNP6aMnndo.

Thuillier, Jacques. *Monsieur Charcot à la Salpêtrière.* Paris: Laffont, 1993.

Truth and Reconciliation Commission of Canada: Calls to Action. Accessed 1 July 2017. http://www.trc.ca/websites/trcinstitution/File/2015/Findings/Calls_to_Action_English2.pdf.

Watson, Lucy. "How Sad Girls Are Finding Empowerment through Being Sad Online." *Dazed Digital,* 2016. http://www.dazeddigital.com/photography/article/28463/1/girls-are-finding-empowerment-through-internet-sadness.

Weiss, Allen. *Aesthetics of Excess.* Albany: SUNY Press, 1989.

– *Phantasmic Radio.* Durham and London: Duke University Press, 1995.

– "Ten Theses on Monsters and Monstrosity." *Drama Review* 48, no. 1 (2004): 124–5.

Wernick, Andrew. *Auguste Comte and the Religion of Humanity: The Post-Theistic Program of French Social Theory.* Cambridge: Cambridge University Press, 2005.

Wherry, Aaron. "Neda Topaloski Explains Why She Went Topless to Protest Bill C-51." *Macleans*, 24 March 2015. http://www.macleans.ca/politics/femen-and-the-theory-of-toplessness-as-protest/.

Yellowbird, Pemina. n.d. "Wild Indians; Native Perspectives on the Hiawatha Asylum for Insane Indians." Accessed 9 December 2019. https://power2u.org/wp-content/uploads/2017/01/NativePerspectivesPeminaYellowBird.pdf.

Index

#metoo, 203–4

Ahmed, Sarah, 204–5
alterity, 8–10, 51
ambivalence, 55, 77, 98
anthropological exhibitions, 17–19
anxiety, patriarchal, 54–100
arc-de-cercle, 4, 22
archive 6, 14, 110, 117
Artaud, Antonin, 166
attack, 22, 26, 43, 137
attitudes passionelles, 80
Augustine, 15, 24, 39, 41, 44, 50–3, 111–8, 132–3, 144, 173; via surrealists, 60
autonomous sexuality, 78. *See also* prostitute; *femme nouvelle*; feminism
Avril, Jane, 6, 134–6, 163
Aygadim Majagalee, Teanna, 191–2

Baartman, Sara, 18–19
Barthes, Roland, 10, 44
Belmore, Rebecca, 190–3
Bernhardt, Sarah, 145, 155–6
Bourneville, Désiré-Magloire, 4, 23
Brouillet, André, 7, 56–60

cabaret, 162
Cabinet of Dr Caligari, 19
café-concert, 51, 162–3
camera. *See* photograph
Canadian Psychiatry Association, 103–4
Charcot, Jean-Martin, 3, 19–21; theatrical tastes of, 149
Cixous, Hélène, and Catherine Clément, 11, 119, 180–1
Claretie, Jules, 37
consent, breach of, surrounding publication of medical portraiture, 43, 51; breach of, surrounding provocation of hysterical attack, 43
crime of passion, 146
cry, 7, 23, 96, 113, 121–30, 161, 190; author's, 198

Dance, Avril's, 135; *rhythmical chorea*, 163–4
Darwin, Charles, 29, 147
Daughters of the Vote, 191–2
Delboeuf, Joseph, 43, 88–91
delirium, 23, 47, 114–15
destabilized spectatorship, 9, 120, 172–3, 175–6
diagnosis, metaphoric, 75
Diagnostic and Statistical Manual of Mental Disorders, 105–6
Dobkin, Jess, 184
doll, hysteric conceptualized as, 106–9, 116
dramaturgy, 8, 94, 200–1
Duchenne de Boulogne, Guillaume-Benjamin-Amand, 20, 147
Durand, Valérie, 69, 201
Duse, Eleanora, 156, 160

emotion, 95
empirical style, 12, 102–6
escape, 173
ethical provocation, 9
ethnographic showcase. *See* anthropological exhibitions
evasion, 46
excess, 47–8, 182

faking, 7, 131, 134–6, 166
FEMEN, 184–6
femininity, nineteenth-century idealizations and demonizations of, 54–5, 64–71, 82; as expressed defiantly, 71–5; expressions of, in Salpêtrière paintings, 56–60; hypnotically induced, 85–96; as performed by hysterical patient, 79; as strategically frayed in performance, 181–2
feminism, 62, 67, 94–5, 176–80, 204–5; Charcot's relationship to, 83
femme nouvelle, 67, 77

Fleury, Robert, 7, 56–60
freakshow. *See* sideshow
Freud, Sigmund, lecture on femininity, 183–4

Geneviève, 143
grande hystérie, 4, 133

hallucination, 49–50, 112; with others 120. *See also* delirium; hypnosis
Hedda Gabler, 154, 161
Hiawatha Asylum for Insane Indians, 194
Hood, Susanna, 178–9
hypnosis, 58, 85–96; as cultural product, 134

Iconographie photographique de la Salpêtrière, 5, 15, 150–5
Impressionism, 71–3
inarticulacy, 109–10, 116–18, 126–9
indeterminacy, 16, 197
Indigenous performance, 189–91
Irigaray, Luce, 102–3, 118–20
Izzy M: The Alchemy of Enfreakment, 193–7

label, photographic, 40–2, 47–8
Lady Macbeth, 147–8
lecture series, 3, 14, 25–6, 46
Levinas, Emmanuel, 10, 51
limits of knowledge, 13
Londe, Albert, 28

McLeod, Dayna, 186–9
medical gaze, 21, 37
medical positivism, 9, 20, 102
melodrama, 12, 150, 157–8
Mojica, Monique, 18, 193–7

naturalism, 41
Nin, Anaïs, 165–6
nostalgia, 84, 97

Olympia, 61–2

pain, 15, 48, 52–3, 88
photography, 39–53; as scenographic, 46; medical, compared to starlet portraiture, 50–4; phenomenological relationships to, 44–6; false, of Augustine, 41
photographic technique, 36, 44
Photographie Médicale, 33–6
physiognomy, 28–31
privacy, 51
projection, 84
prostitute, 68–74
puppet. *See* doll

Qaqqa, Trina, 191

realism, 156, 158–62
refusal, 44
Rejlander, Oscar, 30–1
resistance of the hysterical patient, 6, 39, 96, 100, 175
responsibility, 6, 196, 205
return of the repressed, 99–100
rhetorical style, of Charcot, 18, 101–2; of Delboeuf, 89–90
Robins, Elizabeth, 159

Salpêtrière, 3, 36, 56
scapegoat, 81, 95–6
Scarry, Elaine, 93
scream. *See* cry
sex work. *See* prostitute
Shah, Tejal, 179–80
sideshow, 19–20
Simmel, Georg, 31–2
simulation, 11, 136, 138
Slate, Jenny, 202–4
sound, 126–8
speech, 7
staring, 198
starlet, 141–5
symptom, brought on by hypnosis, 139–42; hysterical, 47, 97; as theatricality, 133; shifting, 171–2

Tarantella, 167–70; theory of, 180

Uterine Concert Hall. *See* Dayna McLeod

Venus Specola, 33
violence of representation, 6, 15
violence, physical, 88, 93
vulnerability, 9, 24, 52, 205

Winocour, Alice, 132–3
witnessing, 27, 171, 191
Wittman, Blanche, 6, 91, 97, 100, 131–2; in Brouillet's painting, 58–60

Zola, Émile, 63, 154, 160